Terror

Terror

The French Revolution and Its Demons

Michel Biard and Marisa Linton

With a Foreword by Timothy Tackett

polity

Originally published in French as *Terreur! La Révolution française face à ses demons*. By Michel Biard & Marisa Linton © Armand Colin 2020, Malakoff. Armand Colin is a trademark of DUNOD Editeur, 11, rue Paul Bert, 92240 Malakoff

This English edition © Polity Press, 2021

Polity Press
65 Bridge Street
Cambridge CB2 1UR, UK

Polity Press
101 Station Landing
Suite 300
Medford, MA 02155, USA

All rights reserved. Except for the quotation of short passages for the purpose of criticism and review, no part of this publication may be reproduced, stored in a retrieval system or transmitted, in any form or by any means, electronic, mechanical, photocopying, recording or otherwise, without the prior permission of the publisher.

ISBN-13: 978-1-5095-4835-4
ISBN-13: 978-1-5095-4836-1 (pb)

A catalogue record for this book is available from the British Library.

Typeset in 10.5 on 12pt Sabon
by Cheshire Typesetting Ltd, Cuddington, Cheshire
Printed and bound in Great Britain by CPI Group (UK) Ltd, Croydon

The publisher has used its best endeavours to ensure that the URLs for external websites referred to in this book are correct and active at the time of going to press. However, the publisher has no responsibility for the websites and can make no guarantee that a site will remain live or that the content is or will remain appropriate.

Every effort has been made to trace all copyright holders, but if any have been overlooked the publisher will be pleased to include any necessary credits in any subsequent reprint or edition.

For further information on Polity, visit our website:
politybooks.com

Contents

Note on the Text   viii
Acknowledgements   ix
Foreword by Timothy Tackett   x

Introduction: The Demons of Terror   1

Chapter 1: *The Terror* – a Concept Imposed by the Thermidoreans   8
1. How the 'system of terror' and the black legend of Robespierre were retrospectively invented   10
2. Developing use of the word 'terror' between 1789 and 1794   16
3. 'Terror as the order of the day': an unsaid, unofficial yet widespread order from the Convention   19

Chapter 2: The Meaning of 'Terror' Before the Revolution   25
1. *Terror* and Enlightenment. A problematic connection   26
2. The concept of 'terror' in the Ancien Régime   28
3. The role of terror in political theory   35

Chapter 3: Terror in the Heart: The Weight of Fears and Emotions   42
1. The spectre of conspiracy and treason   45
2. The flow of emotions and fears   49
3. The impossible combination of virtue and terror   53

Chapter 4: The Revolution and its Opponents: Clashes and the Intensification of Repression — 62
1. Legislation targeting refractory clergy and *émigrés* — 63
2. 'The suspects': how the net of suspicion widened — 69
3. Repression against 'federalism' and the emblematic case of the Lyon revolt — 73

Chapter 5: Creating Revolutionary Law: A Time of Political Exception — 79
1. From ordinary law to 'revolutionary' law — 81
2. 'Revolutionary' institutions and their role in repression — 85
3. The recourse to extraordinary justice — 90

Chapter 6: Terror in the Convention: Political Conflict as an Engine of 'Terror' — 96
1. The Convention and the clubs: from political strife to 'purging' — 97
2. From arrests to political trials — 105
3. Death as a means to eliminate opponents in the Convention — 108
4. The elimination of factions, the apogee of 'terror' or the will to end it? — 112

Chapter 7: Paris and the Vendée at the Heart of the 'Terror' — 119
1. Paris, capital of the *sans-culotte* movement — 120
2. Paris, epicentre of the 'Terror' — 127
3. The 'military Vendée', a zone of civil war — 131

Chapter 8: Who Lived and Who Died? The Difficult Balance Sheets of Terror — 136
1. Working out the death toll — 137
2. Fraternal France and fratricidal France — 143

Conclusion: How the Convention Reconstructed Itself After Thermidor — 157

Chronology for the Years of the National Convention — 165
Maps — 179
Some Further Reading — 188
Notes — 190
Index — 229

In memory of Michel Vovelle (1933–2018)

Note on the Text

This is a shortened and revised version of the original French language editon: *Terreur! La Révolution française face à ses démons*, Armand Colin, 2020, Malakoff, a trademark of Dunod Editeur.

Acknowledgements

Chapters 1, 4, 5 and 8 were originally translated by Élise Trogrlic, with the support of the GRHis University of Rouen, Normandy. All other translations and the rewriting for this edition were by Marisa Linton.

Our grateful thanks to those who generously gave their time to read the original draft of the French edition and gave us invaluable advice and further suggestions (Françoise Brunel, Carla Hesse, Hervé Leuwers and, especially, Timothy Tackett).

Foreword

We can only applaud this cross-channel collaboration between two of the most distinguished and prolific scholars of the French Revolution, the French historian Michel Biard and his British counterpart Marisa Linton. They bring together some of the most recent Revolutionary studies in both English and French for a rich and creative new synthesis. Although their study touches on aspects of the entire period from the late Old Regime through the Napoleonic period, the primary focus is on the phenomena of 'terror' and state-imposed violence in the years 1793 to 1794: the origins, the ongoing dynamic, the broad impact on French society and the prolonged challenge – longer than is often realized – of bringing such 'terror' to a close. The book also presents valuable reflections on the lengthy and contentious historiography of the phenomena in question, on debates whose origins can be traced to the writings of contemporaries of the Revolution itself and that have continued unabated into the twenty-first century.

Few periods in French history have been so afflicted by misinterpretation, deformation and facile oversimplification. The array of explanations for the phenomenon of Revolutionary 'terror', proposed by historians, social scientists, philosophers, literary scholars and novelists is impressive indeed. In their great majority, however, such writers had very little understanding of the actual historical reality of the events they claimed to describe and explain. The majority based their interpretations on a veritable myth concerning the years 1793–4, a myth that originated in the efforts of the post-Thermidorian Conventionnels to distance and exculpate themselves from the period of intense state repression in which they themselves were frequently complicit. 'The Terror' came about, they argued, through the machinations of Maximilien Robespierre and a few of his Montagnard henchmen, who sought to create a dictatorship – some even argued a new monarchy – dominated by 'the monster' Robespierre himself. The Terror was thus a calculated and unitary 'system' imposed by a small minority.

In a series of chapters organized both thematically and chronologically, the authors bring together a range of new research – including many of their own studies – to confront and demolish the ahistorical legend of 1793–4. As they make abundantly clear, the repression of those years was never conceived as a 'system'. Most of the measures associated with the 'terror' were pieced together, adapted and strengthened by the National Convention over a period of several months, in response to the transforming circumstances of foreign war, civil war and popular pressure. Some had precedents dating back to the early years of the Revolution or even to the Old Regime. There was never anything approaching a single pre-conceived ideology at work in this process. And while the role of Robespierre was far from insignificant, he was by no means the dominant force as he has so often been presented. Indeed, in many cases Robespierre's opponents, the Girondins, were at least as complicit in the creation of 'terrorist' institutions as were the Montagnard Jacobins.

Moreover, as the authors also make clear, it is impossible fully to understand the behaviour and political choices of the leaders of the Revolution without taking into consideration the role of emotions. On the one hand, it is important not to underestimate the extraordinary force of the joy and enthusiasm and the collective love of 'fraternity' as motivating factors – and the possible frustration and impatience that sometimes arose when the Revolutionaries were compelled to confront those who did not share the same enthusiasm. But to understand the repression of 1793–4, it is above all essential to examine the multiple manifestations of fear: fear of military invasion, fear of revenge, fear of traitors, fear of conspiracy: a complex of fears that might well be transformed into anger, hatred and cynical efforts at manipulation. The authors provide a graphic demonstration of the extent to which the 'terrorists' themselves might well feel 'terrorized'.

To be sure, and it is to their credit, Biard and Linton are careful not to gloss over the human toll of the 'terror'. They examine the statistics available for the executions ordered by Revolutionary tribunals and military commissions. They do not overlook the terrible repression against the Vendée rebellion and the so-called 'Federalist' revolts; the political 'show trials' against various factional opponents; and the generalized hecatomb in Paris in June and July 1794 arising from the 'Prairial law'. They take note of the impact on the physical and mental health of those compelled to spend long months in insalubrious prisons. They meditate on the extent to which the Revolutionaries chose to set aside the Rights of Man in the face of the perceived necessity of 'violating the law to save the law'.

But the authors also take care to contextualize all such actions in terms of both circumstances and emotions. They are impatient with the utterly inaccurate putative links between the terror phase of the Revolution and the totalitarian regimes and ideologies of the twentieth century. They underline the substantial number of exonerations and case dismissals (non-lieux), often 50 percent or higher, among those individuals brought before the Revolutionary tribunals. And they note the widely varying impact of the repression from region to region, department to department. It is clear that the most intense repression was precisely in those areas that were the scene of major armed counter-revolution against the Convention.

In conclusion, we must express our gratitude for the publication of this enormously thoughtful and nuanced study and for the authors' efforts to come to grips with the phenomenon of French Revolutionary 'terror' in all its complexities and contradictions.

Timothy Tackett

Introduction: The Demons of Terror

Terror ... the word has become synonymous with the French Revolution. When we think of the French Revolution, it is perhaps inevitable that we also think of the demons that came to haunt it and to overshadow its humanitarian project – the demons of terror. In our modern world this association has been intensified by the huge importance that the words 'terror', 'terrorism' and 'terrorist' have assumed for us, and the visceral fears and hatreds that these words invoke. The use of a capital letter for *the Terror* has reified the word, all the more so as it is accompanied by a definite article intended to reinforce it: it has become *the Terror*, sometimes *The Reign of Terror*. By making this word signify a unified phenomenon, we assume that we know what it meant, and what it encompassed. Yet when the women and men of the Revolution used the term 'terror', they almost never gave it a capital letter, or the definite article. However they experienced terror, it was not yet, for them, *the Terror*.

The term, *the Terror* (definite article, capital T) comes primarily from historians who wanted to impose a particular narrative on the past. This process began with nineteenth-century French historians, above all, Jules Michelet. In Michelet's general introduction to his *Histoire de la Révolution française* (published from 1847 onwards) not only did he use this capital letter, but, with his fluent, impressionistic style, he practically personified *Terror*, making it almost another character in his narrative of the Revolution, and giving it the capacity to speak, like a monster lurking in wait to savage the achievements of the Revolution.[1] From that time onwards the practice of using a capital letter for *Terror* was increasingly adopted.[2] A search on the

Internet using the Ngram Viewer linguistic application demonstrates a surge in the use of the term with its capitalization in the decades 1840–60, a peak in the 1880–1910 period (linked to the Centenary of 1789) and then a marked decrease. Another surge, still more spectacular, came with the Bicentenary of the Revolution in 1989, an anniversary that coincided with intense historiographical controversy from historians of both left and right over the meaning and nature of the Revolution.[3] Thus, *the Terror* as a unified and reified entity is a creation of historians, a polemical construction based on antagonistic interpretations, a means for historians to obsessively denigrate this revolution, or, indeed, any revolution.

One of the most problematic features of the term, *the Terror* and, even more so, *The Reign of Terror*, is that these words have so often been depicted as synonymous with a chronological period, although historians do not necessarily agree on when that period began, or when it ended. Whilst the expression *the Terror* has often been used to designate the entirety of the most radical phase of the Revolution, during the years 1793 and 1794, some of it coinciding with the Year II in the new revolutionary calendar (22 September 1793–21 September 1794), there is little consensus on when in 1793 *the Terror* began. To confuse us further, some historians have dated its onset further back, to August 1792, with the overthrow of the monarchy; still others have contended that *the Terror* began even earlier, seeing it as intrinsic to the entire Revolution – a view epitomized by Simon Schama's often-cited pronouncement that: 'The Terror was merely 1789 with a higher body count'.[4] This chronological definition of *the Terror* is particularly misleading because it carries the implication, whether intended or not, that everything within the designated dates (assuming we go along with September 1793 to the end of July 1794) was about *the Terror*, and that nothing outside those dates qualifies as terror. Of course, the years 1793 and 1794 were a time as unprecedented as they were exceptional, but they cannot be reduced to the repressive aspects that for 200 years have commonly been associated with *the Terror*.

In recent years a growing number of historians have been prepared to call into question traditional delineations of *the Terror*.[5] This is not an easy task, not least because the term is such a familiar one, to be found in almost all the older history books, and throughout popular culture. We are faced with a practical question – if we do not call it *the Terror*, then what do we call it, how do we define and explain it? What words do we use that do not become impossibly involved and complicated? Recently, the eminent American historian of the Revolution, Timothy Tackett stated that he continued to use 'the term "Terror" – with the initial capital letter and the definite article ... simply because, like other terms such as "the Renaissance" or "the Industrial Revolution", it has long been adopted by almost every historian.'⁶ As a pragmatic judgement, Tackett's perspective has much to recommend it. Regardless of anything else, the term is a convenient shorthand, and for this reason, if no other, is likely to prove tenacious.

Nevertheless, in this book we shall put the case for changing how historians and the wider public speak of this subject, or at least to give them pause. Our intention is to call into question many of the assumptions that lie behind the easy recourse to speaking of *the Terror*, and to invite readers, as well as to challenge ourselves, to think anew. While this book is in part a synthesis of the most recent works on the question both in France and in English-speaking countries, it is also, of course, based very much on our own researches on a subject to which we have, between us, dedicated a daunting number of years.

We will make the case, therefore, for historians to speak henceforth of 'terror' and no longer only of *the Terror*. We emphasize that this does not in any way mean we desire to minimize the violence of the revolutionary period – as shall become clear, in some locations there was a great deal of violence, as well as widespread threats of violence. Nor are we trying to restate the classic thesis that the revolutionaries were forced by 'circumstances' to adopt 'terror' to ensure the survival of the Republic, making terror a regrettable necessity. One thing that becomes apparent is that, when revolutionaries resorted to terror to defend the moral gains of the Revolution, in an undeniable sense those moral gains were lost anyway. Yet neither do we endorse the thesis that the French revolutionary terror can be conceived as a matrix and model for twentieth-century totalitarianisms. The Jacobins were not the Bolsheviks. Robespierre was no Stalin.

The notion that terror was simply a logical result of circumstances, devised to stave off threats of military violence and the potential annihilation of the revolutionaries and the Revolution itself, by the foreign powers and opponents from the old social elite, is not in itself enough to explain the part played by emotions in revolutionary decision-making; nor why revolutionary leaders turned on one another with such catastrophic effects. The colossal impact of war and civil war accounts for some of this, but it is far from being able to explain everything. Nor can any study of the ideologies of 1789, of liberty, equality and the rights of man, of justice, the general will, or natural rights, do much to help us to understand why revolutionaries, terrified of conspiracy, turned on one another.

We wish, from the outset, to steer clear of historiographical visions that are more related to ideological polemics than to historical research. For that reason, rather than begin our study with a hypothetical date that would mark the supposed beginnings of *Terror*, or with a wide-ranging and possibly nebulous account of its much-debated origins, we will start at a moment that is so often said to have 'ended' *the Terror*, but which, we will contend, saw the beginning of its invention as a unifying concept. That moment came immediately after the overthrow and execution without trial of the revolutionary leader, Maximilien Robespierre and many of his adherents over four days from 27 to 30 July 1794. This was the so-called 'Thermidorian' moment, named after Thermidor, the month in the revolutionary calendar in which it took place.

The men who joined forces to kill Robespierre would become known as the 'Thermidorians'. They were, like him, members of the National Convention, the parliamentary body that had been responsible for the laws that enabled terror. Many of these men, like Robespierre himself, were Montagnards, that is, members of the Jacobin Club who sat in the Convention. Thus, they themselves had been, over many months, at the heart of a wider group (including many non-Montagnards), which had worked together to promote revolutionary policies, including those that enabled terror. They too, therefore, shared in collective responsibility for the violence and threats of violence of the previous months.

Through the ensuing weeks from late July to mid-September, the men who had killed Robespierre, began to systematically spread a vengeful prose intended to cast opprobrium on the 'monster' who had been slaughtered, but also to collectively exonerate the National Convention of its responsibility in the legislation that made it possible to crack down on its adversaries. They then created from scratch the idea of a 'system' or a 'coherent policy' that would have triggered and then implemented the 'terror', the whole blame resting posthumously on Robespierre and his supporters, an episode that was said to have been closed by his elimination in Thermidor. Ironically, many people in regions away from Paris, areas of civil war, federalist revolts, and the frontiers, were barely aware of terror, and learned about it retrospectively from Thermidorian texts, images, pamphlets and prison memoirs which informed them that they had been subjected to a 'Reign of Terror' led by Robespierre and his allies.[7] Not content with self-amnesty, the 'Thermidorians' claimed that the 'terror' had ended, even as they continued to use the machinery of the extraordinary government that had been gradually put in place during 1793 and given the title of 'revolutionary government', encompassing the use of repressive methods and state violence.

This thesis of an end to *the Terror* in the aftermath of 9 and 10 Thermidor was to impose itself durably in historiography, both by minimizing the violence that continued to take place during the remainder of the existence of the Convention until October 1795 (before separating, the deputies voted themselves an amnesty for the actions in which they had taken part) and the succeeding regime, that of the Directory. By positing a neat and convenient date for the 'end to *the Terror*', this thesis had the effect of pushing historians to look for one or more dates likely to mark the 'beginning of *the Terror*', rather than to try to detect terror's deeper, more problematic roots.

The most common date chosen by historians for the start of a system of terror is in September 1793, when it has often been stated that the Convention decreed that 'terror' should become an official policy (made 'order of the day'). In fact, no such decree was passed, either then or at any other date. Should we then look for the beginnings of this 'terror' in legislation passed in response to the military crisis of spring 1793; or a little earlier, in January of that year with the execution of the king; or earlier still, in August 1792 with the overthrow of the monarchy; or even earlier in the Revolution, in line with Schama's pronouncement that terror was already in place with the Rights of Man in 1789? In our judgement, trying to establish a birth date for 'terror' is a vain approach: 'terror' cannot be explained or understood as a chronological sequence limited by a beginning and an end. As Haim Burstin has pointed out, to persist in proposing a birth date of *the Terror* ('one of the favourite exercises of historians', he wrote) is to go down the wrong path in seeking to discover a kind of 'original sin of the Revolution', or even the moment when it 'slipped', to use the verb formerly proposed by revisionist historians, François Furet and Denis Richet.[8]

In order to grasp what terror really meant for the revolutionary generation, it is advisable not to limit our enquiries to its violent aspects alone, but to understand terror in a bigger context of crisis, and, even more, we need to situate the contemporary meaning of terror in the context of a political exception, the same one that brought about the revolutionary government in the autumn of 1793 and which developed out of its beginnings the previous spring. The growing weight of fears and emotions, the progressive aggravation of the confrontations and the parallel radicalization of repressive legislation, the accentuation of political struggles within the Convention, all of these factors contributed to the step-by-step development and maintenance of 'terror'. Linked to exceptional institutions set up alongside the constitutional machinery of power, the phenomenon naturally had its own rhythms and logics, geography and balance sheets, all of which contribute to illustrating the impossibility of speaking of a 'system' that uniformly extended its hold over the entire national territory.

'Terror' is a watchword that has circulated exhaustively, a political concept that has been the object of much discourse and theoretical justification, a process, but also and above all, a phenomenon that has permeated both our understanding of the Revolution and of its revolutionaries. By covering the chronological period of the Revolution in an all-encompassing blanket on which is written 'this was the time of *the Terror*', anything that cannot be designated under that heading is obscured. Whether intentional or not, this can be misleading. We should not lose sight of the extent to which revolutionaries remained committed to liberty, equality and the rights of man, even during the crisis years of 1793 to 1794. The demons of terror should not blind us to this fact. To take just one example, it was revolutionary France that, before Britain and long before America, in February 1794, at the height of the chronological period traditionally designated as *the Terror*, decreed the freedom of all slaves in the French colonies. While this decree followed on from the slave uprising in the colony of Saint-Domingue (later the Republic of Haiti), and the question of rights for all remained deeply problematic in France, we need to acknowledge the achievements of the revolutionaries in all their complexity.[9]

We should also be aware that part of the reason why our minds picture the guillotine and the Revolutionary Tribunal as so powerful and so indelibly redolent of terror – literally terrifying – is that French revolutionaries made it that way. If we still, in the present day, think of the French Revolution as synonymous with the theatre of the guillotine, this is due in large part to the symbolism, rhetoric and imagery deployed by the revolutionaries as a deliberate strategy, presenting themselves as striking back hard at the Republic's many enemies through this spectacular form of revolutionary justice. In this sense, the revolutionary terror was, as Carla Hesse concludes, 'a weapon of the weak'.[10]

Finally, there is the problem that to label what happened in France as *the Terror*, encourages the misleading supposition that somehow 'terror' was specifically and uniquely French, attributable to some endemic characteristic of the French situation or political theory. If we state that only France in the late eighteenth century had *the Terror*, how then do we designate the violence of the American Revolution, or the brutal repression by English forces of the revolt in Ireland in 1798? To quote Hesse again: 'The French Revolution was, it is now clear, *quantitatively*, a no more – and probably a significantly less – violent affair than its sister revolution across the Atlantic'.[11] The American and French Revolutions shared much common ancestry, though they developed in different ways. 'Liberty or death' was a rallying cry for both. It was a phrase that owed much to ideas about love of liberty and devotion to political virtue, drawn and adapted from the common culture of classical antiquity. Its literal meaning, in the words of the American revolutionary, Patrick Henry in 1775, was 'give me liberty or give me death'.[12] For many of the French revolutionaries this would be their fate. They sought liberty, but ultimately the demons of terror brought death. This book is an attempt to explain how that happened.

Chapter 1

The Terror – a Concept Imposed by the Thermidorians

One of the first texts openly attacking the French Revolution, Edmund Burke's *Reflections on the Revolution in France*, was published in 1790. This work by the Anglo-Irish author and Member of Parliament was quickly translated into French and other languages.[1] For some it was seen as a prophetic vision announcing *the Terror*, as it denounced the violence of 1789, especially the killing of two royal guards during the revolutionary days of 5 and 6 October, when a crowd broke into the palace of Versailles, and under the threat of popular violence, the king agreed to move to Paris, to be under the watchful eyes of the populace. Burke not only uses the word 'terror' but also describes the Constituent Assembly as a meeting of deputies trembling before popular violence: 'It is beyond doubt, that, under the terror of the bayonet, and the lamp-post, and the torch to their houses, they are obliged to adopt all the crude and desperate measures suggested by clubs composed of a monstrous medley of all conditions, tongues, and nations.'[2]

A very different view was taken by another British author, Thomas Paine, already known for having politically engaged several years earlier with the independence movement in the American colonies with his seminal pro-revolutionary pamphlet, *Common Sense*. Paine strongly objected to Burke's exaggeration of the extent of the violence of 1789, as well as his comparisons with the so-called 'Glorious Revolution' of the late seventeenth century, which Burke depicted in glowing, Manichean terms. Paine sharply responded to Burke in *Rights of Man*, a work published in early 1791 and translated into French that May. Whilst Paine also used the word 'terror', he saw its purpose and the reasons behind it very differently. For Paine, if the ignorant populace resorted to inflicting 'terror', this was the consequence of them having learned such tactics from the autocratic government under which they had lived. Paine stressed that the violence of 1789 could only be understood if viewed in relation to the cruelty of the Ancien Régime, with the 'terror' that the people suffered provoking the appearance of another 'terror':

> It is over the lowest class of mankind that government by terror is intended to operate, and it is on them that it operates to the worst effect. They have sense enough to feel they are the objects aimed at; and they inflict in their turn the examples of terror they have been instructed to practise.[3]

To this idea of a passive 'terror' (which one suffers under) ripening into an active, vengeful 'terror' (which is directed at one's enemies), Paine added that governments need to be taught about the notion of humanity before asking it of 'the people'. To prove his point, Paine recalled the punishment of Damiens, who had been convicted in 1757 of having attempted regicide against Louis XV. Damiens was subjected to extensive ritualized torture, climaxing in his being 'drawn and quartered'; the sentence carried out as a public spectacle to terrify the populace. Paine concluded that governments make a mistake in 'governing men by terror, instead of reason'.[4] One year later, in late July 1792, just before the fall of the constitutional monarchy, Robespierre took up the link between 'terror' and bad government, assimilating 'terror' with despotism: 'Montesquieu said that virtue was the principle of republican government, honour that of a monarchy, and terror that of despotism. We need to imagine a new principle for the new framework of things that we are in.'[5] Montesquieu was again a source for Robespierre in early 1794 when he attempted to bring together 'terror' and 'virtue' in his speech on 5 February 1794 (17 Pluviôse Year II). Without virtue, terror was disastrous, but virtue was powerless without 'terror'.[6] The despotism of liberty, to take up the bold oxymoron coined by Robespierre, the union between 'terror' and 'virtue', between 'terror' and justice, would be linked to a state of exceptional or crisis government that was by essence transitional – the condition of France in 1793 and in the Year II – and not to a preconceived political project as the ultimate goal in itself. For Robespierre, 'terror' was closely linked to justice – a harsh and improvised justice for a time of crisis, but still justice. After the fall of Robespierre, the meaning of 'terror' would quickly evolve into something rather different, when the victorious Thermidorians started to retrospectively invent the idea of a unified 'system' of terror.

1. How the 'system of terror' and the black legend of Robespierre were retrospectively invented

On the morning of 9 Thermidor Year II (27 July 1794), Louis-Antoine Saint-Just, member of the Committee of Public Safety (the most important of the Committees of the National Convention), rose to make a speech in the Convention in which he intended to support his colleague and friend on the Committee, Maximilien Robespierre. As Saint-Just began to speak, he was interrupted by a fellow Montagnard, Jean-Lambert Tallien, who pushed his way to the rostrum, supported by a concerted group of revolutionaries, many of them also Montagnards, to denounce Robespierre. Tumult ensued. Over several hours accusations spiralled, culminating with the arrest of five deputies: Robespierre, his younger brother, Augustin, Saint-Just, Georges Couthon (also on the Committee of Public Safety), and Philippe Le Bas, of the Committee of General Security. Both Augustin Robespierre and Le Bas had actually asked to be arrested, rather than become party to arresting the others. By nightfall of the following day, 10 Thermidor, all five were dead. This moment, the Thermidorian moment, marked the onset of a sea-change in revolutionary politics, whereby the immediate past would be rewritten and reinvented, in order to blacken the reputations of Robespierre, Saint-Just and their adherents as having been personally responsible for creating a 'system of terror', whilst exculpating many surviving revolutionaries, who had been equally involved in revolutionary government and the recourse to 'terror' policies, but who had chosen the winning side in the conflict of Thermidor.

Bertrand Barère, who had been a close colleague of Robespierre and Saint-Just on the Committee of Public Safety, took an early lead in the frantic rush to distance himself from the fallen deputies. In his speech on 14 Thermidor, Barère separated 'terror' from 'justice', two terms that Robespierre had often tied together. Arguing that 'terror was always the arm of despotism [whereas] justice was the weapon of liberty', he urged the Convention to 'substitute inflexible justice for terror'.[7] Barère knew very well – none better – how the repressive legislation against the opponents of the Revolution, real or imagined, had been conceived and implemented, for he had been at the heart of it. Now, in a remarkable political volte-face, Barère removed any responsibility from the Convention, in particular from members of the Committees of Public Safety and General Security (the Committee of General Security had responsibility for policing, security and prisons). Barère denounced the 'usurpation of national authority' that Robespierre and his followers had committed when they had imposed decrees in response to 'circumstances forced and prepared by themselves'.[8]

Less than three weeks later, on 2 Fructidor (9 August), an exchange between three other Montagnard deputies illustrated the divide within the Convention. Louchet, the Montagnard deputy who had been the first to demand the vote authorizing the arrest order against Robespierre on 9 Thermidor, now took to the floor to defend policies of terror. He underlined the seriousness of the dangers threatening the Republic and the need to combat them, stating that he was 'convinced that there is no other way to do so than to maintain terror as the order of the day everywhere'.[9] With the hall resounding with cries of 'justice, justice!', Louchet clarified his position by associating the two words: 'I understand by the word "terror" the most severe justice'. This position was immediately supported by Charlier: 'Justice for patriots, terror for aristocrats'.[10] A third Montagnard, Tallien, who had led the attack on Robespierre and his fellow Montagnard deputies, Saint-Just, Couthon, Le Bas and Augustin Robespierre on 9 Thermidor, defined 'terror' as a weapon of tyranny, even while supporting the idea that justice must remain severe against 'the enemies of the nation'. According to Tallien: 'Robespierre too constantly repeated that terror needed to be made the order of the day, and while with such language he imprisoned patriots and led them to the scaffold, he protected the rascals that served him'.[11] This was another political sleight-of-hand. In Robespierre's speeches and writings he had always linked the terms 'terror', 'justice' and 'virtue'; whilst the expression *'terreur à l'ordre du jour'* ('terror made the order of the day') was not his doing. Robespierre had mentioned these two words together only four times. In the summer of 1794, he used them to refer not to the repressive measures put in place by the Convention and its committees but to a 'system of terror and slander' targeted towards him, depicting him as a dictator, and attempting to destroy the revolutionary government.[12] It was Tallien, rather than Robespierre, who would develop the political concept of the 'system of terror' just a few days later.

It was on 11 Fructidor (28 August), that Tallien elaborated the concept of a 'system of terror'. While he was not the first to use the term, previously deputies had mentioned it almost in passing, and directing it at different political rivals.[13] In his momentous speech Tallien developed and defined a new theory of a 'system of terror'. In speaking of this system, he coined a new term, one which would haunt our modern world: that of 'terrorism'. He also called it a 'government of terror' and a 'terror agency'. He took great pains to exclude the new – post-Robespierre – revolutionary government of which he was himself a member (he had been rewarded for his part in the fall of Robespierre by a seat on the Committee of Public Safety) from this supposed system. Thus he could better denounce terror as an illegitimate system of the immediate past, whilst safeguarding the legitimacy of the current revolutionary government, which was to serve the Thermidorians' new political agenda. In defining the 'system of terror' he gave a vivid picture of the feelings of fear it engendered: terror took place in the mind's imagination, as well as in reality:

> There are two ways that a government can make itself feared: it can police bad actions, threaten and punish them with proportionate punishment, or it can threaten people, threaten them at all times and for all things, threaten them with whatever the imagination can conceive as most cruel. The impressions that these two methods produce are different: one is a potential fear, the other a ceaseless torment; one is a foreboding of the terror that follows upon a crime, the other terror itself instilled in the soul despite knowing one is innocent; one is the reasonable fear of the laws, the other the stupid fear of persons. The characteristics of terror should be distinguished. Terror is a generalized, habitual trembling, an exterior trembling that affects the most hidden fibres, degrading man and turning him into an animal; it is the disruption of all physical forces, the commotion of all moral faculties, the disruption of all ideas, the upheaval of all emotions . . .
>
> Since terror is an extreme emotion, it is not susceptible of being either more or less. The fear of the laws, on the other hand, can be increased if needed. Which of these two fears supports, consummates, guarantees the revolution? That is what the question boils down to and what I will examine. Let us begin with terror: judge it by the means it is supposed to employ and by the effects it produces. A government can only inspire terror by threatening capital punishments, only by threatening them with it ceaselessly and threatening everyone, only by threatening through acts of violence ever renewed and ever increased; only by threatening all sorts of action, and even inaction; only by threatening with all sorts of proof and even without a shred of proof; only by threatening with the always striking sight of absolute power and limitless cruelty. To make every person tremble, it is necessary not only to link every action with a torment, every word with a threat, every silence with suspicion; it is necessary to place on every step a trap, in every house a spy, in every family a traitor, in the service of a tribunal of assassins. It is necessary, in one word, to know how to torture all citizens by the misfortunes of some, cutting the life of some by shortening the lives of the others; that is the art of spreading terror. But does this art belong to a regular, free, humane government, or is it tyranny? I often hear it asked why the system of terror cannot be limited to

suspect classes while leaving others alone. In response I wish to ask how there can be security for someone where actions are prejudged based on persons, and not persons by their actions. I would like to add that terror must be everywhere or nowhere. The Convention should no longer accept that the republic be divided into two classes, those who create fear and those who live in fear, persecutors and the persecuted. Couthon and Robespierre are no longer here to obstruct the defence of equality and justice. I am also asked if it is possible to strike terror in the hearts of evildoers without troubling good citizens of any class; I answer that it is not, for if the government of the terror pursues some citizens based on presumed intentions, it alarms everyone; and if it only monitors and punishes actions, it is no longer terror that is inspired but another kind of fear that I have already mentioned, the healthy fear of punishment following upon a crime. It is thus right to say that the system of terror presupposes the exercise of an arbitrary power in those charged with spreading it.[14]

Tallien added to the horror by stating that the 'terror' could strike any citizen anywhere in France; that the increasing number of capital punishments came from the very nature of this 'system' that could well fall into excess; that the executions were accompanied by the spectacle of rivers of blood to strike fear even harder into people's minds; that executing different kinds of people together indiscriminately was another means to instil fear; and, finally, that a most cruel refinement was the collective executions of friends or members of the same family sent to the guillotine together.[15] When it came to the guilt of Robespierre and his co-conspirators, there was, for Tallien, no doubt:

> Citizens, everything that you have just heard is but a commentary on what Barère said at this very rostrum on the day that followed Robespierre's death. I would like to add one thing: this was Robespierre's system. He was the one who put it in practice with the aid of several subalterns, some of whom were killed alongside him and others of whom are buried alive in public hatred. The Convention was a victim, never an accomplice.[16]

In the weeks that followed Tallien's speech, another new term would be coined, that of 'terrorist', to define those who had supported the 'system of terror'.

The hunt for Robespierre's surviving 'subalterns' started right away. The next day, 12 Fructidor, the deputy, Lecointre denounced seven former members of the two major committees, among them Billaud-Varenne, Collot d'Herbois, and Barère. The denunciation was timed to follow on from Tallien's speech. While the accusation was rejected as slanderous, it was followed a month later with a second denunciation, made by another deputy, Legendre, against the three former members. Vadier took it up and an investigative committee was created.[17]

Contrary to Tallien's claims, when Barère had denounced Robespierre and his 'co-conspirators' on behalf of the Committee of Public Safety on 11 Thermidor, he had made no mention of a 'system' they had put in place. Rather, Barère's denunciation had followed a standard pattern amongst revolutionary factions, of accusing the four deputies who had been executed the previous day of having usurped public authority to make themselves rulers of France, a triumvirate of tyrants. Such accusations owed much to a common trope in revolutionary politics of accusing opponents of imitating Catiline's conspiracy to overthrow the Roman Republic.[18] According to Barère's hastily-manufactured charges, Robespierre was supposed to 'reign' over Paris and the central part of the Republic, Saint-Just over the North (a fabrication based on his having served as a deputy on mission to the armies on the northern fronts and the Rhine), whilst Couthon and Robespierre's brother, Augustin, would rule over the South.[19] Not one word was said on the fifth deputy who died on 10 Thermidor, Le Bas, who chose to commit suicide rather than have the Convention send him to the guillotine with his friends. Barère's speech contributed to the black legend of Robespierre, the 'new Catiline', stories which started circulating in the summer of 1794, if not earlier.[20] While Barère's speech was fundamentally different from Tallien's in almost every respect, they had one key thing in common: the Convention and its committees (including, of course, themselves) had no responsibility for the 'terror' – it was the fault of other men. Dissenting voices could hardly rise to be heard. Thus Cambon was not heard at all when, in spite of denouncing Robespierre and 'his system of terror', he also pointed out that a number of exceptional institutions had been created by decrees voted in, quasi-unanimously, by the Convention to meet the crisis: 'Take note that we are not in an ordinary time; take note that the Declaration of Rights did not institute surveillance committees, and yet you have unanimously judged them necessary.'[21]

The Convention had given itself an amnesty for its actions in supporting crisis measures enabling terror. It gave itself this absolution by making Robespierre the scapegoat, the so-called sole 'mastermind' behind a 'reign of terror'. As a consequence, over the next two centuries, Robespierre would be remembered as the originator and master of the 'terror', an all-powerful dictator who had stifled all debate by imposing his domination over the Convention and kept adding names to endless interminable lists of undesirables, a tyrant who dreamed of being crowned king by marrying the daughter of Louis XVI so as to be tied in blood to the Bourbon line, a ferocious triumvir who imposed his authority upon Saint-Just and Couthon (Augustin Robespierre, mentioned by Barère, quickly disappeared from the group, not only to refine the formula of a conspiratorial triumvirate inspired by antiquity but also because he was not condemned to death for any reason except his family name, as no crime could be pinned on him). This allowed the Convention to spread the news over the entire national territory and to the armies, presenting Thermidor as the fall of yet another faction that would have usurped the sovereignty of the nation. A flood of letters gushed in to Paris in the summer and autumn of 1794. Written in a language laden with clichés and a limited, stereotyped range of vocabulary, they give an idea of how the news had been circulated to the provinces and how local authorities, popular societies and simple citizens saluted the Convention for its fine deed against 'the infamous Robespierre' or the 'monstrous triumvirate'.[22]

Many pamphlets and brochures came out in the weeks after Thermidor, some waxing on the popular motif of 'Robespierre's *queue*' – literally 'Robespierre's tail' (meaning the remains of his faction, but also a term with a humorous phallic connotation)[23] or the arrival of Robespierre and the Jacobins into hell.[24] Among this mass of writings, the blood spilled in the execution of the 'system of the terror' occupied pride of place, while the sexualized humour offered light relief, attracting readers whilst giving an opportunity to exorcize fear through laughter: thus, 'the revolution's events often give new words to the republican dictionary – and here is one that makes all the women laugh: everyone wants to know his *queue*: Robespierre's *queue*, give me his *queue*, respond to the *queue*, defend your *queue*, cut off the *queue*.'[25]

Mixing the Incorruptible's *queue* with his descent into hell, a supposed letter that Robespierre's ghost sent to his followers from the other side, claims that he explained to the 'tribunal of hell' that he wished to apply a 'policy ... just like yours', sharpening the 'liberticide daggers', robbing fortunes, destroying commerce, spreading famine, protecting brigands, 'immolating so many men in the name of humanity' – in short, 'put terror in power'.[26] As Robespierre's ghost adds that it would have 'taken five mortal years to arrive at [his] goal', the author provides a chronological list of the projects put in place for the 'reign of the terror' between summer 1789 and summer 1794. The political demonstration imparted two ideas to the reader: on the one hand, Robespierre had been moved by an ambition to impose a bloody dictatorship from the beginning of the Revolution; and, secondly, that his execution put an end to 'the reign of the terror', an expression with a long life ahead of it.[27] Tallien's political analysis is confirmed, with the word 'terror' having a widely different meaning in 1794 than it had in 1789, to say nothing of the fact that 'terror as the order of the day' had never been imposed by Robespierre and his supporters.

2. Developing use of the word 'terror' between 1789 and 1794

As we shall see in the following chapter, the term 'terror' was already familiar to the revolutionaries of 1789 from a number of contexts, both political and non-political. In the first period of the Revolution, including up to the crisis point of 1794 when a new political meaning triumphed, these diverse meanings of 'terror' continued to circulate.

In the autumn of 1792, a letter in the newspaper *Le Moniteur* reported how French troops entered Belgium after the victory at Jemappes (6 November): 'Dumouriez is at the gates of Brussels. Terror precedes the republic's victorious armies. The despots and their cowardly servants are on the run.'[28] In the first months of the Vendée uprising in 1793 (on the Vendée, see chapter 7), 'terror' was often used in its military, not political, meaning, as in a terror inflicted by soldiers, as two news items in *Le Moniteur* on 2 July show. The first, a dispatch from the northern front, related that 'the French victory near Arlon had truly instilled terror in the area, so much so that the boat masters of Trier had received an order to keep their boats nearby in order to transport the warehouses further away.'[29] The second item, a letter from General Westermann, announced that 'the terrible example of Amailloux and the castle of Lescure sowed terror among the lost inhabitants'. Amailloux was a town in which Westermann's troops hunted down the Vendéen rebels, burning down buildings and killing a number of inhabitants while the general proclaimed that any village providing aid or recruits to the rebels would suffer the same fate. That same day, he burnt down the castle of Clisson, residence to Lescure, one of the Vendéen leaders. This recourse to terror did not, in itself, seem to raise any doubt, considering that the convergence of these two events, on different military fronts, one exterior, the other interior, shows that the military meaning of the term was well accepted. On the other hand, the fact that the example Westermann wished to give affected not only the armed rebels but also civilians testifies to the horrors of a

The Terror – *a Concept Imposed by the Thermidorians* 17

local civil war. This military meaning of 'terror', furthermore, never stopped being operative, with numerous examples available from debates in the Convention and published writings in the press. On 16 Messidor Year II (4 July 1794) for example, about three weeks before 9 Thermidor and in the middle of the month with the greatest number of executions by guillotine in Paris, Barère used 'terror' in a military sense, not a political one, even if he was careful to employ the fashionable political rhetoric of the time on the notion of the 'order of the day':

> Terror and flight were the order of the day for the odious hordes. The French troops cannot follow the flight of the imperial eagle, and the lands of Belgium are not so wide, and lack enough strongholds, to protect or hide the flight of the confederates ... Ostend was the barbarous warehouse of the royal coalition, the overflowing granary of the armies, the most complete arsenal of tyrants, and the infernal support of the London court, which will also be taught to know terror, just like its satellites make its deadly experience ... Terror and discouragement reign today among the slaves.[30]

The expression 'panic terror' (*terreur panique*) can be found in a considerable number of letters, speeches and other texts, either to describe the disarray of withdrawing troops or to evoke the fears raised by rumours (founded or not) that circulated throughout the countryside as in the time of the Great Fear in July–August 1789 or at the time of the aborted flight of the king to Varennes in June 1791.[31] Similar 'panic terrors' were assimilated to the effects of counter-revolutionary manoeuvres to sow panic and unleash unrest. The fear of running out of bread in Rouen soon appeared to be the result of these conspiracies, an echo of the old belief in the famine conspiracy which made it possible to present a simple, popular explanation rather than a detailed economic analysis of circuits of product and commercialization: 'A *terreur panique* or the manoeuvres of a few malicious people led Rouen into experiencing a fake shortage as in Paris. The doors of bakeries were assaulted for very little reason.'[32] Rumours of troubles near Meaux were similarly explained in a speech by Barère where the word 'terror' is repeated to the point of saturation: he mentions the 'sounds of terror sown in the countryside to frighten the imagination of citizens, causing commotion or trouble'; he urges his audience to 'publish by what exaggerated sounds, by which means of *terreur panique* they infect the countryside, distracting inhabitants from agricultural work, propagating disorder and fear in the cities'; he describes how enemies 'throw fake terrors into our countryside'.[33]

'Terror' can also have a political meaning, though without necessarily relating to a concerted policy of terror. Such use of the word was first linked to the idea of justice and the fact that opponents of the Revolution should fear punishment. Following the September prison massacres of 1792 (for more on the September Massacres, see chapter 7), the minister of the Interior, the Girondin Roland, linked the birth of the Republic with 'the terror of all the traitors' and an alliance of all 'friends of the country'.[34] One heavy symbol of this was the silence of the members of the Commune of Paris, at a time when they were to be targeted by the Girondins, once they had condemned the massacres of September.[35]

Feeling 'terror' while facing justice and the exemplarity of punishment constitute a theme that appeared on a number of occasions, especially during the trial of the ousted king. The trial was conducted by the National Convention itself, with the deputies in their function as 'representatives of the people' to pass judgement on the erstwhile king on behalf of the people. In early December 1792, Robespierre channelled this idea by calling for the creation of a monument to the martyrs of liberty, killed in the assault on the Tuileries palace that resulted in the overthrow of the monarchy on 10 August 1792. This monument was intended to convey a double political meaning: 'nourish in the heart of people the sentiment of their rights and the horror of tyrants, and in the heart of tyrants the salutary terror at the thought of the people's justice.'[36] Other members of the Convention approved of this meaning, as on 16 and 17 January 1793 when every member was given the floor to justify his vote on Louis XVI's fate. The Montagnard Sergent expressed his support for capital punishment in dramatic terms: 'A king's head only falls with a crash, and his torment inspires a healthy terror [*terreur salutaire*].'[37] Does this mean that the origins of *the Terror* lay in the fall of the monarchy and the execution of the king? This was undoubtedly true for the link between 'terror' and 'justice', but it was not the case for 'terror' as a 'system'.

In the early days of the Convention, enmity between the two factions of the Convention, Girondins and Montagnards, went deep, their previous conflicts deepened to a chasm by the trauma of the September Massacres. Each side accused the other of employing 'terror' against them, though they took conflicting views of its meaning. In October 1792, Marat, the last person one would expect in this context, denounced the Girondin Rouyer for having made threats destined to 'keep him away through terror.'[38] Louvet, another Girondin, replied two weeks later in a violent speech against Robespierre, whom he accused of being accompanied everywhere

The Terror – *a Concept Imposed by the Thermidorians* 19

with armed guards and of being, like Marat, the ringleader of a 'dissenting faction, escorted by terror and preceded by the placards of the blood-thirsty man' – the 'faction' being responsible for the September Massacres.[39] Two weeks after this speech, Barère, who sat at the head of the Plain (unaligned deputies in the Convention) before later joining the ranks of the Montagnards, spoke for the first time of a 'system of terror' put in place by those who had ordered the massacres of prisoners and favoured what he called 'anarchy'.[40] Was the case settled when several Girondins denounced the 'terror' fuelled by the Montagnards and the Parisian *sans-culotte* movement? The Girondin Vergniaud used a moving phrase on 10 April 1793, when he stated: 'People have sought to bring about the revolution through terror, I would have liked to bring it about through love', only to return, moments later, to denouncing his political enemies, the Montagnards, once more.[41] It would be a mistake to form any easy conclusions, especially since a number of Montagnards continued to use the word 'terror' against their opponents, like Marat or even Saint-Just.[42] Saint-Just, in his report against the Girondin leaders, attributed policies of terror to them:

> In the provinces it is said that there are slaughters in Paris; in Paris it is said that there are slaughters in the provinces ... This was true in Bordeaux, Marseille, Lyon, the North, and in Corsica, where Paoli spoke out against anarchy. In the midst of these upheavals, the Commission of Twelve was formed to seek out the conspirators, but its members were their supporters. It stripped Hébert of his functions, as the despot had done; it wished to impose terror on the citizens.[43]

The word 'terror' also took pride of place in speeches given upon the assassinations of two representatives of the people: firstly, when Le Peletier de Saint-Fargeau was stabbed by a royalist, enraged by the execution of the king on 21 January 1793,[44] and secondly, that of Marat.[45] It was the assassination of Marat that triggered what historian Jacques Guilhaumou has called a 'return to the terror of the other'.[46] One might say that the situation changed from a 'terror' one suffered under to an active 'terror'.

3. 'Terror as the order of the day': an unsaid, unofficial yet widespread order from the Convention

On 13 July 1793, a young woman from Normandy, Charlotte Corday, bluffed her way into the apartment of the Montagnard and incendiary journalist, Jean-Paul Marat, and stabbed him in his bath with a kitchen knife that she had earlier bought for that purpose. His assassination, along with that of Le Peletier, heightened the sense of fear amongst the deputies, by making evident their own susceptibility to physical attack, a vulnerability made more intense by the ideological conviction that a virtuous politician should be accessible to the public, and not hide away behind guards and palace walls.[47] The assassination of Marat and his very public funeral heightened desire amongst Paris radicals to repress the adversaries of the Revolution. Numerous speeches to that effect were given in the clubs, especially the Cordeliers, and also in the Convention, reinforced by envoys from primary assemblies.[48] Hailing from all over France, these envoys gathered in the capital to lend their massive support to the vote for the new constitution. Some Girondins in hiding in the provinces spread the vision of an Assembly reduced to a sort of 'rump parliament', not unlike the British parliament after the first British civil war.[49] Yet the Montagnards intended to use the presence of these thousands of envoys to project another image of Paris. On 9 August 1793, on the eve of celebrations for the first anniversary of the attack on the Tuileries and the proclamation of a new constitution, Gossuin presented a report on behalf of the commission in charge of gathering the minutes of the validation process for the new constitution. The report showcases the two conflicting representations of the capital by using the word 'terror':

> People's envoys, when you are back in your homes, tell your co-citizens of what is happening in Paris. Have you seen an inhabitant of this great city with a dagger in his hand, meting out vengeful injustice or crying out for anarchy? But this is the picture that was painted to you, just so you would not meet the true Parisians: this amazing city, cradle of liberty, will always be a terror to evildoers.[50]

Two days after the holiday, an orator spoke in the name of the envoys of the primary assemblies to call for a mass citizen uprising and the arrest of counter-revolutionaries. Some members of the Convention, among them the Montagnards, Georges Danton and Robespierre, took up these proposals, seizing on the word 'terror' and linking it to justice. Danton even spoke of a 'terror initiative' from these envoys; his aim was to demand an even more severe justice and above all a mass call to arms – rather than a massive and anarchic arming of the people – as a way to reinforce the Republic's armies:

> The deputies of the primary assemblies have just launched a terror initiative against internal enemies. Let us respond to their wishes. No

amnesty to any traitor. The just man does not pardon the wicked. Let us point to the popular vengeance by the sword of the law against internal conspirators – but let us know how to take advantage of this memorable day. You have been told that the people must rise as one. That is undoubtedly true, but it must be done in an orderly fashion.[51]

Robespierre, for his part, called for a reinforcing of the zeal of the Revolutionary Tribunal so that the guillotine would be able to strike the imaginations of not only opponents of the Revolution but even its partisans:

Let the scoundrels, by falling on the sword of the law, appease the spirits of so many innocent victims! May these great examples destroy sedition through the terror that they will inspire in all enemies of the nation. May patriots, seeing your energy, find their own, so that tyrants be defeated![52]

Once again, the 'terror' one suffered under had been turned into an active 'terror' that one was prepared to inflict on others, but this active 'terror' was combined with an unflinching determination that all popular revenge and violence on the streets would be outlawed in favour of the formal legal apparatus controlled and administered by the Convention. It was also a tactic for the Convention to keep the upper hand at a time when the Paris Commune could have been tempted to use the presence of these envoys from the primary assemblies to reinforce its political role or heighten its demands.[53] Moreover, the two Montagnards, Robespierre and Danton, did not say anything else during the two revolutionary days, 4 and 5 September 1793 – dates long considered by historians to be the key moment for 'terror' being decreed 'the order of the day', though recent studies have shown this to be a myth.[54] When, on 5 September, a delegation of Parisian sections and Jacobins claimed in front of the Convention that it was 'time to frighten all the conspirators', they used the state of exception the Republic found itself in to justify making 'terror' the order of the day: 'So be it! Legislators, make terror the order of the day. Let us be in revolution, because the counter-revolution is hatched everywhere by our enemies.'[55] 'Being in a revolution' is reminiscent of the adjective 'revolutionary' as a synonym for 'extraordinary', a link that was to be theorized in the following weeks. The president of the Convention responded to the delegation by noting that the creation of an *armée révolutionnaire* (a militia composed of *sans-culottes* and charged with ensuring provisions for Paris) had recently been decided by the Assembly. He added that 'courage and justice are at the order of the day', but avoided using the word 'terror', despite popular pressure.⁵⁶ If several of the demands made by the demonstrators of 4 and 5 September ended up being met and decreed into law by the Convention, the Convention nonetheless resisted the pressure of the *sans-culottes* led by the '*exagérés*' (or '*Hébertistes*') and never voted for any decree or law that would make 'terror' into the 'order of the day'. Moreover, in the days that followed, the word 'terror' continued to be used to denounce the fear that counter-revolutionaries were trying to instil in the people, thus as a term for the illicit behaviour of the Revolution's opponents.

The phrase '*la terreur à l'ordre du jour*' (terror enacted as official policy, literally 'made the order of the day') was, for its part, used in a good number of French departments through the intermediary of members of the Convention sent in missions to these departments or to the armies.⁵⁷ The dispatches of these representatives of the people sent on missions, addressed to the Assembly or its committees, contained numerous references to how 'terror' was made the order of the day, a clear sign of how they contributed to spreading the phrase. Dartigoeyte, for example, wrote from Tarbes on 2 October 1793: 'My colleague citizens, terror is the order of the day in the city of Tarbes and in the department of the Hautes-Pyrénées. This is having excellent effects.'⁵⁸ Similarly Laplanche, returning from his mission to the Cher and the Loiret, related his observations to the Convention on 19 September: 'I believed that I had to conduct myself in a revolutionary manner; I made terror the order of the day everywhere.'⁵⁹ Another deputy, Milhaud, on a mission to the army of the Rhine, wrote from Strasbourg on 16 Brumaire Year II (6 November 1793): 'Fellow citizens, on this border, terror is the order of the day.'⁶⁰ Many more examples could be taken from the many dispatches and letters coming from the countryside to Paris or published in newspaper and journal articles.⁶¹ The phrase was most likely used for rhetorical effect and was in no case an application of a decree decided upon by the Assembly. While there was no institutionalization of the 'order of the day', its legitimacy, as Jacques Guilhaumou has noted, was unquestioned, even in the Assembly itself.⁶²

Although no formal decree implementing 'terror' as the order of the day exists, it may still be possible to create a chronological framework to define this period. A major problem, though, is where to set the starting date. Several possibilities include: the summer of 1792, with the creation of the first extraordinary tribunal to judge those who had fought to defend the Tuileries palace, followed by the prison massacres in September 1792 when self-appointed groups entered prisons in Paris to kill people they judged to be enemies of the Revolution; or spring 1793, with the creation of several extraordinary institutions, including the Revolutionary Tribunal, and the passing of the decree of 19 March condemning to death anyone who took up arms against the Revolution; or 17 September 1793 when the decree known as the Law of Suspects was voted in. Or should we set the date much earlier, to July 1789, and the creation by the Constituent Assembly of a new crime of *lèse-nation* (a political crime against the nation)? The difficulty of assigning a fixed date for the start of *the Terror* shows us how nebulous a term it is. Similarly, when setting out the moment when *the Terror* ended, historians have long claimed, in line with the view promoted by the Thermidorians, that this can be pinpointed to the date of the elimination of Robespierre and his partisans.

Yet this interpretation does not hold up. That is, if 'terror' is what was happening before 9 Thermidor, then, by this definition, 'terror' in some form continued after that date. While it is true that the great majority of detainees were let out of prison in the weeks following 9 Thermidor, the use of repressive measures against political opponents did not cease, especially against returning *émigrés* (that is people who had left France out of opposition to the Revolution, but who later returned) who settled in French villages occupied by foreign troops. This was the case in Valenciennes, which fell to the Austrians on 28 July 1793 and was occupied until 15 Fructidor Year II (1 September 1794). A military commission was set up in the weeks after the city was reconquered. In three months this commission ordered the execution of 68 captives, among them 37 priests and 15 nuns, who were condemned as *émigrés* returning to France. The criminal tribunal of Douai was less severe as it judged the fate of 188 detainees, mainly local government employees under the Austrian occupation, and condemned only a single one to death.[63] These figures show continuing harshness against *émigrés* and dissenters.

With Robespierre eliminated, the structures of the revolutionary government served other political goals as the leaders of the Republic intended to strike the two 'extreme' movements of the political spectrum – Jacobins and royalists. The Convention passed successive decrees intended to provide a legal framework for the repression of the former artisans of 'terror', who were now being hunted down. In November 1794 the Convention ordered that the Jacobin Club in Paris be closed down. Suspects were liberated, and the Thermidorian vulgate on the exclusive guilt of Robespierre and his supporters was widely disseminated, as the populace were told that they had been living under *the Terror*, but that this had now ended. Whilst this news was welcomed as a liberation from terror in places where violence and terror had been extensive, in other parts of France people were learning for the first time that they had been living under a 'terror'. While legalized forms of terror were gradually wound down – though not as quickly as the Thermidorian narrative would have it, the Revolutionary Tribunal in Paris, for example, continued to operate and to hand out some death sentences until the end of May 1795 – the settling of scores against Jacobins began in a so-called 'white terror', with up to 30,000 murdered in reprisals.[64]

For these reasons, rather than try to define *the Terror* in chronological terms, it would be largely preferable to understand the phenomenon not only as a succession of particular circumstances or events, but rather as a succession of collective emotions. In this respect, recent work by historians, including Timothy Tackett and Marisa Linton, has highlighted the importance of emotions throughout the revolutionary period.[65] In their different ways they have argued that to better understand the meaning of revolutionary 'terror', it is vital to take into account not just the ideological and tactical basis of terror, but also people's complex emotional reactions to it.

Chapter 2

The Meaning of 'Terror' Before the Revolution

Just when did the 'terror' begin? The answer to this question depends on whom one asks. In the past the French Revolution has been credited by just about every historian and political scientist with the invention of political terror. If we look up the origins of the term in any general study of the history of terror and terrorism, we are likely to come across the phrase 'reign of terror' and to be told that the Jacobins (or sometimes just Robespierre) invented it. According to the traditional line of interpretation, the 'terror' was a new political ethos, forged by the Jacobins into a 'system'. Sometimes such studies will give the 'terror' a specific birthday, most commonly 5 September 1793, the date when Claude Royer called upon the National Convention: 'It's time to terrify all the conspirators. Well, then! Make terror the order of the day'.[1] Certainly, 1793 would see many changes in the revolutionaries' conception and application of terror, changes that we will explore in the course of this book. But the subject of this chapter is rather different. Here we will trace the origins of the 'terror' and ask what people understood by the term 'terror' before the Revolution began. It was not by accident that the abbé Royer and so many of his fellow revolutionaries chose this word to characterize how the revolutionaries should respond to the crises of 1793. If we want to understand the origins of terror, we need to avoid the temptation to read the past backwards, and impose retrospective teleological meanings. The revolutionaries of 1793 had no idea that they would one day, long after their deaths, be credited with having been the intellectual founders of twentieth-century forms of state terror, the intellectual forebears of Stalinism. 'Terror' was one of a repertoire of terms with which the French revolutionaries were already familiar. When they chose 'terror', they chose a word that already had a powerful significance for them. In this chapter we shall explore the intellectual and emotional origins of 'terror'.

1. *Terror* and Enlightenment. A problematic connection

Did the Enlightenment somehow cause *the Terror*? This is a controversy that has raged almost since the moment the Revolution began, starting with conservative commentators such as the comte de Maistre and the abbé Barruel, who claimed that the revolutionary 'terror' had its origins in the philosophy of the Enlightenment. Some historians have taken this idea further, implicating the entire philosophy of the Revolution in the 'terror', arguing that *the Terror* was inherent in the ideology of liberty and equality of 1789, and therefore that *the Terror* was born at the outset of the Revolution. The argument that there was an essential link between 'terror' and the 'ideology' of the Revolution was made principally by revisionist historians, led by François Furet, during the years around the Bicentenary of the Revolution. They opposed the argument that the origins of the revolutionary 'terror' can be found in the context of war, and the specific circumstances of 1792 to 1794.[2] For these historians, 'terror' came out of ideology, an ideology whose roots were grounded in the Enlightenment. Thus, for François Furet, terror 'existed since the start of summer 1789', that is, *the Terror* came into being with the onset of the Revolution itself: 'terror' is synonymous with revolution.[3] The works of Rousseau, above all the idea of the 'general will', are central to Furet's conception of the 'terror'. Yet, in the thirty years since the Bicentenary, the influence of Furet's interpretation has waned. The majority of historians now would agree with the judgement of the American historian, Jack Censer who, in a recent study of works on the intellectual origins of the Revolution, contends that Furet 'by reducing the Revolution to *the Terror*, and blaming all of it on Rousseau's political ideology' makes an overly simplistic and reductionist link between one *philosophe*, Rousseau, and the revolutionary 'terror'.[4]

Keith Baker, who with his work on political discourses has influenced an entire generation of scholars, takes a view that is, in some respects, similar to that of Furet. Baker argues that the National Assembly in mid-September 1789 was already 'opting for the language of political will . . . which is to say that, in the long run, it was opting for the Terror'.[5] Baker also shares with Furet the view that the language of political will emanates, above all, from Rousseau and his concept of the 'general will'. Where Baker differs from Furet is in his argument that the discourse of will was one of three parallel and competing discourses of political power in the late Ancien Régime. The other two discourses that Baker identifies are those of justice and of reason. According to Baker, the discourse of reason is grounded in the idea of enlightened reform imposed by state officials, and involves transposing problems of social order into the language of social science. Baker associates his third discourse, that of justice, with the *parlementaires* (magistrates of the *parlements*, the higher law courts) and their supporters, and writers in that tradition, most notably Montesquieu. Baker exculpates both these discourses from any association with the origins of the revolutionary terror, positing no link between the Ancien Régime discourse of justice, and the revolutionary 'terror'.

Baker's approach has stood the test of time, perhaps, better than Furet's more politically polemical writings. But in several ways recent historians have been venturing beyond Baker's conceptual framework. Historians now are less inclined to confine themselves to the study of discourses as an autonomous subject in themselves; instead, they are asking how people in the past actively chose from a repertoire of available political tropes and languages, and how they manipulated and deployed those tropes and languages, both rhetorically and strategically. Such an approach has the effect of putting individual agency back into history.[6] Baker's original identification of three political discourses of power of will, justice and reason has been widened by successive historians to include several other key political discourses from the Ancien Régime that played a part in the revolutionary conceptualization of politics, including discourses of patriotism, virtue, conspiracy – and terror.[7] Lastly, as we shall see, in recent years there has been much more attention to connections between Ancien Régime concepts of justice, and the concept of 'terror'.

The relationship between Enlightenment ideology and revolutionary 'terror' continues to attract the attention of historians. Whilst controversy about the intellectual origins of *the Terror* shows no sign of abating, it has moved in different directions. Recently the focus of several historians has shifted from Rousseau's concept of the 'general will' to the concept of nature. Mary Ashburn Miller researches the connections between the language of violent nature and revolution, arguing that examples of violence in nature (such as volcanic eruptions) translated into the revolutionary imagination as an idea of terror as violent, sublime, natural – and salutary. Dan Edelstein, for his part, argues that the revolutionary terror emerged from the

Ancien Régime concept of natural right (*le droit naturel*), according to which anyone designated as an 'enemy of the human race' could be executed without need of a trial.[8]

The most controversial recent reworking of the relationship between Enlightenment and terror comes from the pen of Jonathan Israel who, in his multi-volume study of the Enlightenment, argues that there was a 'good' Enlightenment (progressive, modernizing, atheist) and a 'bad' Enlightenment (perverted principally by dogmatic Rousseauism) and that revolutionaries can be divided into devotees of the 'good' Enlightenment project (amongst whom he categorizes Mirabeau, Brissot and the Girondins) and devotees of the 'bad' Enlightenment (Robespierre, once again, and the Montagnards, though not Danton or Desmoulins). Israel identifies the principal culprits as: 'Robespierre and Saint-Just, the men who wrecked the Revolution of 1789 to 1793'. Despite Israel's scholarly erudition, one would be hard put to find a historian of the French Revolution who is persuaded either by Israel's conceptual framework or by his uncertain grasp of the complexities of revolutionary politics, and his work has met with highly critical reviews from some of the most respected historians of the Revolution.[9]

Part of the difficulty in fixing a definite link between the Enlightenment and *the Terror* is that the term Enlightenment encompasses so many things.[10] There is the additional problem that the *philosophes* were intellectuals, not political activists, none of whom actually called for terror to be a principle of government. Indeed, the *philosophes* were highly distrustful of the idea of a government that used 'terror' as its principle. As we shall see below, for Montesquieu '*la crainte*' (meaning: fear or terror) was the principle of despotic governments, and subsequent eighteenth-century thinkers, and even the revolutionaries themselves, were inclined to agree with him.

2. The concept of 'terror' in the Ancien Régime

Recently, attention has been turning away from the nebulous relationship between Enlightenment and *the Terror* to the considerably more precise study of what the concept of terror meant before 1789. The French revolutionaries did not invent the concept of terror.[11] It was a term in widespread use long before the Revolution. It originated in the Latin noun, 'terror, terroris' signifying a great fear or dread, whilst the Latin verb 'terrere' meant to frighten, terrorize or inflict terror on others. Terror could be something that one felt. It could also be something that one inflicted on others. Thus the meanings of terror in Ancien Régime France were complex and multivalent. As we shall see, some of those uses were explicitly political.

Terror had a powerful emotional significance, as the form of fear that people experienced in response to some catastrophic event which they were helpless to avert. Féraud's *Dictionnaire* of 1787 to 1788 defined 'terror' in these terms: 'Dread, great fear. "Throw terror among the enemies. Carry, spread terror everywhere."'[12] The chevalier de Jaucourt in the *Encyclopédie* defined 'terror' (*terreur*) as, 'great dread caused by the presence or by the story of some great catastrophe'. The article on 'fear' (*la peur*) in the *Encyclopédie*, also by Jaucourt, states that there are grades of 'dread' (*la crainte*), namely, 'fear, fright and terror' (*peur, frayeur, et terreur*). Of these, 'terror' is the most devastating because 'it breaks our spirit'.[13] The author goes on to illustrate these different degrees of 'dread' (*la crainte*), using episodes from history. Tellingly, his example of 'the terror' (*la terreur*) is political – the panic-stricken terror of the Romans when Julius Caesar crossed the Rubicon with his army.[14]

The work of several historians has addressed the meaning of terror in Ancien Régime France. In 1980 a pioneering article by the American historian George Armstrong Kelly explored the conceptual origins of the word terror, whilst the French historians Annie Jourdan and Jean-Clément Martin have explored what Jourdan terms 'the discourse of terror' before the Revolution. Most recently, the American historian Ronald Schechter has given us a full-scale genealogy of the multiple meanings and deployment of the term before the Revolution.[15] Between them, these historians have done much to reshape and deepen our understanding of what people before and during the Revolution understood by terror, and the following section will draw on their work.

Schechter begins his book with a paradoxical statement designed to make us rethink what we hitherto believed we knew about the origins of the revolutionary 'terror:' 'The French Revolution gave terror a bad name. This is not a facetious statement. For many centuries prior to the Revolution, the word "terror" had largely positive connotations.'[16] Schechter continues: 'The word was reminiscent of power, legitimacy and glory, and it had something sacred about it.'[17]

The idea that terror can be sacred stems from its close association with the God of the Judeo-Christian tradition. The Bible, especially the Old Testament, had many references to a 'salutary terror' that kept would-be sinners on the true path of being pleasing to God and ensuring their salvation. The God of the Old Testament frequently dispensed terror, through threats, judgements, punishments and salutary violence. He used terror not only against non-believers, as when he caused the Red Sea to overwhelm the Egyptians, but also against his worshippers if they transgressed against his commandments or wavered in their faith. By obeying God's threat of terror, a person could reduce the terror of God's wrath.[18] Schechter notes forty-seven instances of the use of the word 'terror' in the Vulgate version of Saint-Jerome, the most familiar form of the Bible for eighteenth-century French Catholics, whilst the adjective 'terrible' (*terribilis, terribile*) occurs sixty-one times. The sole instance of terror in the New Testament occurred in the context of terror of the Day of Judgement.[19]

Terror of death, of God's judgement, of purgatory and hell, were recurrent themes in some of the powerful and memorable sermons delivered by Louis XIV's most eloquent bishops, including Bossuet, Massillon and Fléchier. Published collections of their sermons continued to be widely read throughout the eighteenth century and reinforced the idea that terror of God's judgement was salutary in its effects. Despite growing scepticism from the *philosophes*, the terror of God's wrath and of hell were still powerful forces for many people in the eighteenth century.[20]

It was not only orthodox Catholics who believed that invoking the terrors of hell could save sinners from their own propensity to sin: Calvinist Protestants, too, were no strangers to the idea of a judgemental God whose implacable decisions inspired salutary terror. The faith of Jansenists could bolster them to challenge the limits of royal authority. The Jansenists (adherents to an austere form of Catholicism) had numerous sympathizers in the *parlements*, and in the judgement of many historians, most prominently Dale Van Kley, Jansenism was a factor in the origins of the Revolution. Yet, when it came to Jansenists' fear of the wrath of God rather than their fear of the wrath of the king, they were every bit as inclined as orthodox Catholics to speak with awe of the salutary terror of God's judgement.[21]

How far were the revolutionaries influenced by these religious dimensions of terror? Many – though by no means all – came to reject the orthodox doctrines of Christianity. Yet almost all had been raised in that faith, whether as Catholics or Protestants. The language and concepts of Christianity were familiar to them, even if they consciously rejected them. As Schechter points out, Claude Royer, priest-turned-revolutionary, curé of Chalons-sur-Sâone and Jacobin, the man who, in September 1793, called upon the National Convention to make 'terror the order of the day', cannot have been immune to the religious resonances and emotional connotations of salutary terror.[22]

Whilst God in heaven used terror to secure the ultimate salvation of sinners, so absolute monarchs on earth, claiming to rule through the divine will of God, used terror to secure the obedience of their subjects. The Bourbon monarchs were meant to embody kingly virtue, in the sense of exercising a paternal authority over their people, to ensure military security, uphold the Catholic faith, ensure justice, and consider the public good.[23] Kingly virtue was not necessarily a moral quality in terms of personal behaviour, for kings, like all Christians, were sinners and might have many lapses in their moral virtue. But kingly virtue was a moral quality in the sense of a king's obligation to make decisions in light of the public good; so that there was an association in the person of the king between virtue and terror.

The impartial administration of justice was seen as an essential quality of a virtuous monarch; an idea that went back as far as sixteenth-century apologists for absolute monarchy.[24] The jurist Jean Bodin described: 'The true marks of a great king'. Such a king would rule in accordance with 'natural justice', and show the following qualities:

> ... what he will do, if he fears God in all things, if he shows pity to the afflicted, is prudent in business, bold in deeds, modest in prosperity, constant in adversity, firm in his word, wise in his counsel, considerate of his subjects, helpful to friends, terrible to enemies, courteous to the good, terrifying to the wicked, and just to all.[25]

By acting forcefully, but justly, with impartiality, and within the laws which he himself had made, a king mirrored the paternal authority of God and prevented his realm from being subject to the most extreme form of monarchy – despotism.

A primary responsibility of a king was to ensure the safety and security of his realm, through the power of his armies. He was the protector of his people. Terror was one of the means in his power with which to ensure that security. Kingly terror, like Godly terror, was depicted as salutary.[26] A king's armies should spread terror amongst France's enemies, bring about their flight or destruction, and by this means ensure the safety and well-being of the king's own people.

The trope of military terror predated early modern monarchies and even Christianity. Works from classical antiquity made many references to wars and civil wars amongst the ancient Greeks and Romans whose armies inflicted terror and massacres on populations. As Jourdan notes, the threat of an advancing army had psychological effects on a population, spreading 'panic terror' (*terreur panique*).

Thus, the threat itself was immensely powerful.[27] The fear that preceded the advance of an army could be more terrible in its effects than actual military force. The rhetoric of military terror was thus a powerful tool in a state's armoury.

From the sixteenth-century religious wars to the Seven Years' War, there were repeated references to French kings using armies to bring terror upon their enemies.[28] Of all the Bourbon kings, Louis XIV was the one most commonly associated with the word 'terror' both during his lifetime and after his death. It was repeatedly said that he instilled terror in his – and by extension France's – enemies.[29] Military terror was not always confined to external foes: sometimes a king used such terror on his own people. Louis XIV provided a notorious instance of this when he used military force to terrorize France's Protestants, by inflicting on them the 'dragonnades', whereby unruly troops were billeted on Protestant households to subdue them. Louis's policy of terror against the Protestants culminated in the war of the Camisards. The events of that traumatic conflict have been compared to the civil war in the Vendée at the time of the Revolution.[30] In Louis XIV's later years, social disruption, famine, war, and the slow decline of the king himself, all served to undermine the notion that kings necessarily uphold the public good.

Louis XIV's successors were supposed to follow his example in ruling with salutary terror. The coronation ceremony of Louis XVI included in its rituals the sword of Charlemagne with its symbolic connotations. The written form of the ceremonial (made available in French as well as Latin) made pious references to the expectation that Louis would continue in the tradition of his predecessors and wield the sword – metaphorically at least – to bring terror to his enemies and to infidels.[31]

As well as being responsible for military terror, kings were meant to have recourse to terror in their dispensation of justice. There was an expectation that kings would use terror to render justice. Justice under the Bourbon monarchs involved harsh penalties, particularly for the poor. Thus, from 1706 onwards, people convicted of smuggling salt could be subject to execution within twenty-four hours without the possibility of appeal; a practice which prefigured those put in place during the Revolution.[32]

Public execution was a highly visible instance of the terror wielded by the sovereign against malefactors. Such executions, often carried out in agonisingly protracted forms such as 'breaking on the wheel', were used to instil terror into both criminals and onlookers. The execution of the would-be regicide, Damiens in 1757, after his attack on Louis XV, followed a prescribed and ritualized form of state retribution enacted on his body. Contemporary accounts referred to Damiens' crime of attempted regicide as meriting the use of 'terror' to deter others from making similar attempts.[33] Damiens was subjected to multiple forms of torture over four hours, including the application of red-hot pincers and molten lead, culminating in him being drawn and quartered. Damiens' punishment was an extreme case, yet throughout the Ancien Régime, the rituals of capital punishment were designed to make a theatrical and terrifying spectacle.

Not all commentators agreed with the argument that punishments for crimes needed to be 'terrible'. Many of the *philosophes* followed the lead of Beccaria, campaigning on both humanitarian and utilitarian grounds against punishments inflicted on the body, including capital punishment. Rousseau, too, despite claiming that criminals who violated the social contract should be executed in order to protect society, stated that such executions should not have the purpose of causing a spectacle of terror.[34] Future revolutionaries would follow the *philosophes* in opposing torture.

Yet there was a point of contact between the idea of judicial terror during the Ancien Régime and the revolutionary concept of judicial terror, a connection that was emotional rather than ideological. According to Schechter, judicial terror functioned 'as a language that induced certain feelings rather than a doctrine that dictated specific propositions'. In the context of the very real dangers confronted by the revolutionaries in 1793–4, 'the language of terror, even if tainted by absolutist traditions and attitudes, was bound to be reassuring'.[35]

Terror was not confined to religious, military and legal dimensions. It was also used in medical contexts, where it was believed that recourse to the curative powers attributed to terror could resolve the crisis point of an illness, either by death or by recovery. Thus a salutary terror could promote a return to health.[36] Terror also had aesthetic significance. Terror was a trope of classical theatre from the early seventeenth century onwards. Aesthetic theory built on arguments derived from Aristotle's formulations on tragedy to show how theatrical tragedy had the power to evoke two fundamental human emotions, pity and terror, often through a sudden reversal of fortunes in the protagonists of the drama.[37]

Not all terror came from God or men. Nature, too, had the power to cause overwhelming terror in humanity.[38] The naturalist Buffon described the first men as terrified and helpless in the face of the immense and overwhelming power of nature and the natural convulsions of the earth itself. Natural catastrophes had made the first men all too aware of the fragility of their existence:

The first men who witnessed the convulsive movements of the earth, still recent and very frequent, having only the mountains for asylums against floods, often driven out of these same asylums by the fire of volcanoes, trembling on an earth which shook under their feet, naked in spirit and body, exposed to the insults of all the elements, victims of the fury of ferocious animals, of which they could not avoid becoming the prey; all equally imbued with the common feeling of a fatal terror.[39]

Edmund Burke explored the cathartic power of terror to transfigure the emotions. In *A Philosophical Enquiry into the Origin of Our Ideas of the Sublime and the Beautiful* (1757), Burke analysed the relationship between terror and the sublime.[40] The sensation of terror heightened all emotions, an intensity which could be either positive or negative depending on the situation. Thus, one might feel both terror and an almost ecstatic awe at the power and grandeur of natural phenomena, such as mountains or oceans. Nature in its most majestic and gloomy forms conveyed a sensation of terror which heightened our appreciation of the sublime. Yet there were risks involved: terror, when it came too close and threatened the person experiencing it, could result in overwhelming fear; one might even die of terror. Diderot agreed: 'Everything that astonishes the soul, everything that imprints a feeling of terror leads to the sublime [. . .]. The darkness adds to the terror.'[41] Ironically, Burke himself, in later years became a founding figure of modern politically conservative thought through his *Reflections on the Revolution in France*, in which he warned that the Revolution of 1789 had the potential to lead to anarchy, violence – and terror. In the very different context of 1789, and Burke's fear that revolution in France might cross the Channel to Britain, he saw the dangerous potential of terror, rather than the positive attributes that he had identified many years before.

The idea of terror as sublime would reach its full flowering in the growing vogue for Romantic and Gothic literature, in which frissons of terror could stir pleasurable sensations in the human heart. The revolutionary Jacques-Pierre Brissot wrote of the 'soft emotion' of terror that wild and gloomy nature inspired in him:

I love the terror that a dark forest inspires in me, and these gloomy vaults where one meets only bones and tombs. I love the whistling of the winds that announces a storm, these restless trees, this thunder that bursts or rumbles, and these torrents of rain that roll in great waves. My heart quivers, moved, crumpled, torn; but it is an emotion that seems sweet, because it cannot be torn away. There is for me in this moment a horrible charm, a pleasure that I can sense more readily than I can define it.[42]

He wrote these lines whilst in prison, with his own fate still uncertain, seeking refuge in his memories of the natural world. He recollected, too, with a pleasurable sensation, the emotions of cathartic terror and grief that stylized tragedies on the stage sought to evoke, though he added wryly: 'At least the blood that flows in the theatre doesn't hurt anyone.'[43]

3. The role of terror in political theory

According to the ideology of absolute monarchy, politics was the exclusive affair of the king. The king's right to be the sole arbiter of political policy on behalf of his people derived from his divine authority. Sovereignty was located within the 'sacred' body of the king. The king was the only 'public' person in France, that is, the only person who was supposed to have the public good as his guiding principle.

Ideas drawn from the classical republican tradition provided an important alternative tradition of political thought to that of absolute monarchy. Classical republicanism furnished a distinctive approach to political ideas, along with a characteristic political culture, a political vocabulary, and models of heroic political conduct.[44] Above all, classical republicanism provided a narrative structure by means of which political players could make sense of events.[45] From the classical republican tradition emerged several key concepts that would significantly influence the political thought of the revolutionaries: these concepts included virtue, patriotism, despotism – and political terror.

Livy, Sallust and Tacitus wrote their histories of the Roman republic at a time when it was already a remote memory. They wrote of the 'republic of virtue' as an ideal political moment; a quasi-mythical golden age, when citizens devoted themselves to the public good. At its very inception then, the virtuous republic was a fading dream of a heroic past, to be held up against the diminished present, whether that present was Imperial Rome or France under the Bourbons. The virtuous republic was more than a political system: it was an ideal community, the *patrie*. In the eyes of these Roman historians, the republic was constantly in danger of being undermined by ambitious and unscrupulous men, who sought power for themselves rather than for the public good. The true man of virtue was meant to be prepared to be 'terrible' in the service of the public good, and in defence of the republic. This was the lesson contained in stories of classical heroes such as Lucius Junius Brutus, who carried out the terrible but necessary action of condemning his own sons to death, because they were conspiring with the former kings to overthrow the Roman Republic.[46]

Terror of denunciation could have a positive role, according to traditions derived from the Roman legal system, above all Cicero. The right to denounce a criminal or corrupt official was an important means to defend public liberty, freedom of expression, and the liberty of the press. Only terror of denunciation kept the audacity of corrupt men in check. In his speech in defence of Sextus Roscius (Pro Roscio Amerino), Cicero argued that 'it is useful to the civil body that there are many accusers, so that audacity is contained by fear'.[47] Personal immorality could be a sign of public or political corruption, and therefore could also be subject to the terror of denunciation. Thus Cicero's denunciation of Mark Antony in the 'Second Philippic' focused on his drunkenness and debauchery as well as on his political corruption, arguing that the two were linked.[48]

Montesquieu was the foremost figure in the eighteenth-century French tradition of classical republican thought. His association of virtue with republics, honour with monarchy, and fear with despotisms, combined with his depiction of the republic as a superior form of government, became the framework through which subsequent generations conceptualized the political order.[49] According to Montesquieu, the court was the place for the pursuit of self-interest, wealth, honour and glory. A republic, by contrast, was founded on the virtue of its citizens. In *The Spirit of the Laws*, Montesquieu defined 'political virtue' as the love of the *patrie* and its laws.[50] This love demanded a terrifying level of self-sacrifice:

> Political virtue is a renunciation of oneself, which is always a very painful thing ... one can define this virtue as love of the laws and of the *patrie*. This love requires a continual preference for the public interest above one's own interest.[51]

Montesquieu warned that such virtue was difficult to achieve, and impossible to sustain in the long term. This is why the ancient republics had been subject to decay, and that was why modern republics, too, would founder.

In his earlier work, *Considérations sur les causes de la grandeur des Romains et de leur décadence* (1734), Montesquieu explored the problem of the fragility of political virtue in a historical context. He saw the decline of virtue as a key factor in the fall of the Roman republic. The men of antiquity were possessed of superhuman virtue; superior to that of any people that now walked the earth.[52] But such virtue came at a cost. A man who held public office who wished to be truly virtuous was obliged to make a choice. His duty was to put the public good before everything else. Ultimately this might mean that a man should be prepared to sacrifice his own life for the public good, or even the lives of those who were personally dear to him – his family or friends. This was the dual nature of political virtue: both 'divine' – and 'terrible'. Montesquieu gave an example of this terrible aspect of political virtue when he described the motives that drove Marcus Brutus to assassinate Julius Caesar, his friend and reputed father, to prevent Caesar succeeding in his ambition to become a dictator:

> It was an overriding love for the *patrie* which, passing the bounds of ordinary rules about crimes and virtues, followed only its own voice, and made no distinctions between citizens, friends, benefactors or fathers: virtue seemed to forget itself in order to surpass itself; and an action that one could not at first sight approve of, because it seemed so terrible, virtue made one admire as divine.[53]

Thus there was a potential link between virtue and terror in the lessons of antiquity. If circumstances arose in which a crisis threatened the existence of the *patrie*, then the needs of the *patrie* overrode every other moral consideration. The need to preserve the *patrie* was above ordinary laws; it even took precedence over the personal ties that bind individuals to one another. In Cicero's words: *Salus populi suprema lex esto*.

Antiquity did not just serve to provide abstract political ideas to future revolutionaries: it fed their emotional attachment to the *patrie*. And it inspired the ways in which they imagined revolution. Most of the revolutionary generation learned about antiquity through their secondary education at the collèges, where much of the instruction was in Latin, and the favoured authors included Plutarch, Cicero, Livy and Tacitus.[54] Heroes out of Plutarch's *Lives* or the re-imagined antiquity of Fénelon's *Télémaque*, gave future revolutionaries models they could use in order to envisage how they too might act in such circumstances; how they could see themselves differently; how they could fashion their own identities as men and women of virtue. In the last years of the Ancien Régime the growing vogue for visual images of classical heroes heroically sacrificing themselves for the *patrie* helped to fire the imaginations of the revolutionary generation.[55]

There was a direct link between the terrible nature of virtue as seen by the Romans, and channelled through Montesquieu, and the ways in which the revolutionaries portrayed their commitment to virtue as a terrible, but necessary, quality for 'the public good' (*le salut public*). At the height of the Revolution, Saint-Just, in his speech denouncing the Dantonists, invoked the same form of terrible virtue as his justification:

> There is something terrible in the sacred love of the *patrie*; it is so exclusive that it destroys everything without pity, without fear, without human respect, in the public interest; it precipitates Manlius; it drags Regulus to Carthage, throws a Roman into an abyss, and puts Marat in the Pantheon, a victim of his devotion.[56]

Although the word Montesquieu used for despotisms was 'dread' or 'fear' (*la crainte*), rather than 'terror' (*la terreur*), it is evident that in his mind the two words were more or less interchangeable in this political context. He himself occasionally used 'terror' (*la terreur*) in place of 'fear' (*la crainte*): 'The severity of punishments is better suited to despotic government, whose principle is terror (*la terreur*), than to monarchy and republic, whose springs are honour and virtue.'[57] The harem at the centre of Montesquieu's earlier book, *Persian Letters*, served as a microcosm of despotic government. At the climax to this book, when the Persian Usbek instructs his eunuchs to retake control of the harem, following a revolt by the women enslaved there, it is 'terror' (*la terreur*) along with 'fear' (*la crainte*) that he unleashes: 'Receive by this letter unbounded power over the entire seraglio: command with as much authority as I do. May fear and terror walk with you ... may all suffer your dreadful tribunal.'[58]

In common with most of his contemporaries, Robespierre adopted Montesquieu's political categories. In Robespierre's *Discours sur les peines infamantes* (1785), in which he spoke against the legal distinctions and culture of shame under which illegitimate children laboured in the Ancien Régime, he mirrored Montesquieu in stating that virtue was the principle of republics. He would continue to use Montesquieu's categories during the Revolution.[59] Montesquieu wrote at a time when democracies and republics appeared for the most part to be in the past. Although he spoke of the republic of virtue as the highest form of political government, and he used the language of virtue as a means to judge current political practice, his principal concern was much more immediate and pragmatic – to guard against the French monarchy becoming excessively despotic. As a *parlementaire*, he constituted himself a defender of the rights and traditions of the noble *parlements* against the encroachments of monarchy.

In the absence of any more representative form of government, the *parlements* were the most powerful focus for opposition to the theory and practice of absolute government. At various points during the eighteenth century, there were struggles between successive kings and the *parlements*, especially the most important of those courts, the Paris *parlement*, most of which centred around one of two issues – the right of the monarchy to extend taxation, and the right of the monarchy to take punitive action against Jansenists. The *parlements* couched their protests against autocratic actions of the monarchy in the form of remonstrances. In the course of these struggles, the *parlementaires* increasingly presented themselves as mounting a defence of the nation against the despotic monarchy. In the eyes of the *parlements*, monarchical terror was far from salutary; rather, it was a form of arbitrary rule.

From the 1750s onwards, *parlementaire* remonstrances, whilst still supposedly a confidential matter between the king and his law courts, were being widely circulated as part of a deliberate attempt to enlist the support of public opinion.[60] The remonstrances helped to provide a political education for people previously excluded from such knowledge, and the political language employed by the *parlementaires* helped to shape the terms of reference within which the nature of politics was conceived.

The most important struggle between king and *parlements* (prior to the final crisis that culminated in revolution) began in 1770, when Louis XV embarked on a series of moves against the *parlements*. The struggle culminated in the disgrace and exile of the Paris *parlement* in January 1771, and the setting up by the chancellor Maupeou in the following month of a new *parlement* (the so-called Maupeou coup); followed by the purging and reform of those provincial *parlements* that protested too vigorously. These changes were accompanied by a storm of protests, from the *parlementaires* themselves, from the lawyers attached to the *parlements*, and from many observers of events who, partly as a result of the effectiveness of pro-*parlementaire* or 'patriot' propaganda, saw the coup not simply as a power struggle between king and *parlements* but as confirmation that the government was despotic, exercising arbitrary power to interfere with the constitutional functions of the *parlements*.[61] The *parlements* and their supporters referred repeatedly to the actions of the agents of absolute monarchy in terms of an unjust recourse to terror. One of the most liberal-minded defenders of the magistrates, and the most outspoken in his denunciation of 'terror' tactics was Malesherbes, *premier président* of the Cour des Aides. In 1770, in remonstrances on behalf of the Cour des Aides over the activities of the farmers-general (who, under lucrative contracts, collected taxes on behalf of the king), he went so far as to accuse the agents of monarchical power of ruling through: 'All this apparatus of terror.'[62]

The terror tactic available to the monarchy that the *parlementaires* feared and resented most was that of public disgrace. Disgrace for a noble was closely bound up with the system of honour characterized by Montesquieu. For a nobleman, disgrace was the ultimate dishonour; in many ways it was experienced as analogous to death: a form of living death.[63] The Bourbon monarchy used disgrace and the threat of disgrace as a way of controlling nobles, above all royal ministers, courtiers, and *parlementaires*. For high-ranking nobles, the issuing of a *lettre de cachet* (an order from the king authorizing arrest and imprisonment without trial) could presage a fall from power, dishonour, sometimes imprisonment, or banishment to the 'living-death' of life on their estates, or, if the king willed it so, to somewhere still more remote and isolated.[64] For such men, before the Revolution, terror meant a *lettre de cachet*.

In reality, the instincts of the noble magistrates were profoundly conservative. The great majority fought for their corporate status, and in defence of their privileges rather than for the good of the nation. Yet the language that some of them were prepared to employ, in protesting against despotic government and rule through terror, was taken up by lawyers and the circles around the *parlements*, and spread beyond them to sections of the reading public. The crisis of the *parlements* opened up a forum where it started to become possible to talk openly of politics. In the course of this crisis, many observers would learn to associate monarchical terror with despotism, a language that would be increasingly deployed in the last crisis of the Ancien Régime.

Terror had multiple meanings before the Revolution. Whilst a few of these meanings had negative connotations – such as the terror wielded by despotic monarchies – the majority of the meanings were positive. In many cases terror had salutary, cathartic and transformative connotations. All meanings of terror were, in one form or another, about power or its lack. Wielding terror could make you feel powerful; whilst terror that you yourself suffered made you feel afraid and powerless. One of the principal rhetorical purposes of employing the language of terror was to intimidate an enemy, and to make one's own people feel stronger and safer as a consequence. By furthering our understanding of the multiple meanings of terror before the Revolution, we are better placed to explain what the revolutionaries meant by the term, and why they chose it. We are also better able to comprehend the emotional significance of the term terror for the revolutionaries.

So, how did using the language of terror make revolutionaries of the Year II feel when they spoke or wrote it? This is a question that

Schechter asks, and his conclusion is that we need to understand the genealogy of terror in terms of the emotions that the word evoked on the part of the person saying or writing it. He claims that for the revolutionaries: 'Using the language of terror made them feel powerful and safe. It functioned as a kind of therapy by which revolutionaries tried to overcome their own feelings of terror.'[65] Paradoxically then, to speak of terror or threaten it, could be a way to ward off (one's own) terror. These conclusions bear out recent work by historians which has been showing that the men who had recourse to terror were drawn to it, not only for ideological and tactical reasons, but also for emotional ones. As we shall see in the following chapter, this emotional dimension demands to be explored further if we want to understand the logic of revolutionary 'terror'.

Chapter 3

Terror in the Heart: The Weight of Fears and Emotions

Revolutions are profoundly emotional events, both for the people who take part, and for those who oppose them. Historians have long acknowledged the emotional dimensions of many spontaneous actions of the revolutionary crowds, such as the momentous moment in October 1789 when working women of Paris gathered to march on Versailles to confront the king for standing by whilst their families went hungry; or when peasants mobilized by rumours in what became known as the 'great fear' turned against the seigneurs who for centuries had dominated the countryside.[1] Yet it is only in recent years that historians have begun to acknowledge the extent to which the Revolution's leaders, most of whom, unlike the urban or rural poor, were well educated and professional, were also subject to strong emotions.[2] This discovery should not surprise us. Anyone who has seen the sudden political destabilization of America and much of Europe in recent years can readily appreciate that emotions count for a great deal in politics, not only on the streets but also in the corridors of power. Why would the emotional experience of the first French Revolution have been any less intense? This does not mean that the revolutionaries themselves were captives of their emotions to the exclusion of their reason or their ideological commitment. On the contrary, we need to acknowledge the interconnectedness of reason and emotion, to appreciate that both these forces act in concert within us, to grasp that: 'Brains can feel, and hearts can think.'[3]

'Terror', too, had an emotional dynamic as well as an intellectual one: it took place in the hearts and guts of those who participated in it, as well as in their heads. As Tackett states in the French edition of *The Coming of the Terror in the French Revolution* (French title: *Anatomie de la Terreur*), we need a major rethinking of the factors that gave rise to terror:

> ... any interpretation of the Revolution and the Terror must take into account the influence of emotions on the psychology and behaviour of revolutionaries ... Revolutionaries were not gods, but men and women struggling to create a new political and social world in the midst of a series of events that they never anticipated and that were often very destabilizing.[4]

To make sense of revolutionaries' emotions we need to situate them in the context of a political situation that was precarious and constantly shifting. Revolutionary leaders, like anyone else, could be caught up in the tide of emotions that frequently engulfed the Revolution, a tide that ebbed and flowed, but at its height could be hard to resist. We need to be wary, however, (a point that Tackett also makes) of reducing revolutionaries to their emotions, as though they were not also reasoning beings, committed to strategic policies and ideological goals. Nor can we understand the emotions of revolutionary activists in a vacuum, in isolation from other factors – ideologies, political culture, networks and the onward drive of events. To see revolutionary activists in terms only of their emotional responses risks reducing them to passive ciphers, fenced in by their own 'emotional regimes'.[5]

Revolutionary leaders were far from being prisoners of their emotions. Within the limits of the possible, they had agency and room to manoeuvre. And they had the ability to make choices, both strategic and moral. Thus they could 'choose terror', or choose to reject it – though during the vertiginous Year II the consequences of making either choice might be perilous. If Robespierre, for example, had been influenced only by fear, either for himself, or for the Revolution, would he have chosen, at some personal risk, to defend over seventy Girondin supporters, imprisoned but, at his insistence, not brought to trial?

There are many difficulties involved in studying revolutionary emotions, many of which relate either to the shortage of source material, or to the related problem of how to interpret such sources as we have. Whilst participants in the Revolution talked tirelessly in public utterances about their cause, their principles, their goals, their opponents, they were rather less forthcoming about their emotions, or the emotions of others. They were more likely to confide their feelings to more personal documents. Yet even private letters present considerable problems of analysis, their degree of openness depending in large part on the writer's intentions and the degree of trust they had in the intended recipient. Personal source material became scarce at the very time historians want it most – the most highly-charged period of the Revolution, during 1793–4, a time when the most active revolutionaries had little leisure to write letters, notes or memoirs, and were often very cautious about what they committed to paper. Many *conventionnels* left memoirs, and these can be invaluable, but must be approached with caution. For every writer had a retrospective narrative to construct, and many were anxious to exculpate themselves from any charge of involvement in the year of the 'Terror'.

Where source material exists, we have the problem of how to interpret it. Ironically, revolutionaries, too, often wondered how to interpret what letters revealed about genuine emotions – including political loyalties. In a context where using the wrong words in the wrong place could make you 'suspect', did people say what they meant? Did they mean what they said?[6] At a time when words could be dangerous, emotions could also be signified by other means, by gestures, facial expressions, or a range of actions, though for historians to reconstruct them, these need to have been recorded by words. Tears were a feature of revolutionary politics: tears of joy, as well as tears of grief, or anger. Laughter was often heard in the Assemblies. According to the *Archives parlementaires*, the deputies of the Convention, even in the crisis months of the 'Terror', laughed often, in fact more than their predecessors in the earlier Assemblies. Laughter had multiple meanings. It could provide relief at times of crisis. It could send a message of defiance towards one's enemies, both external and internal. Laughter could also be a weapon, to mock a political opponent.[7] When revolutionary participants spoke openly about emotions, in the Assemblies, in the clubs, in newspapers, in pamphlets, in open letters to their constituents, how do we know whether they were acting out a trope, a classical reference perhaps, or an episode from a novel, rather than giving voice to their own authentic emotions? Members of the revolutionary generation were familiar with the cult of sensibility, conveyed in novels by writers such Bernardin de Saint-Pierre and Rousseau, and in the work of artists such as Greuze and his fellows; and had become accustomed to express their own emotions in these terms. Some of the writings where revolutionaries dwelt on their own sensibility may come under that category. How can we know the emotions were authentic? We cannot, of course. We can never be sure. Yet the question of how people felt and how their emotions affected their choices and actions are important ones to ask, even if the answers can never be definitive.

The Revolution engendered a plethora of emotions, often changing in quick succession. There were positive emotions: joy, love of the *patrie*, love of virtue, love of *bienfaisance* (desire to help others), enthusiasm, sensibility, loyalty and patriotic fervour. There were also more negative ones: suspicion, enmity, hate and fear. A key emotion was one the revolutionaries sometimes termed 'revolutionary exaltation' or sometimes 'revolutionary enthusiasm'. This emotion was considered essential to the success of the Revolution. This was the dynamic intensity of feeling that gave people the energy to keep working to create the Revolution, and to defend it. Revolutionary activists often seem to have had a heightened intensity of experience; they felt at the centre of events, that they were changing things for the better. There were moments when they felt very alive; and the sensation was exhilarating. Perhaps we would call it more prosaically an adrenalin rush, but it was about far more than the sensations of the individual. The real emotional power of the Revolution came from the sense of interconnectedness it gave its adherents with one another, a sense of fusion, of 'fraternity'. There was no feeling like it. But for the most committed revolutionaries, those who devoted large parts of their lives to the revolutionary cause over the long term, such emotions were hard, if not impossible, to sustain indefinitely. Had the political situation stabilized such passions would have subsided naturally, but as the Revolution spiralled into a succession of political and military crises, the pressure on participants remained intense. Under the pressure of those crises, more negative emotions came to the fore. Behind exaltation, dizzying optimism and the emotional community of the *patrie*, came fear.

1. The spectre of conspiracy and treason

Belief in the existence of conspiracies was prevalent throughout the Revolution. It could be found at every stage and amongst every group. Revolutionaries and counter-revolutionaries believed in conspiracies.[8] Fear of conspiracy was not unique to the Jacobins, nor was it characteristic of a particularly Jacobin ideology or paranoia. In different circumstances all kinds of people can believe in conspiracies. Such beliefs were as prevalent in the early modern world, as they are in contemporary society.[9] Political conspiracy beliefs ebb and flow, but are particularly powerful when joined with fear and political fragility, and in a context where people struggle to explain or understand forces at work in politics.[10]

Conspiracy fears were not, then, unique to the revolutionaries, but they took the specific forms that they did in large part because the revolutionaries were reacting against the system of politics that had preceded them, and which they had consciously rejected. Under the Ancien Régime a vague, contradictory set of governing laws had allegedly allowed corrupt ministers, mistresses and factions to exploit state power 'behind closed doors' for their own selfish ends. The Revolution was intended to regenerate the nation by means of a new politics founded upon liberty, equality, virtue and patriotism. In place of the institutionalized corruption and venality of the discredited Ancien Régime, the revolutionaries sought to fashion a transparent system wherein citizens could voice their opinions by means of an elected legislature, political clubs and a free press. The revolutionaries enacted a new constitution with an explicit delineation of public powers and private rights to ensure that state officials – subject to the scrutiny of public opinion – ran the government exclusively for the common good.

Yet this bold experiment in transparent government was attended from its start by preoccupations with conspiracy. The idea that political stability could be undermined by a conspiracy of ambitious malcontents was familiar before the Revolution. In the enclosed world of the Ancien Régime court, any opposition to the will of the king could be defined as illicit, and therefore conspiratorial. The court was characterized by faction, patronage and intrigue; a culture that provided fertile grounds for belief in conspiratorial activity, with every faction a 'cabal', plotting to empower and enrich itself. Allied to this was popular belief in the 'famine plot', the idea that greedy speculators and hoarders, in concert with officials at the court, were trying to starve the people by hoarding grain to drive up prices.[11]

The education that the revolutionary generation received, with its emphasis on the lessons of classical antiquity based on close reading of such works as Cicero's *Philippics* and Sallust's *The Conspiracy of Catiline*, encouraged the belief that political stability, particularly under republics, was constantly under threat from a series of conspiracies by groups of power-hungry and unscrupulous deceivers. The classical authors saw public denunciation as a public duty and a sign of virtue. Cicero's polemics served as a model of this kind of patriotic denunciation.[12]

It was within this climate of received ideas about political conspiracies that the revolutionaries came to political consciousness. Fear of conspiracy waxed and waned according to circumstances and the sense of crisis they engendered. The events of 1787–9, when for several months the fate of the Revolution stood on a knife-edge, as leading nobles including the king's brother, the comte d'Artois, did their best to block political change, before becoming *émigrés* and avowed enemies of the Revolution, fed the conviction that the Revolution was in grave peril from counter-revolutionaries. As the situation within France stabilized, fear of conspiracy diminished, only to re-emerge in June 1791 when the king himself took flight, and was intercepted at Varennes. Thereafter the revolutionaries had significant reason to see the court as the enemy within.

During the Legislative Assembly, talk of conspiracy escalated as Jacques-Pierre Brissot and his allies, who dominated the new Assembly, played on mingled emotions of fear and patriotism to stir up popular support for war. They seized on pre-existing accounts of a so-called 'Austrian Committee', making this a central part of their case for declaring war against Austria.[13] The Austrian Committee was said to consist of a shadowy group of malevolent counter-revolutionaries, whose patroness was the queen herself. Marie-Antoinette was seen, with some justification, as the proverbial enemy within, her loyalties to her Austrian family dynasty, rather than to France and the Revolution. Amidst the swirling rhetoric of war and patriotism, a new kind of revolution was born, one where the enemy was now the monarchy itself. On 14 January 1792, the Girondin Gensonné declared, to a wildly enthusiastic audience, that anyone who sought a reconciliation with Austria by means of a concert was a 'traitor to the *patrie* and guilty of the crime of *lèse-nation*', that is treason against the nation.[14] In a further move it was decided that such a crime warranted the death penalty. His words met with emotional scenes as deputies, ministers, ushers, spectators (including the women) alike all swore an oath to maintain the constitution.

The declaration of war on Austria in April 1792 escalated into a war with the major powers of western Europe, shortly followed by the overthrow of the monarchy. The birth of the new Republic was accompanied by fear that forces were amassing both outside and inside France to destroy it. March to April 1793 were critical months for the Revolution.[15] A mass uprising began in the Vendée, sparked by resistance to the levy of 300,000 men, and quickly escalated to become an all-out civil war. A succession of military defeats put French forces back on the defensive. Dumouriez, then France's leading general, took the treasonous step of attempting to lead the army with which he had been entrusted against the Convention. When that failed he fled, like so many army officers from the old elite, to become an *émigré*. Dumouriez's betrayal became a major factor in the fall of the Girondins who were accused of having been in collusion with him.

Actual betrayals fed the fear that conspiracies were not confined to foreign agents, that some Frenchmen and women could not be trusted, and were trying to overturn the Revolution from within. Revolutionaries came to fear 'the enemy within' as much as, possibly more than, external enemies. As the Montagnard Billaud-Varenne expressed it: 'The most dangerous assassin is the one who lives in the house.'[16] This raised the problem of how you identified enemies when they shared your national identity and culture, spoke your own language and hid their true intentions.

Were there real conspiracies against the Convention? Undoubtedly yes. The revolutionary leaders had many enemies amongst the foreign powers, *émigrés* and their sympathizers within France. Did the revolutionaries correctly identify the people they accused of being conspirators? Often they did not. It can be hard even for historians today, with access to all the available documentation, including private papers of the accused, and secret negotiations between foreign powers arrayed against France in the Year II, to distinguish between genuine and imagined conspiracies.

The powerful narrative of conspiracy served as a way of imposing meaning upon events. The revolutionaries also 'talked up' conspiracies, purporting to find connections between different groups for which there was little or no objective evidence. There were many instances, too, where the rhetoric of conspiracy was used cynically in order to destroy political enemies. Yet conspiracy also had a powerful emotional impact; there was a genuine fear of conspiracy, even when that fear was often misplaced. We should not underestimate the extent to which the rhetoric of conspiracy expressed a very genuine degree of anxiety, even though those fears were often directed against the wrong targets. Much of Jacobin politics needs to be understood in relation to fears of conspiracy, both real and imagined.

The conspiracy theory that had the most devastating effect on the revolutionaries themselves was the so-called 'Foreign Plot'. This was a kind of uber-conspiracy theory, whereby different groups of revolutionaries, including members of the Cordeliers Club and the Jacobin Club, and deputies in the Convention, were said to be in league with one another as well as with the foreign powers to bring down the Republic.[17]

The foreign wars led to a reversal of the earlier policy of openness towards foreigners who supported the Revolution. These men included the Prussian deputy, and devotee of the universal republic,

Anacharsis Clootz. He and other foreigners in Paris who were close to the populist militant group, the Hébertists, came under suspicion as possible spies for their countries of origin. Several would be denounced as conspiracy suspects, mostly with little justification. To these foreigners were added a number of French revolutionaries who were said to be in the pay of the foreign powers. The factional struggle culminated in the destruction of first the Hébertists, then the Dantonists,[18] in spring 1794, both factions condemned as part of the Foreign Plot. Historians have tried to discover whether there was any substance to the allegations regarding the Foreign Plot. This is a question that is unlikely ever to have a definitive answer. It is clear that some adherents of the Cordeliers and Jacobin Clubs were financially corrupt and had accepted bribes and used their positions to enrich themselves. It is quite possible that a few, at least, had gone further and had knowingly accepted money from foreign agents, but there is little evidence to support the claim that revolutionaries from very different groups, who were themselves bitter opponents, were secretly in league both with one another and with the British and Austrians to overthrow the Republic.[19] Yet the politics around the Foreign Plot were about much more than simple paranoia. Nor were they simply a cynical way of disposing of political rivals, though certainly there was a new degree of ruthlessness in early 1794 about the revolutionary leaders' resort to terror as a means of eliminating real or perceived enemies. Whatever the truth of the Foreign Plot, it seems clear that many leading revolutionaries felt under threat and gave some credence to the allegations. Uncertainty over the identity of the enemy within was perhaps the most difficult thing of all. The traumatic events of the Year II and the way in which the revolutionary leaders destroyed one another cannot be understood without an appreciation that their fear of conspiracy was genuine, all-encompassing and had some basis in reality.[20]

2. The flow of emotions and fears

The revolutionaries themselves were well aware of the effect of uncontrolled emotions in revolutionary politics. Often these were termed 'the passions' and interpreted in a negative light, as feelings that overrode reason. While male political activists were often reluctant to admit how much they themselves were influenced by their feelings, some of their female relatives – at least those who took an active interest in revolutionary politics – were more open about the extent to which the Revolution was an activity that was felt as well as thought. Their enforced position on the sidelines did not hinder, and possibly aided, their understanding of the dynamics involved. Madame Roland, wife of the Girondin minister, and a leading figure behind the scenes of the Girondin group, and Madame Jullien, closely linked to the Montagnard group, despite being in different political camps in 1792–3, had some markedly similar views on emotions. Both saw 'the passions' as intrinsic to the experience of revolution, and both acknowledged how dangerous those untrammelled emotions could be. For Madame Roland:

> It is very difficult to make a revolution without becoming passionate about it; no one has ever made a revolution without that emotion; there are great obstacles to overcome: you can only achieve it by means of a sort of frenzy, a devotion which comes from exaltation or which produces it. But then you avidly seize on anything which can help your cause, and you lose the ability to foresee whether these things could be harmful.[21]

Madame Jullien took the view that the strong passions stirred up by the Revolution could make for a toxic environment. She feared for her teenage son, Marc-Antoine, already an activist, amidst 'the Rolandins, Brissotins, Girondins' who were fiercer than tigers: 'The Revolution has aroused such passions that it's no longer possible to be sure of knowing any man'. She warned her son to keep a lock on his tongue: 'I'm afraid of you making enemies'.[22]

Many revolutionaries, especially the most prominent, made enemies. Their worst enemies were not infrequently former friends and colleagues, people who were well-informed about one another, and often ruthless about employing the knife of denunciation. Especially damaging was the accusation that revolutionaries were motivated by ambition, and that their guise as men of virtue served as a mask for their desire for power. Such denunciations were frequent in revolutionary politics. Marat repeatedly and comprehensively denounced the integrity of the Girondins: they in return sent him to the Revolutionary Tribunal, in an attempt to get him eliminated. Desmoulins, in *Brissot Unmasked* (February 1792), denounced Brissot's secret ambitions, referring to his former friend as 'a real Tartuffe of patriotism and a traitor to the *patrie*'.[23] Brissot in turn intimated that Robespierre's opposition to the war was due to his being secretly in the pay of the Austrian Committee. Louvet went further: in dramatic scenes in the Jacobin Club, he accused Robespierre of secretly plotting to make himself a dictator.[24] Increasingly such mutual accusations could result not just in disgrace and loss of position, as in the earlier stages of the Revolution, but in arrest, and possibly indictment and death.

Even the notional 'leaders' of the 'Terror', the members of the Committee of Public Safety, were not immune from fear and consciousness that their own lives were at risk. Prieur, a member of the Committee, would later recall the atmosphere in the early summer of 1794 as its unity broke down, amidst conflict between Robespierre and other members. As Prieur described it, the Committee's members learned to live with a constant level of anxiety that inevitably took its toll:

> There were days so difficult that, seeing no way to control the circumstances, those most personally threatened abandoned their fate to the chances of the unforeseen ... We ended by becoming so accustomed to these inextricable situations, that we pursued our daily task, so that business should not be left pending, as though we had a whole lifetime before us, when it was perfectly likely that we would not see the sun rise tomorrow.[25]

Such hostilities, rivalries and tensions were replicated in many of the key institutions of government, not least in the War Office.[26] The predominant emotion now was fear.

Revolutionaries became more guarded about what they actually put into words. They also showed increased doubt about how to interpret the words and actions of other revolutionaries. For revolutionary leaders even to show their unease in the face of scrutiny from other revolutionaries could be interpreted as a sign of their own guilt. Innocence was meant to be fearless. Suspected conspirators were compared to Tartuffe, Molière's 'hypocrite', who emulated the words, the appearance, even the emotions of the genuine patriot, but did not share them in his heart. The motif of Tartuffe suggests an underlying anxiety in the revolutionary mentality, a profound, though unvoiced, uncertainty that anyone could ever entirely prove their revolutionary virtue.

There is no doubt that the revolutionary leaders during the Year II had many genuine causes to be afraid. They were afraid of conspiracies and with good cause – even though not all the conspiracies they envisaged were real ones. They were fearful of losing the war. They were afraid of the counter-revolution winning, of the monarchy being restored, and the advances of the Revolution being lost, along with their own lives. They were frightened of the *sans-culottes* and the popular violence that they themselves had benefited from but which, now unleashed, might be turned on them if they lost their credibility. They were anxious about the risks of being assassinated, a danger that might confront them at any moment, in public places, or even in their homes.[27] They were worried about being misled by people with platitudes about virtue on their lips and corruption and enmity in their hearts. They were, with good reason, afraid of each other; after the destruction of the factions in the spring of 1794, it was evident that any renewal of open conflict amongst the revolutionary leadership would almost certainly lead to the extermination of whichever was the losing group. Some of them, at least, were *genuinely* filled with foreboding that they, as the men of virtue entrusted with the defence of the Revolution, were too few and that they would be overwhelmed by the self-interest and ambition of others, united in conspiracy. They were prey to uncertainty about themselves; apprehensive about the mismatch between what they had believed would happen in 1789 and what was happening now. Finally, they themselves were subject to terror, and dreaded that at any moment it might be turned against them.

Nearly forty years after he had played a notable part in the French Revolution as a *conventionnel*, and a staunch Montagnard, René Levasseur published his *Mémoires*. Levasseur claimed that the Montagnard deputies who had been so implicated in directing the terror themselves experienced the fear that this terror could be turned against them:

> The terror that we inspired crept over the benches of the Mountain, as it did into the *hôtels* of the faubourg Saint-Germain. It sat on the benches of the tribunal and taught its members that they could at any moment change from the role of judge to that of the accused.[28]

He added:

> No one, indeed, had ever thought of establishing a system of terror. It had been established by force of circumstance; no will had organized it, but all wills had contributed to its establishment.[29]

We may be tempted to dismiss Levasseur's image of terrorized Montagnards as overdrawn, or a retrospective plea for sympathy. But Levasseur was describing a phenomenon that many revolutionary leaders actually experienced. A surprisingly high number of those who directed the legalized recourse to terror in the Year II, themselves perished in it. This fact has long been known, but historians have tended to overlook it or, if they do remark upon it, to underestimate its significance.

The revolutionary leaders were subject to a specific form of terror, 'the politicians' terror'. This was the terror that revolutionary leaders meted out to one another. In some ways it paralleled the general 'Terror' but it also had particular characteristics of its own. This took two forms. First, revolutionary leaders were liable to arrest under the laws that enabled terror, as successive laws removed their parliamentary immunity and criminalized the 'wrong' political opinions. Second, they were subject to the *emotion* of terror. Fears that they could not openly acknowledge – because innocence was meant to be fearless and fear was a sign of consciousness of guilt – increased in intensity, above all during the critical period between March 1793 and July 1794. The revolutionary leaders' growing consciousness of the danger in which they stood undoubtedly influenced their decisions, even though they were constantly insisting – in public at least – that they did not let it affect them. Ironically, leaders had much more cause to fear the policy of terror than most of the Parisian population. As we shall see in chapter 6, a high proportion of the leaders of the Revolution (above all those who either were or had been members of the Jacobin Club) died violent deaths, either under the guillotine or by their own hand. The 'politicians' terror' climaxed in a series of trials and executions of revolutionary leaders during the Year II. These successive factions were accused of being 'conspirators', whose professed virtue and love of the *patrie* concealed the fact that they were financially and politically corrupt, had sold themselves to the royalists and the foreign powers, and were part of a conspiracy to overthrow the Revolution from within. As the Girondin Vergniaud had anticipated: 'Citizens, it is to be feared that the Revolution, like Saturn, will successively devour all its children.'[30]

3. The impossible combination of virtue and terror

> If the mainspring of popular government in peacetime is virtue, the mainspring of popular government during a revolution is both virtue and terror; virtue, without which terror is baneful; terror, without which virtue is powerless. Terror is nothing more than speedy, severe and inflexible justice; it is thus an emanation of virtue; it is less a principle in itself, than a consequence of the general principle of democracy, applied to the most pressing needs of the *patrie*.[31]

With these words Robespierre sought to reconcile virtue and terror (the latter understood as 'severe, inflexible' justice) in the midst of the crisis facing the *patrie*. His argument rested on the authenticity of revolutionaries' commitment to the public good – literally the authenticity of their own virtue. A revolutionary must be genuinely virtuous in order to be entrusted with power so that he would use it not for himself – not for personal motives such as self-aggrandisement, ambition, vengeance or envy – but for the *patrie*. So long as terror was wielded by men of authentic virtue then it would be morally right, a form of justice. The 'pressing needs of the *patrie*' required the use of terror. The cause was that of the 'public good' (*salut public*). In this way Robespierre sought to rationalize and justify the use of terror to his audience. He was also – and this is crucial to understanding Robespierre – trying to justify it to himself. This was not the argument of a cynical man, using a specious form of words to keep himself in power. This was a man who believed in what he said – even if that effort of self-belief was becoming harder. He really needed to believe in it. The alternatives for a man so committed as Robespierre were unbearable – that the Revolution could fail, or that it might not have been worth the struggle and sacrifice that it had already cost.

Yet the reality was that the fear that Robespierre wanted to use to intimidate the enemies of the Revolution was already in the Convention itself. It hung like a shadow over the heads of the deputies. In early April 1793, the Girondin deputy Birotteau had proposed, and the Convention had accepted, that all deputies who came under suspicion of treason should be liable to arrest.[32] From that time on, the deputies had to live with the knowledge that they themselves had no immunity from arrest, and they were subject to scrutiny of their conduct for signs of corruption and conspiracy. After the shocking spectacle of the Girondins being convicted for treason and publicly executed, every deputy knew that their grim fate might also be his. That fear was consolidated by the arrest, trial and execution of the Dantonists.

Of all the cases that came before the Revolutionary Tribunal, there were none more ruthless than those involving politicians. In most cases brought before the Revolutionary Tribunal, people had some chance to mount a legal defence, and overall, slightly over half the people brought before the Revolutionary Tribunal were sentenced to death. Even after the Law of Prairial was passed on 10 June 1794, nearly one in four of the people who appeared before the Tribunal escaped death.[33] This was not the case with the terror that politicians dealt to one another. None of the deputies who were brought before the Revolutionary Tribunal during the Year II, and virtually none of the other prominent political figures who appeared before it in that time, escaped the death sentence.

The politics of virtue affected the 'Terror' as a whole in two significant ways. Firstly, a key instrument of terror was denunciation. It was seen as a civic duty, which could only be legitimated by the virtue of the denouncer.[34] In this respect, ordinary citizens who denounced people they knew were expected to be motivated by the same devotion to the public good (rather than personal grudges) that was demanded of revolutionary politicians. Secondly, the leaders of the Revolution, by being prepared to submit to terror themselves, by being prepared to denounce their own former friends, and ultimately by being prepared themselves to die for the cause of the Revolution, were also legitimating their use of terror. They were ready to destroy their friends, and even sacrifice themselves for love of the *patrie*: therefore they believed they had the right to destroy other people too.

In order to understand the relationship between the revolutionary terror and fear of conspiracy – and how this rebounded on the revolutionary leaders themselves – we need to consider a key part of revolutionary ideology, that was the belief that virtue was essential for citizenship. Virtue was a concept with a range of derivations, mingling classical republicanism, natural virtue, religious thought and the theme of self-sacrifice for the public good, and owing as much to the political formulations of Montesquieu as to the emotional authenticity associated above all with Rousseau.[35] With the onset of the Revolution the rhetoric of political virtue developed into an ideological imperative underpinning ideas about the ways in which politics should be practised. There was a high expectation that that new class of people, the revolutionary politicians, would set the tone for public life. Virtue was not just something you said, it was also meant to be something that you did. It was not enough for people in positions of public power to mouth the rhetoric of virtue. They were also meant to act with genuine virtue – that is, to serve the public good before anything else, before their own self-interest, and before personal loyalties to friends and family. They should be devoid of personal ambition, egoism or the desire for glory. Virtue was part of a culture common to many people of varying political persuasions. It was not exclusive to Robespierre, nor to the Jacobins, but they bought heavily into it.

The conviction that the Revolution's functionaries were public servants was at variance with much of the actual practice of the Revolution's functionaries, which was all too often distinctly venal. Saint-Just was scathingly critical of revolutionary officials who were exploiting their positions to enrich themselves, speaking of 'factions within the Republic: factions of her external enemies, factions of the thieves who serve her only to suckle on her breasts, but who drag her to her ruin through exhaustion. There are also a few men eager to get jobs, to make people talk about them, and to profit from the war'.[36] He concluded that corruption amongst the Revolution's functionaries, including the deputies themselves, must be rooted out.

Virtue was linked to the concept of transparency. This was the idea that the thoughts and motivation of all political participants should be open to the sight and scrutiny of others. The formation of political factions was seen as inimical to transparency.[37] Factions were considered to be inherently furtive, self-interested and possibly conspiratorial.

Revolutionary politicians sought to cultivate public opinion. They played to the gallery, and tried to establish their authenticity in the eyes of their audiences.[38] Their speeches, their actions and their conduct, were subjected to an unprecedented level of public scrutiny, above all by the revolutionary press and by their fellow revolutionaries. The new men at the forefront of public life were obliged to negotiate this changed landscape in which their own ambition was considered as inherently suspicious, their true identity subject to scrutiny that was often hostile. Every public action, or private action that became public knowledge, was open to judgement. A revolutionary leader's political participation should not be conducted 'behind closed doors' in Ancien Régime fashion, over dinner, in private houses, where public opinion could not judge his sincerity. There should be no gap between what a revolutionary politician said and what he did. Any aspect of a politician's private life which appeared at odds with his political identity could arouse suspicion – such as, for example, injudicious choice of friends,[39] dining with 'suspect' people,[40] living behind high walls in a palace.[41] Anything that suggested personal ambition, or corruption or love of luxury – for example whom one dined with, and what one ate – could be perilous. The revolutionary leaders themselves were judged more harshly than ordinary citizens. There is a profound irony here, for it was not realistic to expect all politics to be conducted in public. Some of what the revolutionary leaders did was necessarily carried out behind closed doors: the Committee of Public Safety itself did not keep minutes of its meetings.

The need to appear as a 'man of virtue' was relentlessly demanding. The attempt to do so involved the revolutionary leaders in a lived contradiction, in which the realities of their lives and the ways in which they actually practised politics could never match up to the identity they professed. The Revolution opened up the possibility of forging a career in politics. It is likely that many of the men who took up a career in revolutionary politics were motivated by ambition as well as by genuine patriotic fervour. Yet it was impossible – indeed dangerous – for them to admit this publicly. They lived with the constant risk of a perceptible gap opening up between what they said and what they did, a gap which would damage their credibility, for how could they ever prove that they were authentically virtuous, as opposed to good at faking it? To have a credible identity as a man of virtue could be a means to power, but it was also a dangerous path to walk.

The English historian James Thompson pointed out long ago that the word 'Terror' was in some senses a misnomer, because it invoked the idea of a whole population cowering in fear under the yoke of the Jacobin government. Certainly, the Law of Suspects was a vague and horrible piece of legislation; nor was everyone who was executed guilty of the crimes with which they were charged. But the revolutionary government was primarily a war government: 'Its policy was intimidation, but its result was not terror.' In practice, as Thompson pointed out, much of the actual terror was directed against a specific group of people – revolutionary leaders and government officials: 'it is often forgotten that the Terror was mainly directed, not against the people, but against the Government'.[42] Whilst we should not forget that the majority of executions were carried out against people who took up arms against the Revolution, and were condemned under the law of 19 March 1793, Thompson makes a valid point, one which we would do well to consider.

The corruption of politicians and government officials was an immense problem for the Montagnard and Jacobin leaders. With little previous administrative experience of any kind, they suddenly found themselves directing a population of some 28 million people, beset by war and civil war. The only governmental system with which they were familiar was that of the Ancien Régime, a system in which venality was central to the structure and function of government. Government still had to continue; men must be found to carry out the administrative tasks of government. The changes to the system, together with the war itself, opened up new opportunities for men from relatively modest backgrounds to enrich themselves. The many official positions necessary to govern civilian life, and to conduct the war, offered ample opportunities for those men who did not hesitate to help themselves to public funds. There were considerable temptations; how then could the revolutionary leadership ensure that men entrusted with power remained honest? To this question Robespierre would reply – by using terror to keep them in check. But who then would ensure that the men administering terror were themselves motivated by genuine virtue?

In a speech on the need to purify the government in the previous October, Saint-Just expressed this problem in fierce terms: 'A people has only one dangerous enemy: its government.'[43] Government was intrinsically corrupt. It was ambition, not virtue, that motivated the great majority of people who held public office, 'public service, in the way it is practised, is not virtue, it is a career'.[44] The only thing that could make it work for the people rather than against them, was the authentic virtue of the people who oversaw the running of government – the revolutionary leaders themselves. The only way to prove beyond all doubt that one's virtue was authentic was to be prepared to make the ultimate sacrifice for the public good – to give up one's own life. Ironically, this idea of self-sacrifice also became a justification for using terror: since one was prepared oneself to die for the good of the Republic, one was also justified in taking the lives of others.

People might, however, have different reasons for saying this. They could be saying that they were motivated by virtue because it was to their advantage to do so. During the time of 'Terror', they might be saying it because they were afraid. The Revolution was a process of political education, from enthusiasm to cynicism. There was a growing consciousness that the words of participants in revolutionary politics were in themselves relatively meaningless if not backed up by actions, and genuine emotions. Hence the emphasis on authenticity and on demonstrating one's virtue through actions. Revolutionary leaders might seek to prove the authenticity of their identities by the way in which they lived their private and public lives; and by remaining relatively poor. Ultimately, however, the only way to prove beyond doubt the authenticity of one's identity was to be ready to die for the cause of the Revolution.[45]

How did leading revolutionaries cope with their fears? Saint-Just, in an undated note (written shortly before his death) sounded bitter but defiant: 'Circumstances are only difficult for those who recoil before the tomb. . . . Certainly it is no great thing to leave an unhappy life in which one is condemned to die either as the accomplice or the powerless witness of crime.'[46] What was in Saint-Just's mind when he anticipated his imminent death and declared he didn't fear it? Guilt over people he had had a hand in killing? Expiation? Pride? Despair? We cannot, of course, know what he was thinking. It is striking that Saint-Just saw his own role in revolutionary politics as that of a powerless and innocent man. The people who crowded the prisons were hardly likely to concur. Yet this was how he expressed his situation to himself. It suggests by the summer of 1794 that even men at the forefront of the revolutionary government were subject to personal despair, and felt helpless to alter events.

In the long years after the Year II, some of the surviving deputies reflected on the time when they, too, had chosen terror. Deciding how to remember this, and how to construct the narrative of their own past involvement, both as men who had supported the recourse to terror, and who had feared that terror would rebound on their own heads, was a difficult and painful process. The memoirs of these former 'terrorists' need to be read with care, for these men wrote partly as a way of exonerating themselves from their own role in having supported the policy of terror. It is suggestive, though, to see the weight they put on the emotions that had stirred them in the Year II.

The former deputy, Baudot in his *Memoirs* repeated the last two lines from Saint-Just's words, quoted above, and then commented on them:

> If Saint-Just spoke with such bitter chagrin of his own powerlessness, judge for yourselves the position of men whose own power was negligible or non-existent. At that time I spoke with my friends amongst the *conventionnels*, calculating that I might have a month to live. They laughed at my presumption that I could count on living a month through such stormy times.[47]

Baudot also observed that it was the best speakers who excited the most jealousy amongst a great number of other deputies who were themselves 'mediocre or inadequate' orators: 'Also almost all of the most eloquent orators perished in the tumultuous battles of the Convention, because they were the most in public view and consequently they were the most exposed to passionate hatreds, such as Vergniaud, Guadet, Gensonné, Condorcet, Danton, Billaud-Varenne, Saint-Just, even Robespierre and others.'[48] In Baudot's view then, there were more emotions that we should add to the lethal cocktail of passions operating in the Convention – jealousy, hatred and vindictiveness.

It was perhaps inevitable that the revolutionaries paid a high price for 'revolutionary exaltation' that had sustained them through long years of struggle. By late 1793 there were signs that many of the most prominent revolutionaries were stressed, exhausted and burnt out by the effort of forging and nurturing the Republic.

Robespierre, who had been involved in every step of the revolutionary process from its outset was already referring to his own physical and mental exhaustion as early as February 1792 (a time when he was energetically, but ultimately unsuccessfully, opposing the campaign to declare war on France's enemies) when he claimed, 'my strength and my health cannot suffice'.[49] Recently, historians, most notably Peter McPhee and Hervé Leuwers, have explored the question of Robespierre's declining health during the last months of his life. Whilst he undoubtedly suffered from physical afflictions, the evidence suggests that it was his state of emotional exhaustion that played the determining role in his partial retreat from active political participation during the weeks preceding Thermidor. He also seems to have made a conscious decision to withdraw from public life in order to restore his damaged public reputation.[50]

At various points during the all-consuming rush of revolutionary politics, Robespierre talked about all that he had sacrificed to the Revolution, but we should appreciate that he was not an isolated case. By 1793–4 many, if not most, revolutionaries showed signs of exhaustion, particularly those who had been actively involved the longest. By this time, even Danton, despite his reputation for physical and psychological strength, showed unmistakable indications of losing heart. According to Levasseur, Danton, in the last months of his life, was exhausted by 'revolutionary exultation' and looking for a way out.[51]

We might think here of Boissy d'Anglas's famous phrase: 'In the space of six years we have lived through six centuries.'[52] He was speaking about the Constitution of 1795, which would deliberately pull back on the Jacobin experiment with democracy. But he was also mindful perhaps of the rollercoaster of emotions that had been the revolutionary experience.

Finally, we need to acknowledge the complex motives of the revolutionary leaders who initiated and maintained the policy of 'terror'. It is against this background that we should seek to understand what people are capable of when fear coupled with strong belief drives them forward. Our approach must be multifaceted because the revolutionary leaders themselves were not ideological automatons but complex human beings, who felt as well as thought about what the Revolution meant. They believed in virtue; they believed in patriotism; they also wanted to make a success of their careers in the new world of revolutionary politics; they were subject to personal loyalties, suspicions, enthusiasms, dislikes and jealousies. The circumstances of crisis would change them. In defence of their Revolution, out of ideological and emotional conviction that they were right, and sometimes out of fear itself, many of them chose 'terror', and must bear their share of responsibility for the deaths that ensued. Yet when we think about their situation, in all its anguish, we should be thankful, perhaps, to have been in our own lives spared such circumstances, such choices and such consequences.

Revolutions evoke strong emotions, *on all sides*. While revolutionaries rejoiced at their plans for a better world, for many others the Revolution evoked quite different emotions – anger, grief and a sense of profound loss. Much of that loss was financial, of course, as a world of privilege, the autonomous power of the Catholic clergy, the status and very existence of the nobility, all were systematically dismantled, first by the Constituent Assembly, then by the Legislative. But that loss was also emotional, a mourning for lost prestige, a lost culture, a lost place in the world. When the decrees of 4 August 1789 were proclaimed, abolishing the old order, some deputies wept tears of joy, but others wept tears of grief and rage. Could these two very different perspectives ever be reconciled?

And how can we fail to understand, finally, to what extent these opposing emotions also played a key role in the gradual radicalization of the confrontations and the concomitant aggravation of repression, with the eventual recourse to a set of repressive measures grouped together under the name of *the Terror*.

Chapter 4

The Revolution and its Opponents: Clashes and the Intensification of Repression

The French Revolution brought sweeping change, and with that change – from the very outset – came resistance. Whilst the Revolution benefitted many, giving them equal political, social and legal rights, along with equality of opportunity, it also gave birth to frustration, loss, discontent and opposition from those who stood to lose under the new regime. The various laws voted by successive Assemblies led to major upheavals in the Church, the army, society, the economy and culture. Could the majority of owners of lordly and feudal rights meekly accept their disappearance and the consequences of lost power, revenue and the very nature of their ownership? Could parts of the nobility unflinchingly witness even the partial loss of what gave them power and a pre-eminent status in society? Could most members of the high clergy welcome the civil constitution of the clergy in 1790 that subjected church to state, or the decision that the Church's properties be placed under the disposition of the Nation and then sold as 'national property'? How could the small administrative, judicial and commercial world that had prospered under the administrative framework of the Ancien Régime transition to the new administrations? Could the disappearance of a world based on particular privileges be accepted without a protest by those who had lost them? To add to this list of grievances, there were the shattering consequences of the decision to enter into war in spring 1792 and the vociferous protests sparked by the drafting of men into the army.

It was to be expected that some of the king's subjects-turned-citizens would actively contest the new order, or at very least, accept it with the greatest repugnance. Their discontent could have remained limited to anti-revolutionary protests – annoying to the new regime, but ultimately containable, but instead, by a process that we shall trace in this chapter, it gradually transformed into counter-revolutionary acts, met with escalating repression by the revolutionary authorities.[1] It was a process that happened by successive stages. There was a progressive and gradual hardening of the confrontation, and the violence that accompanied this was far from appearing *ex nihilo*.[2] The 'terror' represents one of these changes. If the phenomena were part of a planned-out 'system', a deliberate policy targeting opponents (a sort of ancestor, as it were, of the 'totalitarian regimes' of the twentieth century), the 'terror' would not be intertwined with fears that came and went in waves, and it would not have changed so dramatically over time. An analysis of the repressive legislation successively enacted against the Revolution's opponents illustrates the link between the radicalization of confrontation and intensified repression. We will explore this by examining three major categories of conflict: repressive laws and other actions taken against *émigrés* and refractory priests; the gradual expansion of the notion of the 'suspect' (the perfect targets for the 'terror'); and, finally, certain emblematic episodes of violent repression, including the case of Lyon in 1793.

1. Legislation targeting refractory clergy and *émigrés*

The repression against the refractory priests is generally overlooked in historical works on *the Terror*. Yet a significant number lost their livelihoods and positions; some even lost their lives, becoming victims of massacres, or of legalized terror (see map 1).[3] The decision in November 1790 to require the clergy to take an oath accepting the civil constitution of the clergy (the part of the new Constitution that applied to the Church) was a hugely divisive tactic, forcing Catholic clergy to choose between loyalty to the Church and loyalty to the Revolution. When the first oath was taken in early 1791, the Constituent Assembly did not imagine that non-juring priests would be sentenced to death, or even sent to prison. The deputies were gradually led to put in place an ever more severe repression because of the hostile reactions to the Revolution by some of the refractory priests and the rising tensions between them, their elected replacements and the local authorities.

The taking of the oath occurred in the first few months of 1791, resulting in a clergy divided in two, roughly equal groups: those who had taken the oath and those who had not, now considered refractory (or non-juring) priests. The Constituent Assembly did not believe it necessary to pursue non-juring clergymen, thinking they would simply be replaced by the election of a new priest.[4] On 7 May, in the name of the 'principles of religious freedom' and the Declaration of the Rights of Man, the Constituent Assembly decreed that 'failure to take the oath . . . cannot be held against any priest presenting himself in a church . . . solely for the purpose of saying mass'.[5] The adverb 'solely' is very important here, because the same decree ordered the closing of any religious establishment if a speech hostile to the nascent Constitution, or the civil constitution of the clergy were held, a punishment that would involve the speaker in question – clergy or not – being brought before the courts. The manifest desire to avoid trouble while preserving religious freedom was a balancing act. Local authorities, among them the director of the Paris department, had already spoken of tensions and the difficulty of assuring the exercise of the 'public functions of the religious service . . . in conformity with the laws'.[6]

Gradually, hopes faded that the Revolution's opponents would be converted by sheer power of reason. Simultaneously, the behaviour of some refractory priests irritated the authorities, leading them to believe that constitutional and non-juring priests simply could not co-exist. In autumn 1791, with the advent of a new Assembly, the Legislative, disturbing news came into Paris from a number of departments and communes. A letter from the directory of the department of Basses-Pyrénées declared: 'The priests who were replaced refuse to give up their seat to the constitutional priests . . . These priests do not write, but they act, they terrify the weak and seduce and frighten the municipalities. Do something, gentleman, the safety of France is in your hands. Maintain the Constitution or prepare yourself for all the horrors of civil war.'[7] On 29 November a new decree allowed heightened repression, against dissenting, non-juring priests.[8] Refractory clergymen would now be 'suspected of rebellion and of wicked intentions against the nation'. Not only would they be placed under surveillance by local authorities, but if there were any troubles resulting from religious differences, the local directories were required to take them away from their homes. If the refractory priests refused, they risked being sent to prison for one year, a sentence that could be doubled if they had been involved in provoking the initial troubles. One article of the decree ordered that every department draft a list with the names and addresses of all priests who had taken the oath in one column and the names and addresses of all refractory priests in the other column. The refractory priests were, in effect, placed at the margins of what was lawful. Yet if a refractory priest displayed respect for the laws and avoided any speech that could be judged uncivil, the only punishment he faced was being placed on this list. Louis XVI blocked the decree using the veto power granted to him by the Constitution. The news was announced to the Assembly on 19 December. Instead of the expected formula validating the decree – 'the king consents and will implement' – the decree received notification that 'the king will examine', a veto that suspended the transformation of the decree into law, and thus blocked its implementation.[9]

In the spring and summer of 1792 – in a context worsened by the declaration of war on 20 April – legislative repression was reinforced. On 27 May a decree ordered the deportation of a refractory priest if twenty citizens united to make the request. If they evaded the decree or returned to French soil, they risked ten years in prison.[10] The Minister of Justice announced to the Assembly on 19 June that when it came to this decree, 'the king would examine it'.[11] Louis XVI's repeated use of the veto heightened tensions, giving him a share of responsibility for what followed – in July several refractory priests were put to death in Marseille, Limoges and Bordeaux. From Bordeaux, the Assembly had been warned of the risks when the departmental authorities stated in a report on 19 May that masses of angry citizens were ready to wreak vengeance on six refractory priests being led to prison, seen by the crowds as 'enemies, as guilty parties'.[12] On 23 July, after the summary execution of two refractory priests in Bordeaux, the deputy of the department, Ducos, laid the blame for the excess on the executive power rather than those who massacred the priests: 'after he had vetoed the repressive laws on fanaticism, popular executions began to resume ... the two priests, victims of popular fury, had countless times wearied the patience of citizens by their intrigues and villainy'.[13]

On 26 August, shortly after the assault on the Tuileries, a new decree gave refractory priests fifteen days to leave the national territory – but this time the penalty for failing to obey the decree involved deportation to Guyana. Priests over the age of sixty and the infirm were exempted – but in each department they would be brought together and placed under surveillance in a specially-designated house.[14] A number of refractory priests were killed in the prison massacres of September 1792. A map of the place of death for the ecclesiastical victims of the 'terror' indicates a high mortality on pontoons, boats transformed into floating prisons where refractory priests were held while awaiting their deportation to Guyana (map 1).[15] While the Constituent Assembly had tried to find a peaceful solution, the spread of unrest and the gradual push towards repression changed the stakes, without there being a specific policy of 'terror' against the refractory priests. This situation in many ways parallels the experience of the *émigrés*.

The Comte d'Artois (one of the king's two brothers, the future Charles X), the Prince of Condé and other royal princes gave an early and strong political message by leaving France in the immediate aftermath of 14 July 1789. Yet emigration was a relatively limited phenomenon before the summer of 1791 (it would escalate hugely in the summer 1792). While emigration from the beginning elicited commentary and political declarations, since the number of *émigrés* was initially quite low the issue was not so contentious and not made into a punishable crime. Up until the failed royal flight to Varennes in June 1791, crossing the border, even with one's goods and property, was relatively easy. The Constituent Assembly passed a decree on 4 January 1790 that suspended the payment of pensions, gifts, gratifications, treatments and other appointments to all French subjects who were absent from the realm without an official mission.[16] This decree financially targeted mostly members of the high aristocracy like the Comte d'Artois. Before the Revolution he and his wife received, at state expense, a house each and a total of around 3.5 million *livres* from the royal treasury, as well as another 160,000 *livres* of personal money (what we might call pocket money). The Prince de Condé had several pensions that brought in around 105,000 *livres* annually.[17] These high aristocrats did not remain the only targets for long. On 18 December 1790, in reaction to the unrest in Lyon attributed to a 'conspiracy' fomented across the border (the Comte d'Artois was then in Turin), another decree extended this suspension of 'fugitive French' to public functionaries. *Émigrés* were granted one month to return and take the civil oath; failure to do so would result in the loss of their employments and any monies owed to them would be frozen.[18]

But it was the trauma of Varennes that led the deputies to vote, just days later, on 28 June 1791, a decree that de facto outlawed emigration. This decree authorized foreigners, French traders and their agents to leave the national territory, only so long as they had obtained a passport from the Minister of Foreign Affairs (for foreigners) or from the head municipality of the district in which they resided (for French subjects). In addition, one article of the decree outlawed the export of gold or silver money, horses, arms or munitions.[19] Although not explicitly mentioned, the desire to stop emigration was the driving principle of these stipulations, inflamed by a double fear of an 'aristocratic conspiracy' and the flight of capital from the nation. Officers who left the army and crossed the border with their belongings, denounced in numerous letters received by the Assembly, were immediately forbidden to leave the national territory. The reason for this sudden intensification of *émigré* repression was summed up by the *rapporteur* of the decree, Fréteau de Saint-Just, who spoke of 'public safety and retribution for the crimes of the 21st [June], so loudly and unanimously called for by the nation'.[20] This retribution remained uncertain, with the very notion of emigration proving to be ambiguous, as a decree from 1 August showed. Attempting to facilitate the return of the *émigrés*, the wording of the decree was highly ambiguous, shifting from 'French citizens absent from the kingdom', 'emigrants', 'émigrés' and even 'refracteries'.[21] To complicate matters, the passing of the Constitution in September 1791 revoked the interdiction on emigration. As a side measure to the amnesty for judicial proceedings related to events connected to the Revolution, free circulation was re-established throughout the kingdom from the 14th of the month, with everyone able to cross borders without needing either an authorization or a passport.[22]

A new repressive turn was brought about by heightened threat of war and the first rumours about the supposed military clout of the *émigrés* in 'the little army of the princes'. On 9 November 1791 a decree criminalized emigration, but three days later it was met with a royal veto.[23] The deliberation over the decree illustrates how threats and repression were strongly linked – and also how any hope to convert through reason had faded: 'it is finally time to severely punish those individuals who could not be brought to exercise the duties and sentiments of free citizens by indulgence'. Not only were *émigrés* declared to be 'suspected of conspiracy against the nation', but they risked the death penalty if they were still 'in a state of being gathered together' on 1 January 1792 and their income was seized for the nation's coffers. Royal princes and civil or military public servants faced the same penalty if they did not immediately return to France. The decree also held that any French subject, either on French territory or abroad, who incited compatriots to join the *émigré* army also risked the death penalty. While Louis XVI's veto blocked the implementation of this decree, it also, as in the case of the refractory priests, contributed to heightening tensions to a point that ruled out any clemency towards the *émigrés*.

Several months later, the declaration of war and the participation, however marginal, of *émigré* troops in the Prussian invasion in the north, were enough to make repressive legislation irreversible. As soon as the royal power was abolished on 10 August, along with the king's veto power, there was nothing left to stop the intensification of repression. Five days later, the wives and children of the *émigrés* were placed under house arrest, and threatened with police arrest if they tried to escape. By punishing the wives and children of lawbreakers, the Legislative Assembly also violated the principle of individualizing punishment.[24] A final barrier was broken in October 1792, this time by the Convention. The issue was the death penalty that had been threatened to *émigrés* who had taken up arms the previous autumn.[25] On 9 October a decree was passed that held that any captured *émigré* in arms or who had aided France's enemies would be placed before a military commission (a tribunal of 'exceptional' justice composed of military officers) and executed within twenty-four hours. This essentially placed the individual outside the law because the usual legal protections were not granted to them.[26] Then, on 23 October, during a heated debate (in which Camille Desmoulins spoke of a decision more misguided and horrible than the infamous Revocation of the Edict of Nantes – enacted against Protestants by Louis XIV in 1685), another decree banished the *émigrés* from the national territory for life, punishing them with death if they returned – even if they were unarmed and with no distinction as to age or sex.[27] This decree was de facto modified on 10 November by a new text which gave every *émigré* fifteen days to leave France or otherwise face capital punishment.[28]

On 28 March 1793, just after the creation of an extraordinary criminal court that would later be known as the Revolutionary Tribunal, and following upon the decree of 19 March on the outlaw status granted to those opposed to the call to arms (see chapter 5), the Convention ordered that the returned *émigrés* not touched by the measures taken on 9 October be judged by a criminal tribunal in the department where they resided, risking either execution or deportation.[29] Similarly to what happened to the individuals placed outside the law, all that was needed for a guilty verdict within twenty-four hours, with no possibility of a stay, appeal or annulment, was the positive identification of the arrested *émigré* by two witnesses from the same town as the accused. It was an excessively harsh law. The simple fact was that an individual whose name was on the list of *émigrés* had almost no possible way to contest the charge, even if that person had never taken up arms against France. Despite internal discussions on this point in the Committee on Legislation, which was charged with preparing the decree, no particular case was considered capable of leading to an exemption.[30] The Convention and the Committee on Legislation were assailed with petitions from families, and even letters from individuals forbidden to return who pleaded their cases from abroad.[31] Recognizing any particular cases would have meant that this law would be considered an ordinary law. As the *rapporteur* of the committee, who presented the decree when it was put up for debate in the Convention on 28 February 1793, stated on 1 March: 'this law against the *émigrés* is outside the circle of ordinary measures'.[32]

The radicalization of repressive legislation against the *émigrés* was thus inscribed in a context of temporary political exception, when 'revolutionary' (in the sense of extraordinary) laws were voted in – even though the government itself would not define itself as 'revolutionary until the peace' until the following autumn.[33] If one considers that different decrees had, since 1792, targeted the sequestration and confiscation of the property and goods of the *émigrés*, as well as their sale as 'national goods', it is easier to understand why the famous Law on Suspects of 17 September 1793 did not apply to the *émigrés*, whose fate had long been determined by this point. The position of the *émigrés* had taken quite some time to be fixed, in common with the refractory priests, showing again how the multiplication of uprisings and heightened repression went together. The 'terror' was not an overnight phenomenon; it also was not the supposed policy that Robespierre – a very convenient scapegoat for the Thermidorians – had nurtured for a long time and then rapidly implemented. A close study of the various decrees voted in since 1791 shows how repression against the *émigrés* came into being slowly and proved difficult to organize: 13 decrees in 1791, 38 in 1792 (only four of which were passed before the declaration of war), 51 in the first nine months of 1793, 50 in Year II and another 87 in Year III, before the flow gradually dried up in Year IV.[34]

2. 'The suspects': how the net of suspicion widened

Historians have estimated the total number of people arrested or detained as a 'suspect' to be around 500,000, although some estimates go down to 300,000, or even a bit lower. Historian Jean-Louis Matharan, whose doctoral thesis was on suspects and suspicion in Paris between 1792 and 1793, argues that there are no reliable statistics at the national level because the notion of suspicion changed over time. He does, however, provide precise data about Paris: between August 1792 and Thermidor Year II, around 9,300 individuals were arrested as suspects (86 per cent of whom were male). The chronology can be divided up into very different sequences: before July 1793, there were very few arrests; the terrible summer that the Republic experienced in 1793 led to an increase of arrests; two climaxes followed, one in the autumn of 1793 (accompanying the enacting of the

Law of Suspects), and a second in spring 1794.[35] Matharan shows suspects had been arrested in Parisian sections well before August 1792, thus preceding the period traditionally defined as 'the Terror'.

The difficulty of calculating the total figures for people arrested as 'suspect' is compounded by the fact that many were set free relatively quickly. These liberations were not limited to the weeks and months following Thermidor: they occurred throughout the period and thus went in parallel with incarcerations. The period between summer 1793 and summer 1794 was when repression was at its height and detentions tended to be longer (an average period of eight months). All of this illustrates how repression intensified at moments when dangers – whether real or imagined – increased.

The parameters of suspicion changed over the course of the Revolution. The term 'suspect' was in use from the Revolution's early years, though loosely employed by different political groups, and with little consensus over who was intended by the term. Towards the end of 1789 the word 'suspect' made its first appearance in the revolutionary press. The patriotic journal *Révolutions de Paris* gave the term a meaning both wide and vague: thus, in early January 1790, when discussing the plot of the Marquis de Favras to kidnap the king, the journal spoke of a man linked to the marquis as 'suspected of not being a supporter of the revolution'.[36] In September 1790 a decree to ensure the security of the naval arsenal ordered the arrest of 'all suspect men' found entering the site (or on warships) or of inciting workers and sailors. Here suspicion was linked, once again, to military precautions.[37] Similarly, on the day following the arrest of the king in Varennes, measures were instituted, aimed to suspend and replace suspect military officers.[38] Everything began to change drastically on 16 July 1791, the eve of the Champ de Mars massacre. The Constituent Assembly asked the municipality of Paris to authorize the police to make a sweep of suspicious inhabitants. Anyone refusing to be checked would be placed on a list of 'suspects', with a description of their person and their address; those giving false declarations would be noted as 'ill-intentioned'.[39]

The heightening of tensions that accompanied the fight to overthrow the monarchy on 10 August 1792, led to a reinforcing and hardening of measures taken to identify and control suspects, with the Paris Commune increasingly pressing the Assembly to implement such measures. On 29 August the Assembly ordered home visits (searches) in every commune to determine the amount of weapons and ammunitions, as well as horses, carts and chariots. Every citizen deemed suspect would be disarmed; any citizen believed to have hidden weapons would also be treated as suspect.[40] At this time none of this implied an arrest or made it mandatory. The decision whether to arrest suspects was left to local authorities, sharing jurisdiction with the surveillance committees (from spring 1793), but also the deputies sent on missions – and the number of missions throughout the departments multiplied, with some representatives pressed for arrests or placing citizens under strict surveillance in their homes.[41] For the Revolution's supporters, fear was combined with impatience regarding what they saw as a drawn-out and dangerous leniency on the part of authorities towards suspects. Refractory priests, *émigrés* and their families, those who refused the oath, those who made false declarations, citizens who made hostile public declarations towards the Revolution: all of these categories now constituted suspects *par excellence*, to which could be added the speculators threatened with capital punishment.[42]

Yet the limits of suspicion remained undefined until the decree of 17 September – which became known notoriously as the 'Law of Suspects'. This decree attempted to specify and formalize the meaning of a 'suspect', even if it did not order the arrest of all suspects.[43] The decree implemented a principle adopted on 12 August 1793 after envoys from the primary assemblies called for the arrest of all suspects. This proposition was voted on but then sent to the Committee on Legislation so that its practicalities could be worked out.[44] It took the committee over a month to make its recommendations, a sign not only of the difficulties in defining 'suspect' but also of probable disagreements among its members over whether to include the 'federalists'.[45]

Article 2 of the 17 September decree gave a new dimension to suspicion, a widening of scope which does much to explain the increase in the number of arrests. Refractory priests, *émigrés* and speculators were not covered in this decree, save indirectly, because their cases had already been dealt with in prior decrees. The aim here was to identify and deal with new target classes of suspects. Those considered 'suspect people' (not 'suspect citizens', because they were deemed unworthy of that title) included such vague categories as those who could not justify their lifestyle (which could include the possibility of financial corruption), and those who did not do their civic duty and who were refused certificates of civism (literally certificates of good citizenship, attesting to the appropriate conduct of the bearer). Suspects also included those who had been relieved of their functions by the Convention or representatives of the people on official missions, as well as nobles and the parents or agents of *émigrés* who had not 'constantly manifested their attachment to the Revolution'. Finally, the category of suspect included 'those who, either by their behaviour, or their relationships, by their speech or writings, have declared themselves to be supporters of tyranny or federalism and thus enemies of freedom.' Not only did royalists and 'federalists' find themselves under the scope of the same criminal charge, but even an acquaintance or relationship with another could bring about one's arrest. Wealth combined with egoism and selfishness could be seen as grounds for suspicion, and some affluent detainees could find themselves pressured to make 'patriotic gifts' or donate 'revolutionary taxes' to demonstrate loyalty and in hopes of gaining release.[46]

The logistics of holding so many people prisoner were daunting at a time when a 'prison system' existed only in rudimentary fashion. Many buildings, such as former palaces, fortresses, convents, were adapted as improvised places of detention. Conditions varied hugely. On the one hand, many people – the exact figure is unknown – died as a direct or indirect result of crowded prisons and horrible insanitary conditions. On the other hand, wealth could sometimes help with obtaining some comforts, even in a revolutionary context; whilst tens of thousands more were detained under house arrest, rather than in a prison. As Greer points out, a lot of the detentions were 'merely preventative', enacted to 'restrain potential troublemakers'.[47] Yet those who died while in detention were undoubtedly 'victims of the terror'.

Merlin de Douai, the jurist and non-aligned deputy of the Plain, was the chief architect of the decree commonly known as the Law of Suspects, and presented it to the Convention for its approval – which was duly obtained. A fellow member of the Committee on Legislation, who was also deeply involved in drafting this most sweeping of decrees, was Cambacérès, another Plain deputy and a former noble. It is notable that both Merlin de Douai and Cambacérès were among many non-Montagnards who successfully rehabilitated their reputations after the fall of Robespierre. Both would go on to enjoy successful careers as jurists under Napoleon. If there was a taint in having put together the Law of Suspects, it did not stick to them; though Merlin later became known by the ironic name, 'Merlin-Suspect'.[48]

The Law of Suspects was a draconian piece of legislation. There was considerable potential that such a wide definition of 'suspect' could result in arbitrary punishment and the settling of private scores. Articles 3 and 4 of the decree, which gave the power to pursue and arrest 'suspects' to 'surveillance committees', were intended to check such potential abuses. These surveillance committees, made up of twelve members, could not order an arrest without a quorum of seven members and an absolute majority of votes, that is to say, four votes minimum. A national investigation of the surveillance committees shows that precaution was a wise course of action and that a number of committees exhibited a great deal of restraint in tracking down suspects, working more to protect the community rather than to strictly obey orders.[49] This may have held true for rural as well as urban committees, and certainly in the departments where there was little trouble. But it was another case altogether in the four departments implicated in the Vendéen uprising, and for those affected by 'federalist' revolts: here many more suspects were arrested under the provisions of the decree.

3. Repression against 'federalism' and the emblematic case of the Lyon revolt

The so-called 'federalist' uprisings against Paris radicalism broke out in a great number of departments in June 1793 and the succeeding months, following the elimination from the Convention of twenty-nine Girondin representatives on 2 June. While limited in many cases to verbal protests and letters written to Paris (a kind of protest that was quickly shut down), in some departments the protests escalated into taking up arms against the 'Montagnard' Convention. The term 'federalist' is problematic. Historian Anne de Mathan has argued that the common assumption among historians that the Girondins had a real project linked to a federal political system is a misconception; rather the Montagnards and Jacobins used the adjective 'federalist' to discredit the protesters – a political insult that transformed the protestors into opponents of a 'one and indivisible' republic.[50]

The repression to which the Girondins and their supporters were subjected went through several stages. When twenty-nine deputies were served with a decree of arrest on 2 June, alongside two Girondin ministers, they were not thrown into prison but simply placed under house arrest, with a gendarme at each residence. At this time – other than the angry diatribes against them in Hébert's *Le Père Duchesne*[51] – there was no question of bringing the Girondin leaders before the courts, much less sending them to the guillotine. The fact that around two-thirds of the targeted deputies chose to flee Paris instead of submitting themselves to house arrest, and that several others not yet targeted by this purge also fled the capital immediately, led to the first stage of increased repression against the Girondins, an escalation that culminated in the execution of their leaders in Paris on 31 October (a process described in chapter 6). Similar events took place from June to October in a number of other departments, following political information, both true and false, propagated by the Girondins in hiding and their Montagnard opponents alike.

The Girondin fugitives described the Convention as mutilated. Firmly under the control of several dozen Montagnards, no one, the Girondins argued, was able to speak freely out of the fear of the fury of the *sans-culottes*, who saw themselves as all-powerful and were thirsty for blood. Similar stories spread to the rest of France, following the administrative hierarchy as the authorities of pro-Girondin departments wrote to their districts and communes to report on the events. The first two Girondin deputies who fled to Caen, Gorsas and Henry-Larivière, arrived on 9 June – and that same day the authorities of Calvados declared themselves in a state of revolt. Those two deputies were joined by their colleagues, Buzot, Salles and Lesage on 12 June, then Barbaroux, Bergoeing, Duval, Lahaye and Cussy three days later, followed by Guadet and Louvet on 26 June, Pétion on 28 June, and finally Lanjuinais on 30 June.[52] Local authorities did not wait for the events from 31 May to 2 June to adopt a threatening tone. An address sent to the Convention on 2 January already evoked the principle of a call to volunteers who would go to Paris to defend liberty against the threats posed by 'proud and bloodthirsty agitators'.[53] In the days following 9 June, the authorities of several Calvados districts took up their position before sending dispatches to the municipalities in their area. The authorities of Pont-L'Evêque sided with the revolt unleashed in Caen in their 14 June dispatch, entitled 'Insurrection and Resistance Against the Oppression of the Citizens of the Pont-L'Évêque District'. Quickly circulated as a printed sheet, the dispatch made its way to the municipality of Honfleur three days later (Honfleur was one of the few municipalities that refused to support the protest movement).[54] What is striking is that two weeks after their ejection from the Convention, the Girondins in hiding had managed to rally a great majority of the local authorities of Calvados, persuaded by their speeches and proclamations. The phenomenon was seen elsewhere, although it was more serious in places where the Girondin declarations stoked a fire that was already hot.

This was the case in Lyon, a city in a state of revolt, first embryonic and then open, after, on 29 May, militants from various sections overthrew the Jacobin municipality controlled by supporters of Chalier, the main leader of Lyon's revolutionaries. The Girondin representative Birotteau, also on the run, gave a provocative speech on 4 July intended to stir up the rebellion.[55] In his words, 'there is no more Convention' – instead, it was dominated by a handful of Montagnards, some of them former nobles and priests, others guilty of having unleashed the prison massacres in September 1792, but all of them engorged by their thieving and the financial support from the Republic's enemies. This band of Montagnards was, to a man, in support of the monarchy's return and was able to rule only because of the support from two thousand *sans-culottes* from eleven departments. Birotteau's diatribe concluded with him stating that armed men, recruited from Lyon and other departments in revolt, needed to be sent to Paris so that the capital would be 'liberated' from the Montagnard domination ('march on Paris, save the oppressed of this great city; I assure you, you will not meet the least resistance').

A printed version of this speech, published by Lyon printer Aimé Vatar-Delaroche, told the inhabitants of the city that the Convention was now made up of twenty-two nobles, eighteen defrocked priests and monks, and a dozen 'Septembriseurs' (a term for those accused of supporting the September Massacres) – while 'eleven-twelfths of Paris's inhabitants' were waiting to be delivered from this oppression.[56] Such exaggerated charges may be read with disbelief today, but they were repeated in other departments by deputies on the run and through circulated mail and letters – even if the language was more subdued and the rebels took care to deny accusations of federalism. The 'popular commission' spearheading the uprising in Bordeaux wrote on 30 June: 'We are marching on Paris not to wage war on Parisians but to help them . . . We are going to Paris to run into the arms of our brothers, to help them break off the yoke of their oppressors and to swear with them the unity and indivisibility of the Republic.'[57] These narratives played an important role in shaping the momentous decisions taken by the authorities of Lyon as well as in the Convention's decision to intensify the repression towards rebellious cities, in particular Lyon. For their part, the supporters of the Montagnards accused the Girondins of all sorts of evils and transformed them into 'federalists', keen on undermining the foundations of the Republic if not siding with foreign powers, with Brissot depicted as a spy in the pay of the British Crown.[58]

This double game of distorted mirrors was particularly visible when it came to bitterly conflicting depictions of the revolt in Lyon.[59] The city of Lyon had already been suspected in 1790–1 of being hostile to the Revolution, then of being a refuge for counter-revolutionaries in 1792; in 1793 Lyon's image was sullied even further when the Jacobin municipality was overthrown by armed force.[60] In a tragic conflation of circumstances, the revolt occurred on 29 May 1793, only a few days before the elimination of the Girondins in Paris. In June the Convention hesitated on the measures to be taken and sent the Montagnard Lindet on an official mission to advise it on how to re-establish peace and calm. Not only did the new authorities in Lyon refuse to recognize his powers, and thus de facto rejected the Convention's decree nominating Lindet as a representative, but several weeks later two other representatives on official missions passing through Lyon – Dherbez-Latour and Sautayra – were arrested and imprisoned. In other 'federalist' departments, a number of the Convention's official representatives on official missions were arrested, like Romme and Prieur of the Côte-d'Or in the Calvados. But it was the case of Lyon that heightened tensions the most. The former mayor, Chalier, was put on trial; after a swift judgement he was guillotined on 16 July. One week later, a second Jacobin from Lyon met the same death, while another 80 individuals defeated on 29 May awaited their fate in prison. All of them were placed under the safeguard of a 21 June decree by which the Convention made the authorities responsible for their fate.

The entire month of July was spent in a dialogue of the deaf between, on the one hand, the rebels who no longer recognized any Convention decrees voted after 2 June and were convinced that they would obtain armed reinforcement from other departments, and, on the other hand, the Convention and its representatives on missions undertaking fruitless negotiations. On 8 August the first shots were exchanged between defenders of the city and the troops sent to bring Lyon back under the Convention's authority. On 19 August artillery shots from the besiegers opened fire; then on the night of 22 August cannonballs and other incendiary projectiles rained down. Those on both sides who used heightened rhetoric to describe their opponents bore a heavy responsibility for the failure of the various negotiations which had scant chance of succeeding. On 26 August, the *Bulletin du département de Rhône-et-Loire*, controlled by Lyon's insurgents, evoked 'yesterday's frightening bombardment, with no parallel in history . . . From seven o'clock in the evening until four o'clock in the morning, not a single second passed without several enormous cannonballs being launched. The preceding nights had been awful, but last night surpassed them all in its atrocities.' It was a sad spectacle for a French city to be under siege from French troops. The very form of the siege shows that the representatives on official missions and the besieging army had tried for long weeks to break the city through bombardments and isolation rather than risk the human cost of a direct assault.

After two months under siege, on 29 September Lyon was attacked, with the besieging army entering into the city on 9 October.[61] *Vae victis*: the repressive legislation that followed the siege was much harsher. On 12 October, the Convention decreed that Lyon was to be 'destroyed', that it would be known as the Freed-City [Ville-Affranchie], and that the five representatives on mission would be charged with 'punishing militarily and without delay Lyon's counter-revolutionaries'. The adjective 'militarily' (*militairement*) was inscribed in exceptional judicial forms, especially the military commissions charged with judging armed *émigrés*, and the decree of 19 March categorizing the 'rebels' as outside the realm of the law. In other words, the insurgents in Lyon had no reason to expect any indulgence or mercy from several exceptional tribunals that had been successively established. The consequent repression resulted in the execution of around 1,900 captives.[62] Those expectations of severe measures far exceeded the already harsh language of the Montagnard Amar, who said to the Convention on 11 August, after a number of unsuccessful negotiations: 'The time of clemency has passed and that of justice has come. The 200 scoundrels who have put Lyon in a state of revolt must be punished.'[63]

Such ever-expansive and increasingly harsh repression should not be understood as the inevitable consequence of a supposed 'terrorist' ideology that led the Convention and its committees to sending ever more opponents of the Revolution to the guillotine in the name of a supposed 'totalitarian' purity or as an outburst of 'terror' which, like Frankenstein's monster, escaped the control of its creator. The expanding of the scope of suspicion, ever-more draconian measures voted in against *émigrés* and refractory priests, and military violence against several so-called 'federalist' cities or ones thrown into the Counter-Revolution camp, like Toulon after the port was conquered by the British in summer 1793: these all belonged to the field of reaction rather than action proper. These events cannot be understood if they are studied outside their specific context or by examining only revolutionary discourse (especially misleading because of frequent rhetorical excesses). Consider the decree that led Edouard Herriot to entitle his tetralogy *Lyon n'est plus* (*Lyon Does Not Exist Anymore*).[64] The actual text of this decree made for chilling reading, above all, Article 3 which opened with the succinct statement: 'The city of Lyon will be destroyed'.[65] The text that followed pulled back on the extent to which the city would become a literal *tabula rasa*. Rather: 'Every building inhabited by the wealthy will be destroyed. All that will remain are the houses of the poor, the buildings of patriots who were slaughtered or proscribed, buildings specially devoted to industry, and monuments dedicated to humanity and public education.' Furthermore, historians have shown that the actual (as opposed to threatened) destruction of Lyon affected only a small number of buildings and that in some cases the local authorities slyly directed the demolition workers to neighbourhoods that had been targeted for urban renewal projects even before the siege began.[66]

All things considered, the radicalization of the confrontations and the concomitant heightening of repression led the Republic towards a 'terror' that struck citizens who were perfectly innocent – even if they were 'guilty' of ill-chosen words or condemned to death for the simple reason that they embodied the Ancien Régime. To take an example, Madame du Barry was denounced and arrested in September 1793. The countess and last favourite of Louis XV was likened by the public prosecutor at the Revolutionary Tribunal, Fouquier-Tinville, as a 'new Aspasie', a courtesan eager to use her political influence to kill off the Republic.[67] Sentenced to death for supposed (as opposed to proven) intelligence with the Counter-Revolution, Madame du Barry was guillotined on 18 Frimaire Year II (8 December 1793) along with four other prisoners, among them Noël, a Girondin deputy on the run who had been captured at the start of Frimaire near the Swiss border.[68] As *Le Moniteur* put it, Madame du Barry stole the stage in the ultimate, tragic performance that was death: 'She had lived in debauchery and crime. She died without courage. Noël, the ex-deputy, condemned the same day, suffered his punishment at the same time.'[69] At first sight it seems incongruous that two such people – with widely varying political attitudes and who had lived such different lives – should be sent to their deaths together, that the demons of terror should strike down revolutionaries and old-regime countesses alike. Yet the fact was that over the summer, and especially the autumn, of 1793, disputes within the Convention had become bloody and mortal. They were to cost the lives of nearly one hundred representatives, condemned as traitors to the Republic they had served. These dangerous factional conflicts at the heart of the Convention would constitute an engine driving forward the 'terror'.

Chapter 5

Creating Revolutionary Law: A Time of Political Exception

'In the case of an armed revolt or troubles threatening the security of the State, the law can suspend, in whatever place and for the length of time it determines, the supremacy of the constitution. This suspension can be provisionally declared by government decree if the legislative body is in recess, with an article in the decree summoning back the legislature as quickly as possible.' This statement sounds like it could be a key text in the so-called 'system of terror' traditionally dated from 1793 to 1794. In fact, this text is Article 92 from the Constitution of Year VIII (13 December 1799) – the same constitution that served as the institutional foundation for Napoleon's takeover of power and the birth of the French Consulate.[1]

None of the preceding constitutions (1791, 1793, 1795) had featured dispositions rendering constitutional the possibility of a 'state' of exception inaugurating, literally, a 'State' of exception. Before the 1799 Constitution, the French Revolution did not give rise to the State itself becoming exceptional – but the state of political exception led the government to put in place extraordinary measures.

This state/State of exception has occasionally been analysed through the lens of Carl Schmitt's work. He evoked a 'sovereign dictatorship' that tried to create the necessary conditions for a constitution to be created while he also referred to a 'dictatorship of commissars' that temporarily suspended an already established constitution without any pretence of modifying or replacing it.[2] Yet the case of the Convention is infinitely more complicated than Schmitt's conclusions would indicate. The first extraordinary measures took place well before the government proclaimed itself 'revolutionary until the peace', while members of the Assembly were sent out on missions to various departments or armies (as commissars, in effect) before the adoption of the Constitution on 24 June 1793. If this constitution was indeed put on hold due to the extraordinary nature of the circumstances, its framework and articles were never *replaced* by extraordinary measures. The suspension of the Constitution of 1793 was conceived as a temporary measure that in no way transformed the Convention as the constitutive power.[3] A constitutional framework thus co-existed alongside so-called 'revolutionary' measures. In this way, a double legal frame was put in place in 1793 in the decree of 14 Frimaire Year II (4 December 1793), sometimes considered a sort of parallel constitution adopted to justify the revolutionary government.

Far from obliterating the constitutional apparatus, this decree set up a double circulation of the law.[4] On the one hand, the surveillance of 'ordinary laws' remained with the executive Council, under the control of the Committee of Public Safety.[5] These 'ordinary laws' were made up of laws and military measures, as well as the laws that were considered administrative, civil or criminal. Their implementation was the responsibility of departmental administrations, ordinary tribunals (for civil and criminal laws), and general and military tribunals for all matters concerning the armies. On the other hand, the so-called 'revolutionary' laws – conceived to be extraordinary, unlike the 'ordinary laws' – and the measures said to be 'for general security and the public good' were also the object of surveillance and were implemented separately. Surveillance over these laws rested with district authorities, who were also obliged to deliver reports to the Committee of Public Safety every ten days. At the same time, the municipalities and surveillance committees were charged with overseeing the application of these laws, and national agents were charged with ensuring their execution.[6] Another major difference in degree with 'ordinary laws' was that district authorities had only a 'simple, secondary and immediate' surveillance over 'revolutionary' laws – a parallel system of surveillance dubbed 'active and superior' was also in place, which gave the two major committees of the Assembly and the deputies on mission the right to make binding decrees to give 'force to the law'.

In this way, emissaries of the Convention played a major role in implementing political exception. This was not, though, an example of the 'dictatorship of the commissars' as Carl Schmitt defined it, for two reasons. Firstly, even though the 1793 Constitution lay dormant, it did not disappear entirely for the measures taken by representatives of the people on missions because 'ordinary' and 'revolutionary' laws co-existed. Secondly, the role of these commissars allows for a better understanding of how the revolutionary government actually worked and what the response was when the 'terror' was demanded in September 1793. Anne Simonin has even suggested that this 'terror' was subtly transformed into rhetoric so as to avoid it becoming policy.[7] Françoise Brunel and Jacques Guilhaumou have stressed the 'strong ethical dimension that made it possible to simultaneously articulate terror and virtue' and that the Convention was able to maintain political control so as to avoid the call for a 'revolutionary executive power' advocated by the Cordeliers and the Paris Commune.[8] While the members of the committees all belonged to the Convention and the deputies on mission incarnated a kind of 'roving Convention', legislative power remained firmly with the government that had become 'revolutionary'.[9] Such 'legislative centralization', to use Billaud-Varenne's definition, was an entirely unprecedented situation and helps explain Robespierre's efforts to provide theoretical justifications for it. It also shows that the political exception of the French Revolution cannot be reduced to the usual paradigms of the state/State of exception.[10]

The recognition of the exceptional circumstances of the Revolution began in its early days. This does not mean that the 'terror' and the Revolution can be seen as of the same essence. Yet it is undeniable that both the use of the adjective 'revolutionary' as a synonym for 'extraordinary' and the precedents for a number of institutions of exception, including that of the Revolutionary Tribunal, can be traced back to common roots.

1. From ordinary law to 'revolutionary' law

From the earliest moments of the Revolution, the adjective 'extraordinary' was commonly used in debates with its usual political meaning of designating that 'which does not follow ordinary practice'.[11] This was how the word was used in the three successive Assemblies from 1789 to 1792 to describe extraordinary envoys, extraordinary expenses, etc., as well as certain meetings. Yet, even in 1789, the word was sometimes used to describe crisis situations which required the use of extraordinary measures. There was nothing unusual in this – the monarchy had used such extraordinary measures for centuries. The martial law mentioned earlier, for instance, contains in its preamble the notion of 'time of crisis':

> The National Assembly, mindful that liberty strengthens empires but licence destroys them; that far from granting the right to do as one

pleases, liberty exists for obedience to the laws; that if in peaceful times this obedience is sufficiently assured by the ordinary public authority, difficult times can arise in which people, agitated by causes that are often criminal, can become the instrument of intrigues and plots whose deeper meanings they ignore; that these times of crisis require for the moment extraordinary measures to maintain public calm and conserve the rights of all, thus hereby decrees the present martial law.[12]

'Extraordinary' is defined in Article 8 of the decree that ordered that instigators of the disorder be 'pursued extraordinarily' at the risk of capital punishment if weapons (of an unspecified nature) were found in the mass gatherings. This law, which aimed above all at suppressing popular movements, was contested by those who saw in the 'people' a motor of the Revolution and who argued for the Assembly to prioritize rectifying the problems that were causing popular unrest rather suppressing the symptoms themselves. It is telling that not only did Robespierre quickly speak out in the Assembly to criticize the martial law (as did Marat later in his *Ami du peuple*[13]) but he already claimed that social problems had to be fixed by legislation and justice – what four years later would take place when linking 'terror', virtue and justice.[14] A few weeks earlier, when referring to the cost of living, Marat himself defined the 'extraordinary' pursuit incurred by 'offenders' as a weapon of despotism, opposing to that the 'punishment meted out by law'. In so doing, he opposed law and justice to what he saw as despotism.[15]

But over time the adjective 'extraordinary' was to become synonymous with 'revolutionary'. In other words, 'extraordinary' came to define the measures taken to implement laws that would not have been enacted in calmer times. One of the first examples of this was given by Jean Debry, a Legislative Assembly member chosen on 17 June 1792 to take part in a new commission created after the reading of a petition presented to the representatives of the people by a deputation of a Parisian section (of the Croix-Rouge). The petition stated that the king kept vetoing the most salutary decrees, evoking a crisis situation and the need for extraordinary measures. It even used the word 'terror' by proposing to deploy the very weapon used by adversaries to strike against the Revolution:

Legislators, when will our woes end? . . . It is time for you to raise yourselves to the heights of these dangers; bring, through great measures, into the souls of all conspirators the terror that they believe us to be susceptible to . . . We . . . the undersigned petitioners, demand that among the measures the supreme law of the safety of the Empire dictates, that you will decree the permanent meeting of sections of this city.[16]

The Assembly then decided 'that it would name, forthwith, a commission of twelve members to examine, from all points of view, the current state of France, to present its portrait in eight days and propose measures to save the Constitution, liberty, and the Empire.' This commission, of which Debry was one of the twelve members, was then given the title 'extraordinary commission'. The commission remained in place for some time; in July and August the Assembly sent it dozens of subjects to examine.[17] Sixteen days after the fall of the monarchy, on 26 August 1792, Debry proposed to the committee to form a body of 1,200 'tyrannicides', each armed with two pistols, a sword and a dagger, who would be called to take out 'in bodily combat' the generals of enemy armies and kings in the coalition against France.[18] The Assembly first voted in this project, but then a fellow member of the extraordinary commission, Vergniaud, objected to it as immoral and successfully had it annulled.[19] Debry had invoked the extraordinary nature of his proposal from the start:

> Monsieur Jean de Brie [sic] goes up to the tribune. He requires the utmost attention. I will propose, he says, an entirely new measure, *truly extraordinary*; but the war we are undertaking is not like the wars that have taken place up to now. It is not people we are fighting but it is the masters, it is kings, it is the masters of our enemies. Humanity needs to be avenged against tyrants and the masters who wish to kill our liberty.[20]

The case does not end there, for on 29 October, Debry, now re-elected from the department of Aisne to take a seat in the Convention alongside members of the Plain, proposed a definition of 'extraordinary' that would be very similar to the one adopted a year later to describe the revolutionary government:

> It must be noted that *the situation in which we find ourselves is as extraordinary as our mission*; that it would be mistaken to apply to other times what is being done in the present moment and to derive what would be appropriate then from what is necessary today; surely the time will come when the land of liberty will be peaceful and happy, where the law will be loved by all because it is the wish of every person; where these deep disturbances which mark the fall of thrones and the turmoil of human errors will be succeeded by a republican energy that knows its rights and its duties, and above all this wise and regular movement which announces life and health (applause); these times are not yet ours.[21]

The chapter on dictatorship in Rousseau's *Social Contract* may well have proved influential here. Not only did Rousseau argue that 'the order and slowness of forms demand a space of time that circumstances sometimes refuse', which the legislator could not in any case see beforehand and which formed the basis of the Roman dictatorship, but Rousseau also noted that the 'health of the nation' could require the concentration of the government in a small number of hands. He underlined that in such an extraordinary situation 'it was not the authority of laws that are to be altered, but only the form of their administration.'[22] There is little doubt that this passage influenced the men of the Convention when they assimilated 'extraordinary' with 'revolutionary'. Their intellectual formation in Latin had made them familiar with the history of antiquity and its authors, as well as the formula *Salus populi suprema lex esto*, which was quickly taken up in speeches in the Assembly.[23]

Debry, after reading a letter from the former mayor of Strasbourg, Dietrich, who had been arrested and complained of not being tried before the tribunal of his department, linked 'extraordinary' and 'revolutionary' in a speech before the Convention on 27 January 1793: 'You have decided, by a *revolutionary law*, that Dietrich, convicted of fanaticism, will be transferred to the tribunal of Besançon to be tried.'[24] On 10 March, while the Convention was debating the organization of the extraordinary criminal tribunal that had just been created, Robespierre, over the interruptions of the Girondins who cried out tyranny and claimed a veritable inquisition was under way, reminded the members of the Assembly that 'because you have declared *revolutionarily* [*révolutionnairement*] that whoever provokes the re-establishment of the monarchy should be punished by death, I ask that the decree mentions it.'[25] While his proposal was not carried through, the assimilation between 'extraordinary' and 'revolutionary' is nonetheless striking, and would continue until the autumn.

Thus, well before the distinction between ordinary and 'revolutionary' laws in the decree of 14 Frimaire (4 December), the use of the notion became commonplace, especially for Barère. He spoke on 1 August of the 'terrible domain of revolutionary law',[26] and then, three weeks later, evoked a 'revolutionary law commanded by circumstances',[27] before distinguishing on 16 October between ordinary and 'revolutionary' laws.[28] About a week earlier, on 10 October, Saint-Just had laid out the necessary conditions for effectively implementing political exception, obtaining the passing of a decree that recognized the government as 'revolutionary until the peace'. 'It is impossible that revolutionary laws can be executed if the government itself is not constituted in a revolutionary manner.'[29] In this way, 'extraordinary' and 'revolutionary' became synonyms of 'revolutionary' institutions that played a major role in political exception.

2. 'Revolutionary' institutions and their role in repression

'Revolutionary' institutions were constituted in a dizzying array of fashions. Some combined powers not enumerated in the Constitution that had already been occasionally employed but that became generalized throughout the national territory (representatives on missions, surveillance committees, etc.). Others (like the *armées révolutionnaires*) were created *ex nihilo*, even if they seemed pre-ordained before they were formally constituted. Others were already in place (military commissions) or were created out of pre-existing institutions (the Revolutionary Tribunal and commissions of revolutionary justice arising from other judicial courts of exception). Certain constitutional machinery was authorized to employ, temporarily, extraordinary measures (departmental criminal tribunals allowed to judge 'in a revolutionary manner', which in some cases were confusingly called the 'revolutionary tribunal').

Adding to the confusion, the extraordinary government was not limited to the key role given to the two major committees of the Convention, despite these committees being called the 'government committees' [*comités de gouvernment*]. The term is mistaken insofar as the Convention never suppressed the executive power and did not turn the Committee of Public Safety into a governing body (while the latter sprang from a tradition started with the Constituent Assembly of delegating some of the preparatory work for debates and legal proposals to committees it had created). Composed of members of the Convention who were elected (and routinely re-elected) by their fellow representatives, the Committee of Public Safety and the Committee of General Security only had powers thanks to the Assembly, which could choose not to continue to grant those powers or even to abolish those committees. While Robespierre and his colleagues remained, in theory, under the threat of dismissal or expulsion, the twelve (then eleven) members of the Committee of Public Safety remained in place for around a year (from summer 1793 to summer 1794).[30] It was this committee and its sister committee of General Security that were the regular organs of legislative work and the major revolutionary operations centres for everything concerning repressive measures.

Through the decrees they drafted, these two committees did indeed push some of the policies set in place by the Convention, with the decrees standing for, alongside the revolutionary laws, the working of the revolutionary government. The Committee of General Security was created by the Convention but inherited the functions of the Committee of Surveillance (created by the Legislative Assembly in autumn 1791) as well as functions of the committees of Reports and of Research (created by the Constituent Assembly). It took over surveillance and ordered home visits and arrests, and engaged in a close relationship with the police and the legal courts, among them the Revolutionary Tribunal. Membership of the Committee of General Security varied (usually between ten to twenty men; in spring 1794 it had twelve members), and this committee worked closely with the Committee of Public Safety. Reports and legal proposals were frequently presented to the Convention in the name of the two committees, following a procedure in place for other committees (such as reports presented in the name of both the Committee of Public Safety and of War).

The Committee of Public Safety appeared in its first form on 6 April 1793. It had developed out of a preceding committee (the Committee of General Defence), created on 1 January.[31] The creation of the Committee of Public Safety was nonetheless a turning point, partly because of its role in the weeks following in April when the policy of exception came to be institutionalized and partly because of how it was composed. Unlike the Committee of General Defence, the Committee of Public Safety was formed, from the outset, of members elected directly by the Convention, not chosen from other committees. In its early days it had a variable number of members, yet soon its membership stabilized at twelve representatives of the people. Its members became linchpins of the revolutionary government, even if the Committee never transformed itself into a genuine government. But to compensate for the weakness of the executive power – an executive power that the Convention feared – and also to avoid the overwhelming influence of a minister of War linked to the 'Hébertists', the Assembly gradually accepted that the Committee of Public Safety play a major role in the revolutionary government and placed it at the heart of the 'legislative centrality'. Although the Committee of Public Safety was not part of the executive branch, it drew up decrees with the force of law (always provided that the Convention did not reject them). It also adopted executive acts and decided other regulatory acts so that the laws could be applied. In addition, the Committee of Public Safety occupied a privileged place among the revolutionary institutions because its correspondence with deputies on mission allowed it to follow what was happening in the armies and the departments. Due to its role in implementing measures voted in by the Convention and the several hundred employees in its offices (around 500 in summer 1794) who every day handled hundreds of cases, the Committee of Public Safety came to take on *in practice* – though not *in law* – the function of a government. Its decisions were essential in the 'terror'. The working habits of its members attest to its major importance. They were in the Committee's offices from six o'clock in the morning and the day ended with a final meeting between seven and ten o'clock at night, sometimes even later in the case of an emergency. Much work went into the reports the Committee prepared and the draft decrees to be presented to the Convention. Members were aided by 'analysts' (*analyseurs*) who collated and synthesized information, archivists and librarians, designers (for designs, schemes and maps), and secretaries (*expéditionnaires*) who copied and sent out letters and decrees.[32]

A major task of the Committee of Public Safety concerned correspondence with deputies sent on missions. Sending out deputies as envoys on field missions was not a new practice – the Legislative Assembly had used it sparingly, dreading its mixture of legislative and executive powers; while up to early March 1793, the Convention sent eighty-six deputies to the armies or to certain departments stricken by unrest, but in almost all of the cases, these deputies were sent on a single mission, as a temporary stopgap.[33] Yet, beginning in March and April 1793, in tandem with the adoption of other measures of exception, sending out representatives on missions became a systematic practice, showing the Convention's desire to reinforce its control over the national space and the armies. At least 426 members of the Convention, or around half of its members, were sent on missions at some point. Around 900 missions took place between 1793 to 1795 (Year III included). While throughout this period a little less than half of these envoys were Montagnards, they took a prominent part in missions between autumn 1793 and summer 1794, in the thick of the period called the 'terror'. More than 90 per cent of the Montagnards were among those sent to the departments on 9 Nivôse Year II (29 December 1793) to reorganize the authorities and power structures in the departments along the lines laid out by the revolutionary government. The busiest envoys spent up to seventeen to twenty months almost continuously in the field. They were thus absent from the Convention's daily work and could not follow closely the political changes taking place in Paris during their missions.

Historians have often claimed that the deputies sent on missions exercised 'unlimited powers'. This was not the case, though they did have a considerable influence over the departments and the armies, serving as political and cultural intermediaries between the central and local powers, as well as between the government and citizens. This can be seen from a map showing the geographic distribution of deputies sent on mission to various departments (see map 2). The intensity of distribution underlines the urgent need to keep Paris provisioned with foodstuffs and other supplies, a demand linked to 'terror' – seen, for example, in the importance given to the Paris Basin and the Paris–Lyon–Toulon axis. The distribution of deputies sent to the armies (map 3) shows that the need to support the major military fronts weighed heavily – one can see this in comparing the northern front to the Pyrenees. Geographic zones suffering internal conflicts were also assigned representatives to the armies, as can be seen, above all, in the number of deputies sent to the armies near La Rochelle and the Vendée in 1793.

A small – but significant – proportion of the total number of deputies on mission (some several dozen) became involved in mass repression, thereby playing a significant role in the 'terror'. These men would themselves become the target of denunciations. Their roles were later amplified, becoming the subject of thousands of fantastic stories by some historians. Of these, Carrier would become the most infamous for his mission to Nantes and his role in the *noyades* (mass drownings of victims in the Loire). Other deputies are also credited with taking a leading role in local repression. They include: the four representatives who oversaw the brutal repression of the revolt in Lyon in autumn 1793 (Albitte, Collot d'Herbois, Fouché and Laporte); the envoys who coordinated the military efforts to reconquer Toulon in December 1793 (above all Barras and Fréron); the very unaptly-named Lebon who supervised numerous executions in Arras and Cambrai; and others who are today forgotten despite large numbers of executions laid at their door (for example, Francastel in Angers) or who operated in several departments because they were able to exercise their powers over a longer period of time (such as Dartigoeyte and Pinet in the southwest).

These deputies occupied a central place in the 'terror' through their decrees – which had the force of law, provided they were not rescinded by the Convention. Yet a number of checks existed on their power. They were commonly sent out in pairs, to share responsibility, and they were forced to work closely with other commissioners (agents of the executive power, of the Committee of Public Safety, armies, local authorities), their entourage (including their own agents), with local pressure groups, as well as with the Committee of Public Safety and the Convention, which could recall deputies to Paris at any time – with certain call-backs being clear messages of disapproval.

Two other revolutionary institutions served as vectors of the 'terror': the *armées révolutionnaires* and the surveillance committees. The importance of the *armées révolutionnaires*, first created in September 1793, is well known thanks to the remarkable work by Richard Cobb.[34] Nearly sixty such *armées révolutionnaires* existed, assembling around 30,000 men (militant activists, often involved in secularization efforts) and concerning around two-thirds of the departments (map 4) before their progressive suppression starting in Frimaire Year II (December 1793) and concluding definitively in spring 1794. The most important was the Parisian *armée révolutionnaire*, with around 7,000 men, of whom 1,200 were gunners. It was led by General Ronsin, who was linked to the 'Hébertists' and played a major part in the repression of a number of departments or communes (map 5). The decree creating the Parisian *armée révolutionnaire* explicitly mentioned its status as an extraordinary institution because it was from the onset 'intended to suppress the counter-revolutionaries [and] to execute, wherever needed, the revolutionary laws and public safety measures'. Cobb noted that these armies 'represented the ambulant Terror, the Terror in the village; they inspired fear, and that was very much the goal of its creators'.[35] Yet, as Cobb showed, the 'terror' linked to an *armée révolutionnaire* was often ephemeral and not followed by ferocious repressive measures, with rhetoric and symbolic manifestations (notably anti-Christian ones) more prominent than arrests or executions. With the exception of the Parisian *armée révolutionnaire*, especially in Lyon and in the Vendée, or the sinister case of the 'company of Marat' in Nantes, and to a lesser degree the expedition of the *armée révolutionnaire* of the Lot to Aveyron, the *armées révolutionnaires* showed themselves to be an ineffective instrument, incapable of exercising authority in a durable manner, rather than a formidable 'terrorist arm'.

The surveillance committees, too, have often been considered major instruments of the Terror in villages, but recent historical studies and a national survey in preparation now show that the vast majority of these committees did not play a key role in the repression.[36] From their creation in spring 1793 these committees were limited to tracking down 'foreigners' (anyone residing or passing through a commune he or she was not from). In the autumn they were granted the right to draw up lists of suspects. It was after the decree of 14 Frimaire Year II (4 December 1793), which organized the revolutionary government, that the surveillance committees shared oversight over the application of 'revolutionary' laws and measures for public safety or general security with municipal authorities. Most studies indicate that these committees were moderate rather than 'terrorist', with important distinctions in how they operated between the countryside or in cities (their role in the surveillance of suspects was much greater in cities) but also between departments (the degree of internal unrest within departments influencing the role they played). A large number of surveillance committees even defended communities against State demands, especially when it came to requisitions, while their registers noted, in meeting after meeting, that no suspects had been found. What is also striking is how their role changed over time: from spring to autumn 1793, they played a major role against suspects and 'moderates'; after 14 Frimaire, there was a weakening of their power and a marked subservience to district authorities and envoys on missions.

3. The recourse to extraordinary justice

As repression grew against opponents of the Revolution, the limitations of ordinary forms of justice became evident. When sovereignty was transferred from the king to the nation on 23 July 1789, a new form of 'treason' appeared, when the crime of treason against the king (*lèse-majesté*) became that of treason against the nation (*lèse-nation*), yet the very notion of *lèse-nation* as a crime was not defined with precision, and this new indictment was rarely used.[37] The Constitution of 1791 created a new national High Court with jurisdiction over the crimes of ministers and executive agents but also 'crimes that attack the general security of the State'.[38] This new court's first decisions came only in early August 1792, a few days before the assault on the Tuileries overthrew the constitutional monarchy. It was no surprise that a mass of criticism then appeared denouncing the slowness of the court and asking the Assembly to take measures to 'hasten the speed of trials' of those who were in or soon would be in custody (16 August).[39]

On 17 August a new tribunal was established, with a specific remit as a 'criminal tribunal to try crimes committed on 10 August and other crimes so related in either circumstances or vicinity'.[40] This court was proposed by Hérault de Séchelles on behalf of the extraordinary commission of the twelve. From the start, this predecessor of the Revolutionary Tribunal was conceived as an extraordinary court called to try political crimes, even if the very notion of a political crime remained imprecise. Over time, though, the contours of political crimes became more sharply defined with the radicalization of repressive legislation.

Of all the extraordinary courts, the Revolutionary Tribunal, created on 10 March 1793, is considered the most terrible, incarnating the supposed archetype of the 'terrorist' institution. The Convention debates over its formation, marked by lively oratorical sparring between the Montagnards and Girondins, underlined yet again the recourse to the extraordinary: 'We are in a revolution' (Garrau); 'We need to act, not talk' (Bentabole). And then this, from Danton:

> Nothing is more difficult than defining a political crime. But ... it is absolutely necessary that extraordinary laws, taken outside the social body, terrify the rebels and strike the guilty! Here the welfare of the people requires great means and terrible measures. I do not see a middle ground between ordinary forms and a revolutionary tribunal.[41]

This recourse to measures of extraordinary justice was for the Girondin Vergniaud nothing other than creating a new inquisition, while the Montagnard Danton thought doing so was a way of preventing popular furies like those of the massacres in September 1792 ('let us be terrible so that the people do not have to be').[42] The decree voted in included a first article whose words would turn out to have heavy consequences:

> There will be established in Paris an extraordinary criminal tribunal, with jurisdiction over all counter-revolutionary activities, all attacks on the liberty, equality, unity, and indivisibility of the Republic and against the internal and external security of the State, and all plots to re-establish the monarchy.[43]

Despite the imprecise wording that could both limit – and expand – the number of potential targets (as the notion of 'security of the State' shows), the activity of the Revolutionary Tribunal proved to be marked by a respect for judicial forms[44] – at least until the Law of 22 Prairial Year II (10 June 1794), which opened the period of seven weeks remembered as the 'Great Terror' (*la grande terreur*).[45] And while this new decree effectively took away the rights of the accused to a defence and forced sentences to be either capital punishment or an acquittal, it is worth noting that the archival record shows that, even then, respect for judicial forms persisted. Before this decree the Revolutionary Tribunal acquitted around half of the accused brought before it; in the period from 22 Prairial to 14 Thermidor (1 August, when the decree of 22 Prairial was overturned and Fouquier-Tinville, its chief prosecutor, was indicted), nearly one in four of the accused were acquitted.[46] In spite of its noxious reputation, the Revolutionary Tribunal should not be considered the most terrible tribunal of its time. Other extraordinary tribunals in certain departments were much harsher, thanks to the decree of 19 March 1793, a law with military applications, and under which the great majority of death sentences were carried out.

The decree of 19 March 1793 was directed at those who took up arms against the Republic. The work of Eric de Mari allows us to better understand the paths leading to the adoption of this legislative text and how it was used and applied in practice.[47] Following the sources used by Mari, around 22,000 captives were judged to be 'outlawed' (*hors la loi*), 60 per cent of whom were sentenced to death, resulting in 13,000 executions, most of them shot (around 70 per cent of all capital punishments carried out, if one follows the figures proposed in 1935 by Donald Greer).[48] Around 40 per cent of individuals judged to be 'outlawed' managed to escape the firing squad or the guillotine, even if, in principle, being placed 'outside the law' called for inflexible severity. Article 2, adopted on 19 March, for instance, ordered that any armed individual taking part in 'counter-revolutionary revolts or uprisings' against the recruitment of volunteers for the armies or wearing a white rosette ('or any other sign of rebellion') was to be taken before a military commission within twenty-four hours and then delivered to 'the executors of criminal judgements'.[49] The unarmed who were suspected of taking part in revolts (armed or not) and who were arrested were to be sent before the criminal tribunal of the relevant department, also within twenty-four hours. In these two cases, being found guilty through the oral testimony of two eyewitnesses was enough to send the accused to death. These military commissions, theoretically composed of five officers, were operational from October 1792. They were essentially extraordinary tribunals while the criminal tribunals of departments belonged to the ordinary workings of justice created by the Constituent Assembly. In both cases the placement outside the law tended towards an 'extraordinary' justice because, as the fact of being placed 'outside the law' clearly signified, the accused no longer benefited from any of the rights or protections the law offered.

The decree of 19 March, though later nuanced and completed by other texts, thus played a decisive role in the establishment of a justice of exception. Its local implementation admittedly revealed shortcomings and varying interpretations by judges (not all judges stuck to verdicts of either death or acquittal), as well as a surprising leniency given the severity of the cases it covered (individuals judged outside the law but acquitted because they were drunk, 'astray', forced, etc.). Military commissions, commissions called 'revolutionary' or 'popular' (composed of civilians, but with a relatively similar functioning), departmental criminal tribunals judging 'revolutionarily': all of these extraordinary courts sent to death a much larger number of the condemned than the Revolutionary Tribunal of Paris. At least sixty such courts or tribunals appeared, most of them created by deputies on mission and a great number of which did not sit in a fixed locale but were ambulatory (map 8).[50]

In certain places, several such courts succeeded each other, their severity in judgement at times proving to be quite different even though the local conditions remained the same – as was the case in Lyon.[51] On 9 October 1793, the very day that Lyon was retaken by troops sent by the Convention, a military commission was created to judge those captured who were armed, while two days later a commission of popular justice (later called a revolutionary tribunal, to better inspire fear) was to judge other 'rebels'. One month later, on 7 Frimaire Year II (27 November), a third extraordinary tribunal, called the revolutionary commission (or tribunal of the seven), took over. Of the 1,900 detainees executed, the military commission condemned 102 (88 officers and other ranks in the Lyonnais forces), the commission of popular justice 113 (87 for their participation in the 'rebel' authorities), and the revolutionary commission 1,680 (204 officers and 677 soldiers for having fought to defend the city, 271 for working for the local authorities, 319 for 'federalism' and 'counter-revolution', and 209 for the simple reason of being 'ex-nobles' or priests). The revolutionary commission was by far the most sanguine, and not simply because it operated for much longer than the other two. Yet 47.5 per cent of the accused before it were acquitted, compared to 40.7 per cent for the military commission and only 16.7 per cent for the commission of popular justice – evidence that, as with the Revolutionary Tribunal in Paris, the reality of its operation was much more nuanced than appears at first glance.

Other commissions should also be mentioned. There were well-known and sinister ones, like the 'military and revolutionary' commission, also called the 'Bignon committee' that raged in Nantes and judged between 170 and 200 prisoners per day, sentencing over 2,600 to death from mid-December 1793 to mid-February 1794.[52] And there were ones that are entirely unknown today, like the Montudeguy commission in Bayonne, the Bassereau-Bouilly commission in Tours and the military commission in La Rochelle.[53] Other commissions could be cited to illustrate how porous were the distinctions between the different types of commissions. In the Bas-Rhin, for example, deputies on mission attempted, in mid-October 1793, to create an *armée révolutionnaire*, to be supplemented by two 'provisional tribunals'. This *armée révolutionnaire* was meant to be composed of 1,000 regular soldiers taken from the armies of the Rhine and Moselle, while revolutionary justice was handled by civilians, not officers, as in military commissions. The acts of this ambulatory commission in the Alsatian department were often confusingly identified as coming from a 'revolutionary tribunal', which shows the uncertainty and imprecision of the time.[54]

Regardless of whether these commissions were well-defined or not, remembered for their harshness or entirely forgotten, all of these commissions incarnated the extraordinary justice put in place to suppress opposition to the Revolution, and especially to crush those who took up arms against the Republic. The most important thing, rather than attempt to exhaustively detail every single commission, or arrive at the precise number of victims, is rather to understand how the Convention could come to rely upon such extraordinary forms and procedures.

Every revolution is extraordinary, at least at its outset. Yet when the leaders of a revolution dispense with part or all of the previous regime, the new order that is constructed, piece by piece, eventually comes to belong to the realm of the ordinary. An ordinary order born out of revolution, but ordinary nonetheless. For the French Revolution, this process can be seen in the institutions created since autumn 1789 that balanced executive and legislative powers, dealt with territorial and administrative breakdowns, and established a new organization for justice.

Did everything change again after 10 August 1792, a date some historians argue constituted a second revolution? The answer may well be yes, insofar as royalty was abolished and the First Republic was established by the Convention. This new Assembly was faced, in time of war, with the immense task of rebuilding everything on the basis of a new constitution; Michelet would dub it 'the Assembly which never sleeps'.[55] Yet even if the month of August 1792 was undoubtedly a turning point in the radicalization of repressive measures,[56] the birth of the 'terror' cannot be traced back to that summer alone. Two major points are important here: the concept of a political crime and the fact that tribunals were, at first, de facto powerless to judge it; and secondly, the same powerlessness of ordinary institutions to deal with the crisis resulting from political conflicts, war with a coalition of foreign powers, multiple internal resistance to revolutionary policies, as well as the internal contradictions of the Revolution (including the glaring contradiction between the right to property and economic freedom, and the recognition of a natural right to life).

Political exception was born of that consciousness of judicial powerlessness, combined with internal contradictions. The government that became revolutionary had to use different levers of power to govern and steer the ship of state of the Republic. Repressive actions and measures against the adversaries of the Revolution, whether real or suspected, constituted one of the levers that have come to be designated under the name 'terror'. The 'terror' had its own logic, rhythms and a particular geography. Not all of the departments experienced the terror with the same intensity. Some departments, particularly in areas away from the frontiers, and from areas of internal conflict, emerged relatively unscathed. In other places the incidence of terror fell much more heavily. Two cases need to be studied separately: Paris, often seen as the epicentre of the 'terror'; and the geographic zone designated as the 'Vendée' (incorporating four western departments), in which a major conflict tantamount to a civil war took place. We will examine these two cases separately, in chapter 7.

Chapter 6

Terror in the Convention: Political Conflict as an Engine of 'Terror'

Terror was not only something that revolutionary activists inflicted on others – it was also something that they themselves experienced. They inflicted terror, but they were also terrorized. Desperate men had recourse to terror, both to defend the Revolution and, at least in part, to avoid becoming its victims. Here we shall look at how increasingly deadly conflicts played out at the heart of revolutionary politics, within the National Convention.

From the outset of the Revolution the concept of political parties was rejected. In the eyes of the men of the Constituent Assembly, political parties were populated by men who put self-interest and personal advancement before the public good. Inspired in part by the classical republican tradition, the Assembly made a conscious decision not to model the new politics on the British parliamentary system with its nascent political parties, the Whigs and the Tories, which French observers believed, with some justification, were characterized by 'cronyism' rather than public service. The new French system of politics was intended to be founded on political virtue and transparency; that is, each deputy was meant to act with integrity, and to defend the public good rather than the interests of any one party or group. Informal factions were also looked upon with suspicion; seen as secretive networks, whose members worked for their own interests, and were amenable to corruption. 'Faction' became a term of abuse in revolutionary politics.

Yet this ideal was in conflict with the reality, which is that people actively engaged in politics naturally gravitated towards others with whom they shared ideas and goals, along with ties of mutual trust and friendship, as well as elective affinities through their department of origin. From the early months of the Revolution factions were incompatible with the revolutionaries' conception of politics, but they were endemic to its practice.[1] During the time of the Constituent Assembly confrontations between factional groups in the national representation were largely confined to words, spoken and written; on the whole, and with the exception of occasional duels, deputies tried to discredit, dishonour and disempower, rather than to kill one another.[2] The principle of inviolability for deputies from arrest or prosecution was first set out on 23 June 1789 when Mirabeau called upon the deputies to proclaim their inviolability in a bid to protect themselves from the sweeping executive powers of absolute monarchy; this inviolability was confirmed by the Constitution of 1791. For nearly four years the principle that deputies were entitled to special protection by function of their office was maintained, though not definitively established.[3]

Soon after the Legislative Assembly first met, in October 1791, tensions arose over whether France should go to war with Austria. Jacques-Pierre Brissot, a key figure both in the Assembly and in the Jacobin Club, gathered around him a group that supported his contention that such a war would result in French victory, whilst bringing out into the open the Revolution's internal enemies – that is, the king and queen. This reckless policy was opposed by Robespierre in a series of debates within the Jacobin Club. He had intermittent support from some other Jacobins, including Marat, Danton and Desmoulins, but at times he cut a lonely figure, as support for the war policy, couched in a rhetoric of fervent patriotism, escalated both in the Jacobins and in the Assembly. Robespierre and others who opposed war were attacked as 'unpatriotic'.[4] This initial split over the war became the starting point for bitter divisions within the Convention.

1. The Convention and the clubs: from political strife to 'purging'

When the Convention met, it faced the task of establishing the Republic, whilst ensuring that France remained militarily undefeated by the invading foreign powers and the *émigrés* who fought alongside them. At the same time the *conventionnels* were confronted by a series of daunting problems within France: the entrenched opposition of counter-revolutionaries, supporters of monarchy and the non-juring clergy; social and economic turmoil and shortages that ensued from the war; the question of what to do with the king currently imprisoned in the Temple; and the unrest of the *sans-culottes* who had played a crucial role in overthrowing the monarchy and now expected a stake in the new regime. In these tumultuous circumstances, achieving political stability was an all but impossible task.

Further problems confronted the Convention from within its own membership. The new rallying cry was 'the Republic one and indivisible'. The *conventionnels* were brought together both by their consciousness of their shared mission and by the urgency of the ongoing war crisis. Yet from the outset there were two opposing groups or factions in the Assembly: they became known as the Girondins and the Montagnards. The Girondins loosely coalesced around Brissot, and for several months they dominated much of the business of the Convention. Many in this group were former Jacobins, though by autumn 1792 the majority had abandoned the club or been formally expelled. Several members of the group, notably Brissot himself, along with deputies from the Gironde region, including Vergniaud and Gensonné, were amongst the 49 deputies who had dominated the Legislative Assembly.[5] Linked to this group (though outside the Convention) were several men who had served as ministers in the spring of 1792, and returned to the ministry after the fall of the monarchy. The most prominent of these 'Girondin' ministers was Jean-Marie Roland, Minister of the Interior. Brissot's group became known variously as 'Brissot and his friends', the 'Brissotins', the 'Rolandins 'or simply 'the faction'. It was only in late 1792 that they become identified by the name that was later taken up and widely used by historians – the 'Girondins'.

We need to bear in mind, however, that the naming and identifying of the 'Girondins' (as well as other revolutionary factions including the 'Dantonists', 'Hébertists' and 'Robespierrists') is deeply problematic. In many cases names of factions were invented and imposed on men (some of whom were connected and some of whom were not) by their opponents. Factional identities became terms of abuse, part of a war of words used to vilify opponents. During the most intense periods of infighting, for a revolutionary to be labelled as part of a faction could be tantamount to a death sentence. Deputies repeatedly denied being members of a distinct faction, repudiating attempts by their opponents to label them as factious.

It is not an easy matter for historians to establish beyond doubt some fundamental facts about the 'Girondins' – who and how many they were; whether they had a coherent specifically 'Girondin' political philosophy or line of thought, and, if so, what that was; whether they were ideological or even tactical 'federalists'; and even whether, beyond a small inner circle linked by friendships, they actually existed as a group at all. Michael Sydenham argued that the idea of a unified political faction of Girondins was largely a myth, created by the Montagnards in order to condemn the Girondins as a conspiratorial group. Its members were only loosely allied politically, nor did they share a consistent set of political ideas clearly distinguishable from that of Montagnards. Alison Patrick, in her detailed study of voting, tactical operations and alignments in the Convention, took a slightly different view. She showed that there was an inner group of sixty men whom she identified as being made up of 'Brissot and his friends', who often worked closely together, but who still exercised considerable independence over ideological positions.[6] The Girondins have often been labelled as ideological 'moderates', but this was certainly not the case in the summer of 1791. Immediately after the flight to Varennes, Brissot and his group were amongst the first to embrace the call for a republic, whilst Robespierre was still hesitating over the repercussions of such a policy. They were also strong opponents of slavery. Throughout 1791, Brissot's group were no more squeamish about popular violence than were other Jacobins, and they were eager to court the support of the *sans-culottes*. Gorsas (along with other members of the group around Brissot) was one of the very first to invent and use the new political term *sans-culotte* between September 1791 and May 1792. There was a tragic irony in the fact that the same men who fell victim to real *sans-culottes* in June 1793 had themselves invented this political term, profited by it, but then proved unable to control it.[7]

Friendship networks and personal loyalties played a major role in shaping political choices and allegiances.[8] Insofar as the Girondins had a collective identity, it was primarily through their friendships. Brissot was never the official leader of the group; rather, he was the central connecting point of a series of friendship groups. An inveterate networker, he dominated partly through his facility for forging connections. He himself confided in his *Memoirs*, 'I have always loved to bring my friends together.'[9] Roland and his wife formed another connecting point at the heart of the Girondin network, through Roland's ministry and Madame Roland's salon.[10]

Pitted against the Girondins were the Montagnards (literally 'the mountain people'), a group named from the elevated position of the seats they occupied in the Convention, whilst also evoking symbolism associated with mountains (fiery volcanoes, Mount Sinai, etc.). More of a unified group than the Girondins, most of them were habitués of the Jacobin Club. After the departure of the Girondins from the club, it became the undisputed power base for the

Montagnards. Twenty-two deputies for Paris formed the nucleus of the Montagnards, including Robespierre, Danton, Collot d'Herbois, Desmoulins and Marat.[11] Not all those who aligned themselves with the Montagnards were representatives of Paris departments, and Montagnard deputies were scattered throughout the country: Saint-Just, for example, was from Aisne, Couthon from Puy-de-Dôme, Le Bas from Pas-de-Calais. Nonetheless, the Montagnards identified themselves with Paris and in support of the *sans-culottes*, together with the principle of popular violence as a legitimate form of direct democracy. As a consequence, they drew a great part of their strength from the support of the Parisian militants.

Historians used to claim that there were major social, class and ideological differences between Girondins and Montagnards.[12] But in fact, there was very little to distinguish between them. They came from similar social and cultural backgrounds, had many friendships in common, read the same books, and shared the same ideals. In 1792 both groups were committed republicans; both conceptualized revolutionary politics in terms of a struggle between men of virtue who defended the Republic, and the conspirators who opposed it; and both sides would be prepared to break the ideological principle of immunity of deputies in order to eliminate their opponents.

Friendship was important to revolutionaries. Revolutionary politics was a minefield; having friends could help you to negotiate its risky terrain. Friendship was a natural way of conducting politics in a cultural milieu in which there was no formal party structure to bring people together. Friendship could be advantageous, providing a way of making connections that could give access to administrative and governmental posts. Friendship was central to the informal networking through which much of the business of revolutionary politics was conducted. On a personal level, friendship played a part in shaping people's allegiances and choices. Many friendships were forged in the ferment of revolutionary politics. People were drawn together by shared purpose, hopes and camaraderie, as well as the risks that they faced together. Revolutionaries often idealized friendship, using Rousseauist language to describe their love for their friends. But there was a decidedly negative aspect to friendship in revolutionary ideology, one that was closely allied to the idea of 'faction'. Friendships could be regarded with suspicion, as a conduit for private self-advancement in a manner that recalled the practices of the Ancien Régime. Informal networking could mean secretive politics. In certain circumstances friendships were seen as linked to the dangerous notion of conspiracy. Loyalty to a friend could be portrayed as a betrayal of the imperative to serve the people as a whole.

Friendship between individuals could potentially be in conflict with the demands of political virtue. Personal enmity also played a part in factional divisions: in some cases, the most bitter enemies were people who had once been friends.

Many of those who later divided into 'Girondins' and 'Montagnards' had previously been friends; choosing to turn one's back on former friendships could result in a betrayal no less personal than political. Thus the Montagnard Camille Desmoulins would later admit that many of the deputies labelled in 1792 as 'Girondins' had formerly been his personal friends. Many had been present at his wedding in December 1790. Amongst their number was Brissot himself who, along with Robespierre, was one of the 'witnesses' of Desmoulins' nuptials. Three years after his wedding, when Desmoulins himself was under intense pressure at the Jacobins Club, he frantically tried to excuse himself for having chosen the 'wrong' friends:

> I was always the first to denounce my own friends; from the moment that I realized that they were conducting themselves badly, I resisted the most dazzling offers, and I stifled the voice of friendship that their great talents had inspired in me.[13]

What distinguished 'Girondins' and 'Montagnards' beyond anything else were the choices that they made at some critical points of the Revolution.[14] The first divisions began over the war debates. The conflict escalated into accusations over financial – especially ministerial – corruption, integrity and motivation.[15] A further issue, one that grew to overshadow the others, was that of Paris. During 1791 Brissot and his group were closely linked to Paris militants, but over the following year this connection disintegrated. The September Massacres became a dividing point: several Girondin leaders later became convinced that their own lives had been endangered, though whilst the massacres were taking place the Girondins did no more than future Montagnards to intervene to stop the killings.[16] Fear and bloodshed divided the two factions beyond hope of reconciliation. Whilst many of the subsequent actions of the Girondin leaders were reckless and precipitate, their actions should be understood against the background of their understandable fear that popular violence would be turned on them, inflamed by the incendiary words of Marat, Hébert and other journalists popular with the militants.[17] Whilst the Girondins wanted to move the Convention out of Paris, there is no indication that they espoused a 'federalist' ideology.[18]

The majority of the *conventionnels* remained politically unaligned and sat in a metaphorical and literal middle space known as the Plain or Marais (the marsh). Some of these deputies sided with the

Girondins on occasion – especially when the dominance of Paris was at issue – or with the Montagnards; or fluctuated between the groupings. Many of the deputies new to national politics were attracted to the Girondins' banner by their anti-Paris stance. Over the ensuing months, however, the balance of power shifted as a sizeable section of unaligned deputies, who began by offering fairly consistent support to the Girondins, gradually switched to supporting the Montagnards. This was not because they identified themselves as Montagnards, but because they were increasingly sceptical of the Girondins' leadership, and they came to see the Montagnards as having a more pragmatic grasp of the political and military realities of the situation. These unaligned deputies voted for the laws that enabled terror, and their support would be crucial for maintaining those policies.

Revolutionaries kept a watchful eye on one another; they frequently criticized or even denounced one another's conduct. Both sides maintained, and seem to have sincerely believed, that their opponents were traitors, conspiring with the foreign powers. The best orators could rouse up their audiences into excited outbursts of approbation or disapproval. Since the early days of the Revolution, all parties had learned much about the power of the press and how to negotiate it. Some deputies were also editors of their own newspapers. Whilst the Girondins were incensed at the antics of the pro-Montagnard crowds in the public galleries, the Montagnards were equally furious at the hostile reporting of the Girondin press, and particularly exasperated by Roland's recourse to ministerial funds to sponsor newspapers that took a Girondin line.[19] Both sides engaged in political calumny, attacking one another's integrity, secret motives and underlying ambition.[20]

Amongst the Montagnards, Marat was the most vitriolic opponent of the Girondins, whilst they, for their part, openly detested him. Robespierre, too, though with less frenzied language, played a leading part in the war of words, claiming that leading Girondins were ready to assassinate him for his resolution in exposing their perfidy.[21] Desmoulins wrote two influential pamphlets that did much to construct the narrative of Brissot and his group as conspirators, secretly working to oppose the Revolution: *Brissot Unmasked* (February 1792) and *Fragment of the Secret History of the Revolution* (later also known as *L'Histoire des Brissotins*) (May 1793).

Yet it was the Girondins who mounted the first challenge to the principle of inviolability of deputies. On 17 December 1792 they attempted to have members of the Bourbon family exiled. This was a blow aimed at Philippe d'Orléans, the immensely rich erstwhile duke and cousin of the king, who had disavowed his privileged background, taken the name 'Philippe-Equality', and now sat with the Montagnards. The Montagnards defended the inviolability of national representation and succeeded in defeating the proposal.[22]

The Convention decided to put Louis XVI on trial. The deputies themselves, on behalf of the people, would stand in judgement of their former king. There was no doubt that he would be found guilty of treason: it was unthinkable that the Convention, which had already formally deposed him, would come to any other conclusion. The question of whether or not he should be subject to an immediate death penalty was, however, much more divisive. The Montagnard deputies tended to take a harder line than the Girondins, arguing for the king to be put to death. But the divisions were not clear cut. Whilst some Girondins sought a form of public referendum to decide the question (an *appel au peuple*), other deputies linked to the Girondins argued for death. The debates illustrate the difficulties of trying to pigeon-hole deputies into factions.[23] The verdict that the king should be put to death was carried, amidst scenes of knife-edge tension. The decision to execute him established the principle that the public good overrode all other considerations.[24]

March 1793 brought renewed crisis after a series of military reversals, culminating in the outbreak of conflict in the Vendée, and the battle of Neerwinden.[25] It was in the face of this burgeoning crisis that a series of measures 'of political exception' were passed, and which we discuss in the next chapter. They included: the decree of 19 March declaring armed rebels to be outlawed (declared '*hors la loi*') and subject to execution within twenty-four hours; and the setting up of an 'extraordinary criminal tribunal' in Paris, soon to be named the Revolutionary Tribunal. Both Girondins and Montagnards supported these measures.[26] In defining a 'political crime' for the new tribunal, no distinction was to be made between representatives of the people and ordinary citizens.[27] The definitions of 'conspiracy' and 'treason' were dangerously vague.[28] At this time Robespierre still had reservations about the dangers of using the nebulous term 'conspirator' without a rigorous definition of what it meant. He addressed the Convention: 'I ask that it be specified what the Convention, what the friends of liberty mean by conspirators, counter-revolutionaries'. If these terms are not clarified, he continued, 'the best citizens' risked being brought before a tribunal which had been instituted with the aim of protecting them.[29]

The crisis intensified with the treason of general Dumouriez. The Girondins had strongly supported him, leaving them vulnerable to accusations that they were implicated in his treason as 'enemies within'. Treason in time of war has meant death in most times and cultures; the revolutionary wars were no exception. There is no evidence that the Girondins were party to any plot with Dumouriez: they were guilty of recklessness and incompetence in conducting a war that they themselves had done so much to bring about, rather than treason. Ironically, there is rather more evidence – albeit circumstantial – implicating Danton in Dumouriez's activities. Danton had visited the general at the front, just prior to the latter's defection. The Girondins accused Danton of being in league with Dumouriez, though Danton denied it strenuously.[30]

When news broke in Paris of Dumouriez's betrayal, Marat declared to the panicked Convention that the conduct of deputies, generals and ministers should be examined. A Girondin, Birotteau, went further, and obtained a decree stating that the Convention, 'regardless of the inviolability of a representative', had the right to indict any of its members suspected of collusion with the 'enemies of liberty, of equality, and of the republican government'.[31] This decree ended the inviolability of deputies: it would have grim consequences. A few days later, on 6 April, Danton managed to get this decision modified somewhat, at a time when his own relations with Dumouriez were in question. It was agreed that the assent of the Convention itself was needed to authorize the arrest of anyone serving as a deputy, general or minister.[32]

The Girondins were the first to deploy this decree against their rivals; they denounced Philippe d'Orléans and the former marquis de Sillery (who also sat with the Montagnards) as accomplices of Dumouriez, and succeeded in obtaining their arrest.[33] It was the Girondins, too, who on 12 April, on a proposal by Boyer-Fonfrède, used the new decree to obtain the assent of the Convention to a decree of accusation against Marat for an incendiary address put forward by the Jacobin Club which he had signed as president. Had the Girondins succeeded in their move against Marat, he would have been the first deputy convicted by the Revolutionary Tribunal, but their plan backfired, and he was acquitted on 24 April, amidst scenes of enthusiastic support by the crowds.[34] The Girondins' attempt to eliminate Marat was a serious blunder. It set a precedent for deputies to use terror against one another, thus heightening the stakes in the factional conflicts.

Throughout April and May the tension intensified: scuffles and physical confrontation broke out between deputies inside the Convention. The Girondins set up a Commission of Twelve to look into the activities of the Commune, leading to the arrest of Hébert and other Commune officials. Brissot and his friends called for armed militias (*armées départementales*) to be created to march on Paris and the *sans-culottes*. They made repeated attempts to rouse their constituents against the Parisian militants. Early in May, Vergniaud wrote to his constituents (*ses mandats*) in the Gironde, urging them, 'Rise up! Strike with terror at the men who provoke civil war.'[35]

Popular pressure on the streets of Paris brought down the Girondins. During April the Paris sections continuously petitioned both the Convention and the Jacobin Club with two main demands: the removal of the deputies associated with Dumouriez, and the setting of a maximum price on essential supplies, above all bread. Day after day tens of thousands of people surrounded the Convention. Women played a prominent role and there is evidence that they led some of the demonstrations.[36] On 15 April, a petition was presented to the Convention by thirty-three sections, sanctioned by the Jacobin Club and the Commune, demanding the exclusion of twenty-two 'Girondin' deputies (the number would become symbolic).[37] It was not the Montagnards themselves, but *sans-culotte* leaders who planned the insurrection, though most of the actual leaders were from the more affluent classes rather than genuine *sans-culottes*.[38]

2. From arrests to political trials

On 31 May and 2 June, militants from the sections organized a full-scale insurrection with mass demonstrations around the Convention to intimidate the *conventionnels* into agreeing to the exclusion and arrest of the leading Girondins. Despite protests from deputies at this violation of the national representation, the insurrection culminated in the purging of twenty-nine deputies, along with two ministers, Clavière and Lebrun. The Montagnard deputies did not take an active part in these events, though some of them, including Robespierre, gave tacit support to the *sans-culotte* proposals. There is evidence that the Montagnards themselves were in fear of the crowds that day; like the Girondins before them, they were riding the tiger of popular militancy.[39]

The excluded deputies were placed under loose house arrest; others had already absconded. There was considerable uncertainty as to what should be done with them. At this stage there was still room for negotiation, and several Montagnards, including Danton and Couthon, offered themselves as hostages, an offer refused by Girondins still in the Convention. It was hoped that the arrested Girondins would eventually be readmitted to the Convention, which voted for them to continue to receive their salaries. The initial report on the arrest of the Girondins, given by Barère on 6 June on behalf of the newly-formed Committee of Public Safety, was judicious and conciliatory. But the flight of two-thirds of the deputies placed under arrest in their domiciles, and their engagement in a series of armed revolts against the Convention was to rapidly extinguish the possibility of compromise.[40]

A more comprehensive report was produced on 8 July by Saint-Just for the Committee of Public Safety. This went further in outlining a Girondin conspiracy to use violence against the Montagnards, to put Louis XVI's son on the throne, and make his mother regent. The report spoke of terror as a weapon used by the Girondins, whose plan was to 'confound the government by terror and declamations'.[41] The Convention needed to exercise caution: 'public safety' (*le salut public*) was the highest law. Notwithstanding:

> Not all the prisoners are guilty; the greatest number were only led astray; but as in a conspiracy the salvation of the *patrie* is the supreme law, you may have confused for a moment error with crime, and wisely sacrificed the liberty of a few for the salvation of all.[42]

Saint-Just's report reassured its listeners that the Convention would not be 'terrible' towards those who submit to its laws. His conclusions were fairly pragmatic:

> However it may be, freedom will not be terrible towards those whom it has disarmed and who have submitted to the laws; proscribe those who have fled from us to take up arms; their flight attests to the lack of rigour of their detention; proscribe them, not for what they have said, but for what they have done. Judge the others, and forgive as many as possible: error should not be confused with crime, and you do not like to be severe. It is time for the people to hope for happy days at last, and for freedom to be something other than party fury.[43]

The report attempted to marshal evidence to prove the charges. It was also careful to limit the numbers of men accused of actual involvement in the conspiracy. Saint-Just continued:

> Now pronounce. You must differentiate between the detainees: the greater number were deceived, and which of us can flatter ourselves that we were never deceived? The real culprits are those who fled, and you owe them nothing, since they are desolating their homeland.[44]

Nine men who had fled from arrest to instigate the revolt were decreed 'traitors to the *patrie*', the equivalent of 'outlawing' under the decree of March. This was a major step, as it indicated that these men need only be apprehended to be put to death. There were said to be grounds of accusation against a further five men suspected of complicity with those who had fled. Roland was not mentioned. Nor was Brissot, despite Saint-Just's description of him as 'a Monk amongst you' (a reference to General Monck who played a role in ending the English 'Republic', and was rewarded with a pension and a dukedom).[45] Brissot had escaped arrest, and been recaptured, but had not been involved in the armed uprising.

Still the Montagnards hesitated to use this rhetoric to kill. Saint-Just's speech showed they were still capable of differentiating between the leaders amongst their political enemies and the rank and file who were 'misled'. Yet within a week the policy of compromise would be jettisoned. It was sealed by an act of violence – the assassination of Marat by Charlotte Corday on 13 July (see the account in chapter 1). In death Marat was transfigured, becoming a revolutionary martyr. The embargo against visual depictions of political leaders in a way which might glorify them did not apply to a dead man.[46] Soon David's iconic painting of the dying Marat would hang in the Convention, alongside his depiction of another assassinated *conventionnel*, Le Peletier, a constant reminder to living representatives that they too might be called upon to die in the cause of the *patrie*. Fear of assassination would haunt the Montagnards.[47]

Corday's action, which she had believed would put an end to terror and violence, had the opposite effect. The Montagnards, convinced that no woman would devise such a plan unaided, believed she had acted at the instigation of the Girondins. Other *conventionnels* also came under suspicion, including Fauchet and Deperret (Lauze de Perret) whose help Corday had sought when she arrived in Paris. Fatally, in Deperret's pocket was found a list of 75 deputies who had signed a secret protest against the expulsion of the Girondins.[48] The ongoing federalist revolt also had serious consequences for the fate of the Girondins. On 13 July the Girondin insurgents in Normandy were defeated with relative ease. But federalist protests spread to other parts of the country, and in some areas, most notably Lyon, Marseille and Toulon, shaded into outright counter-revolution.

By the time that Billaud-Varenne spoke on 15 July, his account of the Girondin conspiracy had become much more sinister. There would be no more compromise. He identified a concerted, active and long-standing conspiracy, and widened the net of suspects, tracing 'a conspiracy plan that evidently embraces the entire republic'. He conceded that there were few formal proofs, since the conspirators were 'working in the shadows, and meditating on their crimes at leisure, material traces are almost always missing', but their plots could be uncovered by means of 'simple moral conviction' and by observing how far their plans were in conformity with those of other conspirators.⁴⁹

Nevertheless, the Montagnards remained reluctant to cross the Rubicon and send the Girondins to their deaths. The Girondin leaders remained in prison over the summer and early autumn. During that time the Republic struggled under a series of military disasters. On 2 September news arrived in Paris that Toulon, with its naval bases, had been delivered up to the British by royalists; an event which offered confirmation of the links between (some) federalists and royalism. The revolutionary leaders were under intense pressure from the Paris militants and populist journalists led by Hébert to demonstrate their own commitment by taking a hard line on the 'conspirators'. On 20 August Hébert was defeated in an attempt to become Minister of the Interior. He thereafter redoubled his efforts to make himself the leading spokesman for the Paris militants, replacing the dead Marat. Through his domination of the Commune, the Cordeliers Club, and his journal, *Le Père Duchesne*, Hébert was rapidly becoming a major force. Moreover, over the summer and into the autumn of 1793, spokesmen for the militants, first the 'Enragés', then, after their elimination, the 'Hébertists' (see chapter 7) repeatedly attacked the Convention, the Committee of Public Safety, and even Robespierre. In the words of one pamphleteer, the time for mercy was over: 'Do not say "liberty or death" but "death to all those who stand in our way". No more pity.'⁵⁰ Under intense pressure, the Convention finally agreed to put the Girondins on trial.

3. Death as a means to eliminate opponents in the Convention

As Michel Biard shows, three types of decree could be used against deputies in the Convention.⁵¹ Each had to be voted by the Convention itself, with the Committee of General Security detailed to oversee the executive process of carrying it out. The first decree was for a deputy to be put under arrest (*décret d'arrestation*). This could be a house arrest, or a place of detention such as the Luxembourg Palace. The second form of decree was to issue a formal indictment (*décret d'accusation*). If this was done, the deputy was transferred either to the Conciergerie prison to await trial before the Revolutionary Tribunal or, in a few cases where the deputy had been apprehended outside Paris, to another tribunal. The third form of decree was to declare a deputy outlaw (*décret de mise hors de la loi*). If this happened, he was effectively branded as a traitor in time of war and subject to death. No other form of trial was called for, and if the deputy was apprehended, all that was left was to confirm his identity, and he was to be put to death within twenty-four hours.

For the deputies already under arrest, it remained to decide who was to figure on the list of those to be sent for trial. There was much uncertainty about whom to include, with names added and struck off up to the last minute. Several of the men who figured late in the day as members of the 'Girondin party' had had limited political connections with the Girondin leaders.[52] In some cases, friendship (above all the brave decision to be publicly loyal to proscribed Girondins) was a factor in whether or not individuals were listed among the 'Girondins'. This was the case for Ducos and his brother-in-law, Boyer-Fonfrède, both of whom had often voted against 'Girondin' measures, but they were intimate friends of Vergniaud, and had courageously defended him in the Convention after his arrest.

On 3 October Amar appeared in the Convention on behalf of the Committee of General Security to present the formal indictment which would form the basis of the legal case brought against the Girondins at their trial. As he began to speak, the doors to the Convention were locked, so that no one could escape.[53] The numbers of those accused had climbed to forty-one; plus twenty others declared 'traitors to the *patrie*' and thus outlawed. The seventy-five men who had signed the secret protest learned that they too were to be arrested. They had had no prior warning. In harrowing scenes, deputies were hauled from their seats. The Girondin Dulaure later described the distressing sight of stunned deputies being led away, with no chance to speak in their own defence, 'like lambs destined for slaughter'.[54]

There were now thirty-six more men implicated than in Saint-Just's report. The additional names were those of men who had not been involved in the federalist revolt, and who were only marginally associated with the Girondins' inner network. Yet they were all, said Amar, part of the conspiracy.[55] They were accused of being party to the federalist revolt, of involvement in the assassination of Marat, of being implicated in the revolt in the Vendée, and of being agents in the service of Pitt – an altogether nebulous charge for which no plausible evidence was offered.[56]

Even so, there were limits beyond which Robespierre, for one, chose not to go. At this same meeting of the Convention, Robespierre opposed Billaud-Varenne's demand that there be a vote by roll call (*appel nominel*) on the grounds that it would polarize the Convention into those for and against the arrests: 'I do not see the necessity ... to assume that the National Convention is divided into two parts, one of which is composed of friends of the people, and the other of conspirators who have betrayed it'. Some Montagnards called for the seventy-five deputies who had signed the secret protest to be indicted too, and sent before the Revolutionary Tribunal. Robespierre opposed this demand: 'The National Convention should not seek to multiply the number of the guilty; it should focus on the leaders of the faction; the punishment of the leaders will frighten the traitors and save the *patrie*.' He warned, 'be aware that among the men you have seen dragging the chariot of the ambitious, whom you have unmasked, there are many who have been led astray'. He persisted through shouts of angry disapproval from the galleries that threatened to drown out his voice.[57] The true defenders of the people, he said, are 'those who have the courage to tell the truth, even when circumstances would seem to command their silence'.[58] The seventy-five remained in prison, but were not put on trial. Robespierre's stance on that day probably saved their lives. He continued to defend them subsequently. Ironically, though understandably, some of these men would seek retributive vengeance on surviving Jacobins after Thermidor.

The first deputies to be executed were on the list (in Saint-Just's report) of those who had escaped arrest to engage in armed revolt, and been declared 'traitors to the *patrie*' and thus 'outlawed'. The first was Gorsas, captured when he returned to Paris to visit his mistress. After his identity was formally established, he was sent to his death on 7 October. Hébert, speaking in the voice of his alias, the *sans-culotte*, *Le Père Duschesne*, mocked Gorsas's apparent stoic indifference en route to the guillotine, which Hébert claimed was due to his having consumed several bottles of wine in an effort to escape the mockery of the *sans-culottes*.[59] This long calvary endured by a national representative, sent to his death amidst the taunts of onlookers, would be repeated many times over. The second execution was that of Birotteau, captured and sentenced as 'outlawed' in Bordeaux. His reported message to the Convention was: 'I know that the guillotine is waiting for me, you would not have evaded it, nor would all the partisans of the Mountain, if we had been the strongest.'[60]

Thus the conflict between the factions had escalated into a ruthless fight to the death, with men on both sides prepared to destroy one another. The conflict was not just about the conduct of the war, or the relations between Paris and the provinces. There was also a personal dimension to the struggle: enmity, mistrust, rivalry, betrayal and, above all, mutual fear, fed the cocktail of toxic emotions in the Convention. The poisoned atmosphere was compounded by the worsening legal situation of the *conventionnels* and the erosion of their inviolability, leaving them vulnerable to arrest, trial and execution.

The trial, conviction and condemnation to death of twenty-one Girondins provides devastating evidence of just how vulnerable national representatives had become. The purpose of the trial was not to establish the guilt or innocence of the accused, but to procure their deaths. It is hard to speculate with any certainty on what might have happened had the Girondins and not the Montagnards been the victors; but is likely that a similar scenario might well have developed, though one in which the identities of accused and accusers would have been reversed.

The trial of the Girondin leaders was thus a 'political trial'. It was characterized by fear on the part of the men carrying it out. If the Montagnards failed to convict, their own lives could be at stake. A man whose virtue was vindicated could easily retaliate by turning the tables and accusing his accusers. This had happened when Marat had been acquitted by the Revolutionary Tribunal; the verdict in his favour rebounded on the Girondins who had engineered his arrest. This knowledge made the Montagnards ruthless. It also led to an increase in the numbers of people included in the trial. Once the Montagnards decided to exterminate their political enemies, any friend of their enemies who was left alive was likely to seek revenge. It would be safer then, to kill anyone who might pose a threat in the future. This was the brutal logic behind the trial of the Girondins. A similar rationale would characterize all the decimations of political factions during the following months. The point of the trial was not to prove the guilt of the Girondins, but to bring about their deaths, and to make the case look vaguely credible.

The Girondins tried to organize their defence. Vergniaud, on the question of whether he had been part of a faction, wrote, 'Relations based on mutual esteem, never coalitions of views'.[61] It was a hopeless effort. The Girondins were accused of complicity in a conspiracy alleged to have begun with the Revolution itself, 'a conspiracy against the unity and indivisibility of the Republic, against the liberty and security of the French people'.[62] There was no way out of the tangled web of conspiracy charges: the opinions of one were assumed to be the opinions of all. Hearsay and personal and circumstantial evidence were admitted. The crux of the trial came down to the question of authenticity of motives, who was the 'patriot' and who was the 'conspirator' disguised in false patriotism? Amongst the witnesses who gave evidence against the Girondins were former colleagues and friends amongst the Jacobins, fellow deputies including Fabre d'Eglantine, Chabot and Léonard Bourdon, and leaders of the Commune, Chaumette and, above all, Hébert, all of whom used their personal knowledge of the Girondins to inform against them, to accuse Brissot and his friends of being motivated by personal ambition and corruption.

To cut short the proceedings, the Convention voted that after three days a jury could opt to hear no more evidence. Antonelle, spokesman for the jury obligingly confirmed that 'the conscience of the jurors is sufficiently informed'.[63] After three hours of deliberation, all twenty-one of the accused were found guilty, amidst scenes of stupefaction and horror. One of their number, Valazé, stabbed himself in the dock. The others were guillotined the following day, 31 October. It was the largest number of representatives of the people sent to the guillotine on the same day. The body of Valazé was taken along with the twenty others to the foot of the scaffold (though not decapitated), to demonstrate that even in death there was no evading the judgement of the Revolutionary Tribunal.

4. The elimination of factions, the apogee of 'terror' or the will to end it?

The official line was that, with the elimination of the Girondins, the Convention was united. In reality, the politicians' terror was not so easily ended: in the following months it emerged again, this time in the form of divisions within the Mountain itself. The Jacobin Club reached the height of its influence during Year Two. Now that their leaders dominated executive power, controlling posts, patronage and the wealth of the state, many Jacobins hoped for, indeed expected, rewards for their years of loyalty and sacrifice to the revolutionary cause in the form of career advancement and personal success. To some extent this would be fulfilled: the Republic needed men who had the appropriate patriotism and could be trusted to undertake administrative tasks. Those who were disappointed in their expectations were often angry and resentful of more successful revolutionaries. It is one of the ironies of the Jacobins' politics that they reserved their bitterest antagonism not for royalists, or *émigrés*, or politicians who did not frequent the Jacobins – but for one another. Of the deputies who perished in Year Two, a very high proportion had at some time been members of the Jacobin Club. Most of the other deputies were left alone so long as they kept out of the ferocious disputes within this group. Even during the height of the recourse to terror, it was very rare for deputies to be penalized for political independence.[64]

Corruption was a deep-seated problem. The many official positions necessary both to govern civilian life and to conduct the war, offered ample opportunities for those men who had no hesitation in helping themselves to public funds. Robespierre was particularly concerned that public officials should be politically virtuous.[65] Many Jacobins did take pride in conducting themselves with honour in positions of trust, and were scrupulous about the money that passed through their hands. Others seemed to have succumbed, more or less willingly, to the opportunities that lay open to them to acquire wealth and office. Some engaged in outright theft. In response, the Jacobin Club engaged in a process of 'purifying scrutinies' in an attempt to establish the financial and political integrity of its members, with those who failed to convince their listeners of the authenticity of their commitment and integrity being expelled.

There was an assumption that financial corruption was linked to political corruption; that is, that public officials, including deputies, who were venal and took bribes, were open to being bought by agents of the foreign powers. It was this conviction that underpinned belief in the Foreign Plot, a meta-conspiracy said to involve both the foreign powers and revolutionary traitors. There is little objective evidence for the actual existence of such a conspiracy, though there are indications that some individuals were accepting payment from the foreign powers.[66] The narrative of the Foreign Plot would be used to bring about the elimination of two groups of revolutionaries, that became known as the Hébertists (or Cordeliers) and the Dantonists (or Indulgents).

Both these factions, for different reasons, opposed the rule of the Committees. They were also fiercely opposed to one another. Hébert's group dominated the Commune and the Cordeliers Club; and was seen as being on the extreme radical edge of the Revolution, calling for an intensification of terror against counter-revolutionaries and 'aristocrats' and a policy of dechristianization.[67] They had personal grudges too against rival Jacobins.[68] How far these men formed a coherent faction is difficult to say.

The faction around Danton is still more problematic. As with the Girondins and the Hébertists, much of the narrative of this group, including the names used to identify it, was constructed retrospectively by the people who destroyed it. The identity of the 'Dantonists' was subsequently deepened and mythologized. The trial of the Dantonists became one of the most iconic moments of the Revolution. For many observers in the 230 years since the Revolution, the 'Danton affair' epitomizes the dark heart of the revolutionary terror. Dramatists and novelists have repeatedly tackled the subject; and it has frequently been equated with show trials under twentieth-century totalitarian dictatorships. Despite this continued interest, the nature of the factional trials is not well understood. The mythologized version rests on the idea that Danton and Robespierre represent polar opposites, inevitably fated to come into conflict. The reality is rather more complex. Robespierre for a long time defended Danton, publicly at least, and when he eventually turned on Danton, it was in large part in a desperate and ill-fated attempt to preserve revolutionary unity at a time of exceptional crisis.[69]

Insofar as the Dantonists existed as a coherent group, they appear to have consisted principally of Danton, Desmoulins and several friends. They are said to have campaigned for an end to terror, with the goal of setting up a commission of clemency to hear cases of people arrested under the Law of Suspects, with a view to releasing the vast majority; and to breaking the power of the Committee of Public Safety. Whilst Danton is credited with having been their leader, he kept a comparatively low profile during the months of the group's activity. The most overt vehicle of the group was Desmoulins' journal, *Le Vieux Cordelier* which, over the winter of 1793–4, interspersed attacks on Hébert (which were returned in kind) with attacks on the Committee of Public Safety. It is hard to state with certainty exactly what Danton's motives were, though ties of friendship were almost undoubtedly a factor. The idea that Danton in early 1794 was the leader of a group opposed on principle to *the Terror*, is hard to sustain. Much of it was a posthumous invention.[70] Stories of Danton's financial corruption had circulated for years, and there is compelling evidence to substantiate the rumours.[71] Up until December 1793, Robespierre continued to defend Danton against these allegations.[72] Robespierre read and approved the first two issues of *Le Vieux Cordelier* before publication and, for a brief moment, lent tentative support to the idea of a secret commission to examine the cases of the Lyon rebels, to see if injustices had been committed, before backtracking several days later, probably after intervention from Billaud-Varenne and other members of the two leading committees.[73] Thereafter Robespierre adopted a position distinct from both Hébertists and Dantonists, depicting himself – and probably genuinely seeing himself – as a man of virtue, whose sole concern was maintaining the unity that he saw as essential to the survival of the Revolution.

For some time Robespierre was reluctant to move against the Dantonist group, not least because he had been on friendly, though not intimate, terms with Danton, and had counted Desmoulins as his close friend.[74] Ironically, Billaud-Varenne confirmed Robespierre's reluctance when he himself denounced Robespierre on 9 Thermidor, stating that when first he denounced Danton to the Committee of Public Safety, Robespierre had leapt up in fury, saying that he understood Billaud-Varenne's intention: 'So you want to destroy the best patriots?'[75] Once Robespierre agreed to the destruction of the two factions, however, he did not hold back. The decision to annihilate both factions seems to have been a kind of trade off, or quid pro quo, designed to show that the Committee of Public Safety and the Committee of General Security were not under the sway of either group. The committees acted in concert to bring about the arrest, trial and execution of the Hébertists, including disparate individuals in their number as 'suspect' foreigners, one of whom, Clootz, was a *conventionnel*. The Hébertists were arrested on the night of 23–24 Ventôse (13–14 March), subjected to a form of trial in which they had scant chance to defend themselves, and in which several of their former friends and associates from the Cordeliers, including friends of Danton, testified against them. They were executed on 4 Germinal (24 March), convicted of having been part of the Foreign Plot.

The arrest of the Dantonists came just days later. The process was much swifter than that which engulfed the Girondins. Fear for themselves and the precedent set by the destruction of the Girondins meant that the men who ordered the arrest of Danton, Desmoulins and two other deputies had already decided they must die. The committee members worked together, only two declining to sign the arrest warrant.[76] They took the additional precaution of pre-empting the right of the Convention to decree the detention of its members by arresting the Dantonists themselves during the early hours of the night of 30–31 March. When Robespierre ventured to maintain that it would be the legally correct thing to do to denounce the Dantonists before arresting them, Vadier of the Committee of General Security is reported to have answered:

> You can run the risk of getting guillotined, if such is your desire; for myself, I prefer to avoid this risk, by getting them arrested at once, because we shouldn't be under any illusions about what we're doing here; it all comes down to these words: *If we don't guillotine them, we'll be guillotined ourselves.*[77]

Robespierre played a leading part in preparing the denunciation, providing detailed notes based on his personal knowledge of the men accused to enable Saint-Just to write the formal denunciation. Robespierre's notes and Saint-Just's report contained little in the way of substance or hard evidence; even Danton's financial corruption was swiftly passed over. The charges were based on the contention that none of the people under accusation was a true patriot, all had been involved in a conspiracy to undermine the very revolution they purported to defend. They were linked to other factions who had already been condemned as conspirators, making them guilty by association.

When, the next morning, it looked briefly as though Legendre and other friends of Danton could successfully challenge the committees' right to arrest them without giving them the right to address the Convention, Robespierre intervened to state that no privilege should apply to Danton that had not applied to other *conventionnels*. He presented the action of the committees and himself as a refusal to be intimidated into supporting Danton out of fear for themselves, or out of loyalty to former friendship: 'Who indeed are these men who sacrifice the interests of the *patrie* to personal connections, perhaps to fear . . . And they have tried to instil terrors in me too'.[78]

According to Robespierre, he had put his zeal for liberty and the public good before fear or friendship. These chilling words had their effect. Legendre and the others backed down, fearful of the consequences for themselves if they appear to put friendship before virtue. After hearing Saint-Just's report, the Convention voted to confirm the arrest of the Dantonists.

The trial of the Dantonists was not about justice: it was a political trial, one that was atypical of the great majority of trials conducted before the Revolutionary Tribunal, but one which had many elements in common with the trials of the Girondin and Hébertist factions.[79] The legal proceedings were manipulated by the committees who put pressure on Fouquier-Tinville and the judicial officials, with the aim of obtaining a conviction for treason against the defendants. For the trial itself, the committees brought together disparate groups of men to join the accused, in order to cloud the proceedings, including other Montagnard deputies, already under arrest, who had been implicated in financial corruption, including the scandal around the liquidation of the East India Company. Several foreigners were included to add credibility to the idea of the Foreign Plot. There was little to suggest a common thread uniting most of these men except in terms of the narrative constructed by their accusers. Indeed, some of the men in the dock had previously denounced one another. All were fighting for their lives. When Danton and some of the other defendants made concerted efforts to defend themselves in the courtroom, Saint-Just obtained a decree from the Convention stating that any of the accused who insulted national justice should be excluded from the court. This decree, voted by the members of the Convention, was used to cut short the trial, above all to silence Danton. The

Dantonists were convicted as traitors and sent to their deaths on 5 April, just six days after their arrest.

Robespierre and other members of the Committee of Public Safety sought to reassure the *conventionnels* that this trial would be the last such traumatic event to rupture the Convention. But the atmosphere of fear hung heavier than ever over the Convention, augmented by hate, bitter resentment, distrust and a desire for vengeance. The Law of Prairial (see chapter 7) was regarded with acute anxiety by some in the Convention who believed it could ease the path to their own arrests.

Over the early summer of 1794 a new conflict would emerge within the Mountain, one that climaxed in a struggle to the death between opposing groups, resulting in the deaths of five deputies: Robespierre, his brother Augustin, Saint-Just, Couthon and Le Bas, along with over 100 members of the Commune, over three days in Thermidor (see chapter 1). There have been many interpretations of the coup of Thermidor, which has been seen variously as being about ideological differences, or the power machinations of Robespierre. But the best way of understanding the conflict is as a further step in the process of the politicians' terror, a struggle precipitated by mutual fear, distrust and hate, pursued by men who could find no way to emerge from the demons of terror that were enveloping them. A generation later, the *conventionnel* Thibaudeau looked back on Thermidor as a fight to the death between the Revolution's leaders, brought on by mutual fear, and in which all sides acted ruthlessly: 'The terror didn't end because its leaders were weary of bloodletting, but because they were terrified of one another and divided amongst themselves. You had to be the first to attack, because whoever stayed on the defensive was lost.'[80]

The trials of political factions during Year II constitute some of the most infamous episodes of the Revolution. In contrast to the majority of the cases heard before the Revolutionary Tribunal, there was very little question of legally establishing innocence or guilt. In the trials of factions, revolutionary leaders actively intervened in the legal process, initiating arrests and charges, writing accounts of them, criminalizing the accused as 'conspirators', appearing as witnesses, and exerting pressure on the Tribunal to secure convictions. Likewise, the accused, when given the opportunity to speak, did so in the same terms of virtue, authenticity and corruption, asserting their own integrity and calling their accusers power-hungry hypocrites. Almost without exception in the Year II, every leading revolutionary figure (deputy or political leader) called to appear before the Revolutionary Tribunal was sentenced to death, a rate of attrition that contrasts sharply with the figures for the majority of cases heard before this extraordinary court.[81] The practice of denunciation, itself interwoven with the rhetoric of virtue, had a lot to do with it. Of course, fear was not the only motive for the factional trials: it must be placed alongside other motives, ideological, strategic and personal. Revolutionary leaders on trial, former colleagues and friends in many cases, were motivated in part by their belief that factionalism and disunity were signs of a 'conspiracy'. In many cases, they appear to have been genuinely convinced that their political opponents were, at best, financially and politically corrupt and, at worst, in the pay of the foreign powers. But it was their own fear that made them so ruthless in their treatment of their opponents.

A large number of deputies died violent deaths as a direct consequence of their political engagement. The former deputy Baudot stated in his memoirs that eighty-six deputies perished in this way.[82] In fact there were sixty-one executions, sixteen suicides (in almost all cases, to avoid execution) and six assassinations during the period of the Convention.[83] Death was not the only risk: nearly a third of the deputies were arrested at some point between 1792 and the dissolution of the Convention in October 1795, and endured months of deprivation, fear and uncertainty about their future in the revolutionary prisons.[84] Moreover, the death of Robespierre did not put an end to this situation: arrests and purges continued even after Thermidor. Though the death rate declined, some *conventionnels* were executed, victims of the failure to establish a form of political stability.[85] The former deputy, Thibaudeau, at the time of committing his memories to paper, considered the violence that had decimated the most active revolutionaries to have been a tragedy, though one which subsequent generations would find it difficult to recognize as such:

> The terror was more deadly to the friends of liberty than to its enemies. The enemies had emigrated because of a false sense of honour, out of hatred of the revolution or for their own safety. The friends of liberty, strong in their consciences and patriotism, remained faithful to the soil of their homeland even when it was devouring them. In this great hecatomb, fewer priests and nobles perished than plebeians. After the terror, the memory of the former was sustained by a crowd of unofficial avengers, the shades of the latter had only secret tears and silent regrets to console them.[86]

In his view, the revolutionary leaders had been true 'friends of liberty' who had sincerely hoped to make the world a better place and had finally paid a terrible price for their commitment during this time of political exception.

Chapter 7

Paris and the Vendée at the Heart of the 'Terror'

Paris played a unique role in *the Terror*, mirroring its status as France's capital. It was the location of the most politically important trials, of the Revolutionary Tribunal, and of the terrible spectacle of the journey to the scaffold, all along the route between the Conciergerie and the successive locations of the guillotine. The most important clubs – the Jacobin Club (at the centre of a national network of Jacobin clubs) and the Cordeliers Club were based there. Paris was home of the *sans-culottes*, a group credited with providing the shock troops of revolutionary militancy. The Paris Commune was both the institution responsible for the administration of the city, and a powerful political force in its own right. The forty-eight 'sections' into which the revolutionary city was divided provided a fundamental framework for the political commitment of those who have been grouped together under the generalized name of the *sans-culottes*. The demographic weight of the city with its 600,000–650,000 inhabitants,[1] the burning question of its supply of subsistence and various materials, the presence of the organs of central power, the political importance assumed by the Commune after 10 August 1792, the increasing impact of the revolutionary 'great days' that had been taking place there since 1789, the influence on the national territory of what was printed there, particularly newspapers, all contributed to making Paris a unique place.

The special position of Paris was even more evident during the period of the Convention, which first met immediately after the massacres of September 1792 and in dramatic conditions far removed from the opening of the Estates-General at Versailles in 1789 or the

Legislative Assembly in 1791, against the turbulent backdrop of the war, the fall of the monarchy and the inauguration of the Republic.[2] When the Convention met on 20 September and abolished royalty the next day, about half of its members were present to approve this entry into the republic (89 per cent on the 30th and 97 per cent one month later).[3] From whatever department they were mandated, these men could neither ignore the power of the *sans-culotte* movement and that of the insurrectional Commune that emerged on 10 August, nor the bloody violence in the prisons, even though very few voices condemned that violence outright. Even more so than the two previous legislatures, the Convention was an Assembly deliberating under the pressure of the public galleries, heedful of the echoes from the streets that issued in the name of the right to insurrection 'for the people and for each portion of the people'. Unsurprisingly, therefore, the portion of the population living in the capital had an infinitely greater weight than people elsewhere

By contrast, nothing predestined the 'Vendée' to become a symbol of the Counter-Revolution, nor was it a geographical area where violence was so endemic that one would have anticipated the outbreak of a civil war. Nevertheless, the fierce and protracted fighting and the repression that erupted in the departments concerned transformed the name of a single department into a political designation intended to stigmatize 'rebels' who had to be annihilated. As such, should the 'Vendée' be included in a study of *the Terror*, when what took place there was a ferocious repression of which other countries and eras could, alas, provide many examples? We make this choice for two major reasons: on the one hand, the political repercussions that this 'war in the Vendée' had in the capital, some even seeing it as a decisive factor in the factional struggles; on the other hand, and above all, the fact that this territory was transformed into a 'region of memory' to be durably associated with *the Terror*, to such an extent that even today historiographical debates on the subject are often linked to contemporary political quarrels.[4]

1. Paris, capital of the *sans-culotte* movement

Without the participation of the people of Paris there would have been no Revolution. Without the readiness of ordinary Parisians to risk their lives on the streets there would have been no storming of the Bastille, no march of market women to confront the king at Versailles, and, nearly three years later, no pitched battle at the Tuileries palace to overthrow the monarchy and install a republic. All of these events involved violence. But does that mean that ordinary Parisians were engaged in the 'terror'? To address this controversial question, we need to look at who the popular militants of Paris engaged in revolutionary activism actually were; their aims, their social origins and the patterns of their activism. We also need to look at their relationship to violence and 'terror'. Was the violence that some militants employed a form of 'popular terror'? Did it stem from ideas of popular justice and retribution, together with rumour and fear on the streets? We also need to examine the relationship of the Paris militants to the policy of terror adopted by the Convention during the period from 1793 to 1794, and consider how far the revolutionary government was pushed into deploying 'terror' out of fear of, or sympathy for, the organized popular militants.

The problem of the true identity of the people who participated in mass protest and insurrection has long dogged historians. It is a question with political connotations. For the nineteenth-century historian, Hippolyte Taine, no admirer of the aspirations of the common man, they were the nameless, faceless rabble ('*la canaille*'); whereas for Jules Michelet, the Revolution's great advocate, they were 'the people', still nameless, but great-hearted, bearing the destiny of the Revolution on their shoulders, and, for Michelet, the days of their participation were the 'great days' (*grandes journées*) of the Revolution. It was not until the historian George Rudé, that painstaking archival work began to discover the identities of the people who participated directly in revolution on the streets of Paris.[5] As Rudé found, many were skilled artisans and shopkeepers. They were not the lowest of the low; nor were they mindless puppets of revolutionary demagogues; they had their own concerns, economic, political and legal. The price of bread and other basic commodities was important to them, but so too were political aspirations – popular sovereignty, economic subsistence as a political right and direct democracy. The political processes of the Revolution, and the opening up of the franchise in 1792 gave many adult males a political voice for the first time, putting popular sovereignty to the forefront of revolutionary politics. The concept of 'pure' or direct democracy, that is, the right of ordinary people to act in the political realm without needing to use their elected representatives as intermediaries, found its strongest expression in claims to popular insurrection as a democratic right.

The name '*sans-culottes*' (acquired over the course of 1791–2) is sometimes applied to the urban lower orders of Paris en masse, but it belongs more specifically to the activists who identified themselves as *sans-culottes*.[6] Whilst many thousands of people turned out for mass street protests, a smaller group became political activists or militants.[7] These committed activists attended meetings of the forty-eight sections (around 13,000 of them in late 1793, about 10 per cent of the working men of Paris), they formed the backbone of the popular societies and clubs, and were a major force in the Commune.

Many historians have been drawn to the complex universe of the *sans-culottes*. Albert Soboul's *Les sans-culottes parisiens de l'an II* still stands as the pre-eminent and most detailed study of the Parisian popular movement during the zenith of its political influence.[8] Yet historians of eighteenth-century Paris, including Arlette Farge, Daniel Roche and David Garrioch, have thrown new light on the experience of the 'fragile lives' of the urban poor, and the functioning of neighbourhood communities.[9] The work of Haim Burstin explores ways in which people proactively went about making a space for themselves in politics, organizing, networking and identifying themselves as '*sans-culotte*'.[10] Historians have looked at the ways in which the urban populace was affected by collective emotions, often spread by rumour. Fear was a driving force for the *sans-culottes*, as it was for so many participants in the Revolution. Longstanding fears of a 'famine plot' to starve the people developed in the revolutionary context into fears of an 'aristocratic plot' on the part of the rich and privileged to crush the ordinary working people who had made the Revolution.[11] Historians have also gone beyond the traditional focus on the *sans-culottes* as representatives of an economic group, to examine how people chose to identify politically and culturally as *sans-culotte*; they point to the fact that some of the leading figures in the sections were from social elites or middling groups, rather than from the urban poor.[12]

In the eyes of hostile observers, the *sans-culottes* were the embodiment of street terror. This image was popularized and perpetuated by a series of caricaturists, many of them English, such as James Gillray and George Cruikshank, who depicted *sans-culottes* as half-starved cannibals, frenziedly feeding on the butchered bodies of nobles and the clergy, exulting in the spilling of blood. The *sans-culottes* themselves and their advocates took a diametrically opposed view of their nature and authentic motives, a view epitomized by such images as 'the good *sans-culotte*', which depicts the *sans-culottes* as virtuous men and women, living a simple life, hardworking, and devoted to the well-being of their fellows and to the *patrie*.[13]

What about the relationship between revolutionary activists on the streets and violence? Were they violent? Sometimes, yes. And where street violence took place, it was brutal, terrifying and spectacular. The murders of the governor of the Bastille and six of his troops, followed by that of Jacques de Flesselles, the *prévôt des marchands*, and, a few days later, of the intendant of Paris, Bertier de Sauvigny and his father-in-law, the minister, Foulon, shocked observers from the social elite, even those sympathetic to the hunger and frustration of the urban poor, their suspicion of 'the famine plot' and their desire for retribution. Bertier and Foulon were lynched, then decapitated, on the Place de Grève, traditional site of public executions, a location chosen by their killers to bolster the idea of their deaths as an example of retributive justice. The king had formerly dispensed justice through public executions, a form of 'salutary terror'; now it was the turn of the people to enact rough justice, 'the people's justice'.

The most shattering instance of 'the people's justice' was the 'September Massacres' which began on 2 September 1792. Driven by fear of foreign invasion and counter-revolutionary conspiracy, following the seizure of Longwy by the Prussians, an event attributed by some to treason, groups of self-appointed *sans-culottes* (their names remain for the most part unknown) formed impromptu 'popular tribunals', entered the prisons of Paris, interrogated around 2,700 prisoners, and condemned about 1,200 of them to death – a sentence promptly carried out with knives, swords and pikes.[14] Like so many violent actions in the Revolution, fear inspired the massacre – fear that aristocrats and other counter-revolutionaries were biding their time in the prisons and in hidden tunnels, to emerge once the volunteer soldiers had left to fight the invading armies, to cut the throats of the soldiers' families, left defenceless in Paris. Such rumours spread panic on the streets. These fears were not confined to the uneducated populace – bourgeois Parisians shared many of these anxieties.[15] Madame Rosalie Jullien, for example, closely connected to the Montagnards and a woman of bourgeois sensibility, wrote to her husband that she had been profoundly shocked by the massacres, 'my spirit is afflicted', but maintained that she accepted the need for 'a terrible justice': 'The people have risen, the people, terrible in their fury, avenge the crimes of three years of the most cowardly betrayals ... I weep, but I cry out, "France is saved".'[16]

The dreadful spectacle of the massacres inspired further fear – not only amongst royalists and supporters of the non-juring clergy (around 240 of whom were killed in the massacres), but also amongst the national representatives, even those – and at the time there were many – who saw the massacres as a cruel necessity in the context of what they feared at the time to be the imminent collapse of the French armies before the onslaught of the invading forces and the *émigrés*. As the immediate danger to Paris receded following the military victory at Valmy, many revolutionary leaders, including Girondins, who had done nothing to intervene at the time to stop the killings, now drew back in horror at what had taken place. Those amongst the *sans-culottes* and in the Convention who continued to defend the massacres, became known as 'drinkers of blood'. Though nothing on the scale of the massacres was to occur again in revolutionary Paris, these events cast a long shadow.

When the *conventionnels* decided to take the dispensation of exceptional revolutionary justice into their own hands, passing a series of laws that enabled a recourse to terror, they did so in part to ensure that there would be no repetition of the improvised terror wielded by *sans-culottes*. There was no place, according to the Convention, for extra-judicial killing, retributive violence, improvised interrogations with no legal basis, no provision for defence and summary executions. If there was to be terror, the *conventionnels* believed it ought to be situated within the framework of the law, a framework organized and controlled by the nation's elected representatives. When Danton spoke in favour of setting up the Revolutionary Tribunal, on 10 March 1792, he summed up this feeling with the phrase, 'let us be terrible so that the people do not have to be'.[17] It was one of several occasions when Danton invoked the word 'terrible' in relation to the revolutionary government's obligation to dispense harsh justice on behalf of the people.[18]

Even amongst the *sans-culottes*, actual violence remained very much the exception. Micah Alpaugh shows that most of the political activism of the *sans-culottes* took non-violent forms, such as peaceful demonstrations and processions, petitions to the Convention sent by deputations from the sections, fraternal banquets, meetings of the popular societies and attendance at revolutionary festivals.[19] According to Alpaugh, the *sans-culottes* were developing peaceful participatory means of protest, but these new democratic practices took time to be learned; political education was needed to form a new people. Yet, despite the non-violent nature of most *sans-culotte* activities, given the precedents for crowd violence, the *threat* of violence remained implicit in mass protests, and was a far from negligible force in revolutionary politics.

For the Montagnards and other revolutionary leaders, riding the tiger of the popular movement could be empowering for those who claimed to speak on behalf of the people, but it was also a risky affair. Some of the most influential journalists were those who constituted themselves as spokesmen and champions for the *sans-culottes*. Denunciation was seen as a civic duty which, in principle, was meant to be wielded with virtue. A culture of denunciation of suspects was widespread among revolutionary activists: Marat and Hébert were amongst a number of journalists who regularly denounced political opponents on behalf of the *sans-culottes*, escalating the atmosphere of fear.[20] After the murder of Marat, Hébert exerted a growing ascendancy over the *sans-culottes* and their adherents through his editorship of *Le Père Duchesne*. Hébert himself, like most of the self-appointed spokesmen for the *sans-culottes*, was from a higher social class than the people he represented.[21] But in his journal he assumed the persona and plebeian language of a *sans-culotte* in a calculated populist move to appeal to the militants.

Some *conventionnels* imitated the dress, speech and manners of the *sans-culottes*, the better to garner their support. Madame Roland described such antics in a contemptuous portrait she penned following her arrest, 'the deputies, after 31 May, dressed like navvies, in trousers, short jackets and bonnets, their shirts open on their chests, swearing and gesticulating like drunken *sans-culottes*!'.[22] Yet there had been a time when future Girondin leaders, too, had adopted some of the manners associated with 'the people'.[23] Robespierre was an exception to this kind of tactic: he was resolute in his support of the *sans-culottes*, but that did not mean that he wanted to be seen as one of them. His image was dignified and meticulous, far from that of a 'man of the people' – rough, uncouth, prone to swearing, drinking – and violence. Robespierre kept himself aloof from that kind of persona, and was limited in his direct contact with the leaders of the sections. Robespierre and Saint-Just (in common with other Montagnards) used a network of intermediaries, including, in Robespierre's case, his landlord, Maurice Duplay, the printer Nicolas (who served on the Revolutionary Tribunal), and the Polish patriot, Lazowski, to maintain links with the *sans-culottes*, get consensus and obtain their support.[24]

Fear of the *sans-culottes*, as well as sympathy for their cause, influenced the choices of successive revolutionary leaders. The *conventionnels*' desire to control and contain the demands of the *sans-culottes* became, in the eyes of many historians, a decisive factor in steps to adopt the legalized recourse to terror as a state policy.[25] The critical years of 1793–4 saw the apogee of *sans-culotte* power and political leverage. Over the summer of 1793, a group came to prominence among the *sans-culottes*. They became known collectively as the '*Enragés*' (literally: *the enraged ones*), although there is little evidence that they were a unified group with a concerted policy. Some individual *Enragés* put intense pressure on the Convention to enact both price controls and a policy of terror. They demanded that the Revolutionary Tribunal be used against the rich 'who have profited from the advantages opened up by the Revolution', against monopolists, bankers and those who engaged in financial speculation.[26] Hébert, Chaumette and their allies at the Commune engaged in a power struggle with the *Enragés* over the organization and articulation of *sans-culotte* anger and grievances. *Enragé* leader, Jacques Roux, one of the revolutionary 'red priests', deeply distrusted Hébert and Chaumette, whom he saw as ambitious and cynical exploiters of the poor who had placed their trust in the Revolution.[27]

Women played a vital part in the *sans-culotte* movement. Although denied the rights of political participation accorded to men, they made up a significant proportion of the spectators in the public galleries at the Convention, at the Commune, at the Jacobin Club and Cordeliers Club, also at the Revolutionary Tribunal.[28] Some popular societies admitted women as participants, and over the summer of 1793 some of the sections admitted women as members.[29] Around 170 women attended an exclusively female club, the Society of Revolutionary Republican Citizenesses.[30] The leaders of this club, Pauline Léon, a chocolate maker, and Claire Lacombe, who had worked as an actress, were connected with the *Enragés*, with whom they shared economic and political goals, including the demand for 'terror'.[31] The political importance of women *sans-culottes* increased after many of the most committed male *sans-culottes* volunteered to fight in the Republic's armies, whilst others joined the Parisian *armée révolutionnaire*.[32] Women *sans-culottes* kept a watchful eye on the national representatives, accusing some of lacking authentic political virtue, of looking too well-nourished, of being corrupt. Many of the most activist women *sans-culottes* were willing to embrace tactics of violence and terror, either urging men in power to deploy 'terror', or sometimes seeking to wield it on their own account. One of the rights to which the Revolutionary Republican Citizenesses laid claim was that of women to bear arms against counter-revolutionaries, including in the war in the 'Vendée'.

One aspect of this female 'terror' which may well appear unsettling to us is that substantially more women than men attended the executions by guillotine. It is a disturbing fact, yet it also reflects the reality that the eighteenth-century urban poor – including women – were habituated to scenes of violence. Throughout the eighteenth century, public executions drew numerous women spectators.[33] There may be a kernel of truth, therefore, in the terrifying stories of *sans-culotte* women as the 'Furies of the guillotine' or 'the *tricoteuses*' – women who industriously knitted garments while watching the spectacle of the guillotine. Yet, as Dominique Godineau argues, the preponderance of women around the guillotine can also be seen as a consequence of women's lack of direct political power: attendance at the guillotine, or at the Revolutionary Tribunal, enabled women of the people to see themselves as having some share in a power that they otherwise lacked, the power to be part of something bigger than themselves, part of popular sovereignty in action, expressed through the judgements of the sovereign people against their enemies who had tried to oppose them.[34]

2. Paris, epicentre of the 'Terror'

By the summer of 1793, Hébert and his allies, the 'Hébertists', had an entrenched power base in the Commune where Chaumette[35] was the *procureur*, and Hébert his deputy. They also dominated the National Guard, now led by Hanriot. On 5 September 1793, mass *sans-culotte* demonstrations called upon the Convention to: 'Make terror the order of the day . . . let its blade rise indiscriminately over all heads'.[36] Immediately, and over succeeding days, the *conventionnels* passed key laws associated with 'terror' – the Maximum on prices, establishing the *armées révolutionnaires* and, on 17 September, the 'Law of Suspects', which provided for whole categories of people deemed 'suspect' to be detained indefinitely, putting increased powers into the hands of the surveillance committees to draw up lists of suspects and carry out arrests.

The deputies bowed to popular pressure. Yet the demands from the *sans-culottes* made most revolutionary leaders, including Montagnards, uneasy. The Convention decided to delay the implementation of the egalitarian and libertarian Constitution of June 1793, on the grounds that in time of war the priority was to ensure the survival of the Republic and the revolutionary government. During the autumn of 1793 the *conventionnels* moved to curb the popular movement. Jacques Roux, and other *Enragé* leaders (Leclerc, Varlet) were arrested, the meetings of popular societies and clubs were subject to controls, and meetings of the sections were cut back. Following a brawl between market women (the *'Dames des Halles'*), and the Revolutionary Republican Citizenesses, Amar of the Committee of General Security obtained a decree from the Convention on 30 October 1793 to close down the Revolutionary Republican Citizenesses along with all women's clubs, stating that the natural place of women was in the home, and that they should not meddle with politics.[37]

After the exclusion of the *Enragés*, Hébert, with Ronsin, Vincent and Chaumette, moved in to become the chief power-brokers on behalf of the *sans-culotte* movement. They took up many *Enragé* demands, calling for the intensification of 'terror' against counter-revolutionaries and 'aristocrats', support for *sans-culotte* economic and political measures, and a policy of dechristianization, a form of religious terror directed against the Catholic Church and its adherents.[38] They had personal grudges too. After his failed attempt to become Minister of the Interior, Hébert used his journal, *Le Père Duchesne* to criticize the leadership of the committees.[39] The factional activities of the Hébertist leaders were as much – or more – about personal power politics and frustrated ambition as they were about sympathy for the economic plight of the ordinary people of Paris.

On 4 March, the Hébertists attempted to incite the Cordeliers Club into an insurrection against the committees. The threatened insurrection itself did not go much beyond a lot of bluster in the Cordeliers; but there was a clear implication of threat towards the members of the Committee of Public Safety, including Robespierre.[40] Vincent spoke out against Robespierre's continued defence of the men who had signed the petition against the arrest of the Girondins, a defence which had protected them from the Revolutionary Tribunal. The Montagnard leaders were not prepared to take the risk of another popular demonstration before the Convention; they decided that the safest policy was to eliminate the Hébertists. The destruction of their faction marked a further step towards the disarming of the *sans-culotte* movement. The Commune was purged and placed more closely under the control of Montagnards.

At the beginning of July 1794, nearly 7,900 people were crowded into the prisons of Paris as a consequence of the concentration of trials in the capital.[41] The numbers increased as the revolutionary leaders made concerted efforts to close down tribunals in the provinces. Additional buildings had been pressed into service as improvised prisons. The former palace of the Luxembourg held a number of high-ranking prisoners from the old social elites, and was seen as a potential hotbed for a 'prison plot', so recently warned against by Hébert and his *Père Duchesne*.

The Conciergerie served as the holding prison for those about to appear before the Revolutionary Tribunal. The Tribunal itself was located on the upper floor of the *Palais de justice*, in the same chamber that had once housed the *Parlement* of Paris. In place of Ancien Régime justice, revolutionary justice. The Revolutionary Tribunal publicized its judgements, opening its sessions to the public, and printing pamphlets and placards. The *Bulletin du tribunal révolutionnaire* gave accounts of the questioning of witnesses and the accused, detailed the cases presented by the court officials, and published the final judgements. By these means this extraordinary tribunal engaged with public opinion, especially in Paris, and 'ensured that justice was a *public spectacle*'.[42] The legal procedures adopted by the revolutionaries gave opportunities to the accused, whilst in detention, to print and publish their own versions of events. Many prisoners availed themselves of this opportunity to protest their innocence vociferously.[43]

The guillotine, that new invention, became the logical instrument for carrying out death sentences pronounced by the Revolutionary Tribunal. On 20 Prairial (8 June 1794), it was dismantled from its position on the Place de la Révolution (the present-day Place de la Concorde) in preparation for the Festival of the Supreme Being, when crowds passed through en route to the Champ de la Réunion (formerly the Champ de Mars). As Jonathan Smyth has shown, the Festival was a much bigger and much more popular affair than has often been acknowledged. Previously, the standard account, derived from Thermidorian literature, depicted it as the fruit of a personal religious obsession on the part of Robespierre.[44] In contrast to the Festival of Reason (the atheistic festival celebrated in Notre Dame on 10 November 1793), the Festival of the Supreme Being celebrated nature, families, virtue and the deist concept of a benign providence. It also took place on a day that was still, in most people's minds and despite the revolutionary calendar, Whitsunday. The Festival was seen as indicative of a first step towards religious reconciliation, a sign that the ferocious policy of dechristianization pursued by the 'Hébertists', the Commune and the *armée révolutionnaire*, was over. It is evident, too, that some of the enthusiasm with which people embraced the Festival arose from a widespread assumption that the dismantling of the guillotine signalled that the policy of 'terror' itself was about to end. Two days later, these hopes were dashed, when the Law of Prairial (22 Prairial) was passed. This new law inaugurated seven weeks of intensified executions in Paris, in what would be termed the 'Great Terror'. It was during these weeks that almost half the total of those executed in Paris met their deaths.

Controversy still surrounds the circumstances whereby the Law of Prairial was brought into being. The role of Robespierre, in particular, is much disputed. He had supported the decree, which was presented by Couthon, his close ally on the Committee of Public Safety, but then withdrew from most spheres of public life (he still spoke occasionally at the Jacobins), only returning for what became the final climactic factional struggle between the Montagnards. Robespierre also withdrew altogether from meetings of the Committee of Public Safety and left the implementation of the Law of Prairial to others.[45]

As with other seismic events that led to 'terror', fear played a part in the genesis of the new law – fear of an uprising in the overcrowded prisons (echoing the fears that led to the September Massacres), fear of assassination of revolutionary leaders, sparked in part by attempts on the lives of Robespierre and Collot d'Herbois, and possibly, and most ominously, continuing conflicts between factions in the Convention – therefore fear that the new law might be applied against other *conventionnels*. Recently, Annie Jourdan has argued that the Law of Prairial was primarily intended to expedite the judgements of prisoners incarcerated in Paris, with judicial process enforced through *commissions populaires*, but that the actual application of the law was much more chaotic and less rigorously carried out than had originally been envisaged, leading to an increase of executions in Paris, even as they declined in the provinces.[46]

After the removal of the guillotine from the Place de la Révolution, it was installed briefly in the Place de la Bastille, before being moved further away from the city centre to the Place du Trône-Renversé (now the Place de la Nation), in order to make 'terror' less of a visible presence in the city that had become its epicenter (map 6). The adoption of the guillotine as the new form of state execution had been an attempt to make the death penalty more humane, swift and egalitarian than under the Ancien Régime. But, originally conceived as a 'non-spectacle', the guillotine itself became a public theatrical performance. Attention was concentrated on the attitude of the victims on their prolonged journey in the tumbrels, and whilst awaiting their turn to climb the steps of the scaffold. The attitude and demeanour of those about to die would be observed and commented on by the crowds that turned up to watch the ghastly show.[47] Unlike some protracted public executions of the Ancien Régime, the actual killing was quick; nevertheless, it was profoundly shocking for those close enough to witness the almost instantaneous transition from life to death, as the severed head of a victim fell, whilst a fountain of blood spurted from the severed arteries. Nor could the red paint that coated the guillotine and the baskets disguise the smell of blood that lingered around the scaffold.[48]

For many Parisians, especially those who lived nearby, the guillotine was a machine for the butchery of human beings, an object of horror and disgust, especially when the escalating number of bodies posed the pressing problem of the ensuing 'vapours' that were believed to poison the surrounding neighbourhood.[49] The sinister sight of mass graves covered in quicklime was a feature of the 'Vendée' too, though on a completely different scale, and there the guillotine was far from being the primary means for killing people.

3. The 'military Vendée', a zone of civil war

The risk of civil war was something that revolutionaries grew increasingly concerned about. Sowing the seeds of civil war, fanning the flames of civil war, provoking all the horrors of civil war – such statements resounded dozens of times in the spring of 1793 during the oratorical combats between Montagnards and Girondins, with both sides accusing one another of fomenting civil war.[50] In the event, France endured one full-scale conflict which can be counted as a 'civil war'. This was the 'war in the Vendée', which began in March 1793.[51] This conflict, as we shall see, was brutal in the extreme; but it remained geographically limited, confined to a region in western France (the Vendée and neighbouring departments) without the revolt managing to spread and, above all, without linking up (or federating) with other more scattered counter-revolutionary movements.[52]

The first act of the uprising took place at the beginning of March 1793 when, in several communes, disturbances broke out during operations to recruit volunteers for the armies of the Republic. In fact, the raising of 300,000 new soldiers, decreed in February, imposed for the first time on each department a quantity of troops to be found, determined according to the number of inhabitants, and especially taking into account the number of volunteers recruited in 1791–2. The method was high-risk, since the lower the number of volunteers, the less enthusiasm there was for defending the nation with arms in hand, and the greater the number of troops required from the reluctant territory. If there were not enough volunteers to reach the quota distributed among the communes by the departmental authorities, the requisition must nevertheless be provided, at the price of a violation of the very principle of voluntarism, a violation aggravated by the possibility of buying a replacement (for those who could afford it). Moreover, the decree left the authorities of each commune free to choose the recruitment methods if the number of volunteers proved insufficient.

However, opting to choose by means of drawing lots among single men or childless widowers between the ages of 18 and 40, or selecting them by election, was frequently contested. Thus, in Saint-Florent-le-Vieil (Maine-et-Loire), on 10 March, disturbances caused several arrests of young people hostile to recruitment, before, two days later, an armed mob invaded the place, this time causing deaths on both sides (again in Maine-et-Loire, in Beaupréau, a week earlier, other people opposed to recruitment had also already fallen under the bullets of the National Guard). In one of the neighbouring departments, Loire-Inférieure, on 11 March, at least 1,000–1,500 armed men swarmed into the small town of Machecoul, again to oppose recruitment, and several dozen 'patriots' were massacred there; the killings continuing until April with at least 150–200 deaths.[53] On the 14th, a first important town, Cholet (Maine-et-Loire), fell into the hands of the 'rebels', then, on the 19th, in the Vendée department, a column of 3,000 soldiers was forced to flee before the rural insurgents.

The 'Vendée' had just been born, with a 'rebellious' territory stretching over four neighbouring departments: most of the eponymous department, the south of the Loire-Inférieure, the south-west of Maine-et-Loire and the west of the Deux-Sèvres.[54] Although many other protest movements against the levying of the 300,000 men broke out all over France at the beginning of spring, sometimes powerful movements as in Brittany, nowhere else did they take on the lasting scale of what was happening in the 'Vendée'. The situation was all the more serious as fear of this 'inexplicable Vendée', as Barère put it, was compounded by the military setbacks on the northern borders. Indeed, on 18 March, Dumouriez's army was defeated at Neerwinden, then, two weeks later, the General himself passed over to the enemy and handed over to them the Minister of War as well as four representatives of the people who had been sent by the Convention in order to hold Dumouriez to account.

The spectacular act of the treacherous general and the defeats in the rebellious West seemed to Republicans to be the result of the same conspiracy fomented from abroad, thus raising, once again, the spectre of civil war. At the Convention on 16 April, Barère spoke in explicit terms:

> Civil War! At this word the European despots smiled with hope; they saw in it the political fuel that could ignite terrible blows to the Republic; it is to the internal divisions that all the combinations of our enemies are joined; their strongest auxiliaries are the culpable hopes of uprisings produced in some maritime departments. It is on the banks of the Loire that they have planted part of their abominable plots.[55]

This thesis of a territory rising up against the Republic, inspired by nobles and refractory priests, and supported by the powers coalescing against France, was a political invention, one that for a long time was maintained by two opposing historiographical currents, one based on the idea of a counter-revolutionary plot at the origin of the 'Vendée War', the other on a vision of 'Vendéens' spontaneously insurgent for God and the king (despite the flagrant contradiction of an uprising in March to save a king who had been guillotined in

January).⁵⁶ Neither thesis has any serious basis: most of the noble chiefs, far from triggering the uprising, were called upon by the rural people to lead them; while the refractory priests certainly blessed it, they did not provoke it. As for the description of the region as a sort of small paradise of the Ancien Régime disturbed by the Revolution, this too does not stand up to analysis.

In reality, the 'Vendée War' stemmed from a series of factors that were also to be found in several other departments, but which came together in this location to start a fire of singular intensity and, above all, great endurance: the major role of the parish priests as sociocultural intermediaries and the vigour of opposition to the 'intruders' who replaced the refractory priests from 1791; rural hostility towards the urban bourgeoisies at the time when the new administrative divisions of 1790 were being set up; frustrations arising from the sale of 'national goods' (in the district of Cholet, traders appropriated some 40 per cent, farmers about 9 per cent); disappointments arising from the distribution of taxes and in the Vendée department accentuated the imbalance of the fiscal pressure between the *bocage* (terrain of small fields with high hedges and woodland characteristic of the region) and the 'plain' (region in the south); social differences in the peasantry (in the *bocage* about 20 per cent were day labourers, against 80 per cent in the 'plain'); labour conflicts in the dispersed manufacturing areas opposing rural weavers and urban bourgeois (as in the Mauges); the question of maintaining order in the countryside where the urban National Guard intervened against the rural population from 1791 onwards; and lastly, and most obviously, the major role played by determined resistance to the requisitioning of men in March 1793.⁵⁷ These factors certainly help us to understand why an uprising took place here, though they do not account for its scale, its duration and even less the brutality of its repression.

The terror this provoked in Paris became the direct cause of the 'hors la loi' decree outlawing armed rebels, voted on 19 March, and must also be measured against the initial successes of the 'rebels'. Indeed, from March to June, the 'rebels' carried everything or almost everything in their path, strengthened by the weight of their numbers (often at least a ratio of one to four, or even more) as well as by the flexible nature of what was called the 'Catholic and Royal Army' (quickly dispersed, quickly reformed). Moreover, the weak permanent presence of the military in this area, far from the land borders, which left the National Guard and then a heterogeneous troop of volunteers from other departments to absorb the first shocks, but also the initial divisions of the command of the republican forces, with, in addition, strong rivalries between generals and deputies *en mission*, also help to account for the first 'Vendée' successes. At most, republican forces were handicapped by the weakness of their cavalry and their inability to conduct a real siege in front of a city (following the example of Nantes, where they were defeated on 29 June 1793).

Over the summer, and especially into the autumn, the balance of power on the ground changed, with the defeat of the 'rebels' at the battle of Cholet (17 October) followed by the 'foray of Galerne'[58] and its failures in front of Granville and Angers, and finally the two most decisive defeats in December (at Le Mans on 12 and 13 December and at Savenay on the 23rd). In addition to the brutality of the fighting, there was mass repression using some of the instruments of the 'terror' (deputies *en mission*, extraordinary courts, etc.), marked in particular by the infamous mass drownings of prisoners at Nantes under the authority of the representative *en mission* Carrier, the shootings in Angers under the aegis of his colleague Francastel, as well as by the 'infernal columns' sent to cover the insurgent territory, who pillaged and killed in a sometimes indiscriminate manner, including in communes that had remained outside the uprising.[59]

These episodes are classically assimilated to *the Terror*, understood as its bloodiest manifestation (170,000–200,000 deaths, far more than the executions in Paris), or even analysed as an alleged 'genocide'.[60] However, in a more commonplace way, this was a ferocious brutalization strategically applied to a defeated territory in order to eradicate any hope of a new revolt, a method that was used in other states and other periods in the eighteenth century, not to mention previous cases and *a fortiori* colonial repressions.[61] Despite this, and in a manner that seems paradoxical, far from 'destroying the Vendée', this repression contributed to its survival, even though 'Vendée' troops no longer existed by the beginning of 1794, reduced to bands of a few hundred men gathered behind chiefs like Charette and Stofflet, now practising 'small war' (or guerrilla warfare) and hunted down by republican troops.

Although the treaties of La Jaunaye and Saint-Florent, in February and May 1795, allowed a lull, the fighting resumed with the landing of *émigrés* and Englishmen at Quiberon in June.[62] Other episodes of the 'Vendée Wars' would continue until the nineteenth century (and beyond) the living memory of the uprising of 1793, while uprisings (*Chouannerie*) also affected Brittany and part of the Normandy departments under the Directory. In June 1795, a date when, according to the Thermidorian narrative, *the Terror* was considered to have been over for nearly a year, General Hoche had some 750 armed *émigrés*, who had landed in Quiberon, summarily judged and shot.

What is the difference between these subsequent events, and the executions of outlawed *émigrés* who were shot in 1793–4? Is there a condemnable *Terror* here and a trivialized military terror there? Or is it not more appropriate to consider the 'Vendée' under its two major aspects: on the one hand, a space of civil war where the ferocity of the fighting and repression were equal to the fear provoked by the initial successes of the uprising, including of course the fear of the republican soldiers engaged in this hostile space with enemies described as ferocious 'bandits' to be dealt with without giving quarter;[63] on the other hand, a strong political symbol, as important for counter-revolutionaries as for republicans?

In this respect, the 'Vendée', once established as 'public enemy number one' in the words of historian Jean-Clément Martin,[64] became more of a political issue in the rivalries between Girondins and Montagnards, but also between the Convention and the most radical political movements in the Parisian *sans-culotterie*, than a simple territory in which to exercise repression, however terrible that might be. As Martin convincingly explains, the 'Vendée', the symbolic counterpart of Koblenz to stigmatize the Counter-Revolution, was indeed atrociously *brutalized*, but not *terrorized*,[65] and the duration as well as the atrocity of this civil war were intimately linked to the fears as well as the political rivalries between revolutionaries, in Paris as well as in the field.

Chapter 8

Who Lived and Who Died?
The Difficult Balance Sheets of Terror

It was a great thing to be one of the survivors of the Year II: they had a chance to tell the story and to shape it. Two men with very different fates, turning on choices they made over a few hours in Thermidor, illustrate this point. Both served for a year on the Committee of Public Safety, where they played major roles in directing the military efforts of the Year II, culminating in Fleurus and other victories of the early summer, bringing to an end the fraught situation over two years when France had been fighting a defensive war against invading armies. Both men were also implicated in 'terror', not only terror to support military endeavours, but also political terror against the Committee's opponents. As testament to this, the signatures of both men are on the order for the arrest of the 'Dantonist' deputies. The first man was Lazare Carnot. He survived to reinvent himself and his actions over the previous year, absolving himself from terror, and creating the narrative that he had been concerned solely with military matters. He would be rewarded with the heroic name of the 'organizer of victory'. The second man was Saint-Just, who chose to stand by Robespierre in Thermidor, and died as a consequence. His memory would suffer under the black legend attached to Robespierre and his friends, in which he himself was dubbed the 'Archangel of Terror'. On 4 August 1889, when France's leaders were seeking an acceptable way of celebrating the centenary of the Revolution, and Carnot's grandson, Sadi Carnot, was president of the Third Republic, the remains of Lazare Carnot were transferred in pomp to the Pantheon, resting place for France's most revered heroes. The remains of Saint-Just had long since disappeared in a common grave along with the others executed at Thermidor. The demons of terror had demanded a sacrifice perhaps – a way to escape from terror.

Popular history likes its heroes and its villains. That is acceptable if all we want is to keep things simple, to commemorate, rather than understand. But a better way to comprehend the past is to do justice to the good and the bad, and recognize that both can exist in the same people. Similarly, France has never known quite what to do with the Year II, the First Republic, and the 'Terror'. In what follows, we will try to offer a more accurate understanding of what occurred, and why. The first way to do that is count the number of victims, especially the dead.

Considering the great number of those condemned to death, accounting for the human toll of the 'terror' is a necessary exercise. Yet it is hard to be satisfied with this since the 'Terror' never existed as a political or autonomous system. Repression can no longer be separated from the state of political exception and the extraordinary government associated with it. It is also important to add to the human toll political, economic and social aspects; and especially military ones, since the situation at the borders was closely linked to the heightening of repressive legislation as well as the 'terror' in the armies that certain deputies implemented in order to re-establish discipline. This does not mean that the tragic events of summer 1793 entail an easy explanation for the origins of the 'terror' or function as attenuating circumstances. But it would be impossible to understand the military recovery from winter 1793 to spring 1794 without taking into account those deputies of the Republic – like Saint-Just and Le Bas to the Army of the Rhine, or Milaud and Soubrany to the Pyrénées Orientales – who called for an exemplary and visible severity to police the behaviour of officers and soldiers who undermined the fighting efficacy of French soldiers on these external fronts. The military balance of power with regard to foreign armies cannot be understood without taking into account how internal revolts were crushed, notably the decisive victories in December 1793 over the 'Vendéens', as western departments in revolt had for months diverted resources and soldiers from the fronts at the borders.[1]

1. Working out the death toll

The incidence of the terror fell very unevenly across France. As map 7 shows, across large swathes of the country executions were very limited, with many departments suffering fewer than nine. These were the regions where, as Howard Brown states, people in

1795 learned for the first time from Thermidorian literature that they had been living under a 'reign of terror' supposedly orchestrated by Robespierre and his associates.[2] The overwhelming number of executions took place in frontier regions, where the presence of hostile armies heightened tensions, and in places where there were armed uprisings, whether royalist or 'federalist', above all, in the Vendée and its neighbouring departments. Also in Paris, where many people were sent for trial from other parts of France, especially after the Law of Prairial was decreed with its aim of centralizing the handling of exceptional 'revolutionary' justice and bringing it under tighter control.

The data collected by American historian Donald Greer, published in 1935, indicate that between 1793 and 1794 a total of 16,594 individuals were sentenced to death.[3] About 75 per cent of these sentences concerned individuals who were armed or who had taken up arms against the Republic. To that figure one needs to add around 20,000 summary executions of captives in areas where uprisings occurred. After much dispute that even took in claims of genocide, serious demographic studies have now produced trustworthy figures for the human cost of the War in the Vendée: around 170,000 Vendéens were killed with anywhere from 26,000 to 37,000 casualties for Republic forces.[4]

The geographic distribution of capital punishments (map 7) shows very clearly the ravages in Paris of the Revolutionary Tribunal.[5] Six of the departments in the West were strongly touched by the Vendéen uprising.[6] In the North, and especially in Pas-de-Calais, the deputy Lebon set up in Cambrai and Arras two tribunals to judge 'revolutionarily' in a hostile context, with enemy armies just several dozen kilometres away.[7] There were three major geographic zones of the so-called 'Federalist' uprisings. The first was the Gironde, with a revolutionary commission in Bordeaux and Libourne. The second was the Rhone, with Lyon, renamed a Freed Commune (or Freed City), awash with blood by three commissions of extraordinary justice. The final geographic zone consisted of four departments in the south-east: the Var, with repression following upon the siege of Toulon; the Bouches-du-Rhône, with two extraordinary tribunals set up in Marseille; the Vaucluse, where the notorious commission of Orange, introduced late on, sentenced, in six weeks in spring 1794, 332 individuals to death;[8] and the Gard, where the criminal tribunal in Nîmes sent to the guillotine 135 of the 295 cases before it from December 1793 to August 1794.[9]

Military commissions, with the exception of Paris, played a major role in these condemnations, as too did popular or revolutionary commissions, not to mention the decisive role played by so-called revolutionary tribunals (in Lyon, Orange, Arras and Cambrai, for example). Criminal tribunals at the departmental level, with some exceptions (as in Nîmes), played more limited roles, as Donald Greer had already noted (he estimated that they contributed to 12 per cent of capital sentences across France) and as several recent studies have since confirmed.[10]

In cases when a first instance of repression did not involve any judgements but then a military commission and a criminal tribunal authorized to judge 'revolutionarily' entered the scene, the figures speak for themselves. After the recapture of Toulon, which had been handed over by rebels to British and Spanish ships, a thousand individuals were condemned to death: more than two-thirds were summarily executed as soon as the city was regained, the others being condemned by a military commission.[11] That violence can be compared to the actions of the criminal tribunal sitting in Grasse, which was authorized to transform into a 'revolutionary tribunal' by a decree from Montagnard deputy Barras. With this new status it began to try counter-revolutionaries on 15 Frimaire Year II (5 December 1793). For five long months the court sat almost every day. Out of 200 accused, only 29 were condemned to death (14.5 per cent of the total), while 131 were acquitted, and the others were either kept in detention or, in seven cases, were deported. This relative leniency can be explained in part by the harshness of the initial repression or the fact that many counter-revolutionaries had fled the area. But the clemency accorded by this tribunal was also due to the fact that those working at the tribunal, and especially the public prosecutor (Vachier), sought to moderate the sentences passed, at least in comparison with what a military commission would have ruled.

There can be no surprise that the geographic distribution of military commissions was related to the presence of internal unrest – and external borders (map 8). There were two notorious exceptions. In the Bas-Rhin, a commission initially planned to be associated with a revolutionary army impacted different communes in addition to Strasbourg.[12] In the eastern part of the Nord department several military commissions came into being quite late on (late summer/early autumn 1794) after French troops recaptured cities that for many months had been controlled by foreign armies.[13]

For the rest, almost every army installed, at one time or another, at least one military commission. From Charente-Inférieure to the Breton departments and the Sarthe, the War of the Vendée led to the establishment of numerous military commissions of the coastal armies and the Western army. The Loire's strategic role – the Vendéens were to be contained south of the river – was already apparent with the successive deputies sent there.[14] Nearly a dozen military commissions were set up close to the Loire's banks, some of which turned out to be particularly severe in the justice meted out. In the Loire-Inférieure department, thousands of prisoners were executed, most of them sentenced in Nantes or Savenary by the Lenoir or the Bignon commissions.[15] The military commission set up in Noirmoutier, in the Vendée, after the island was wrested back from enemy control by force in early 1794 and then renamed Île de la Montagne, condemned more than 1,000 prisoners to death by firing squad. The Montagnard deputies Bourbotte and Prieur de la Marne wrote a letter to the Convention on 14 Nivôse Year II (3 January 1794) that laid out the unambiguous task they had assigned to the commission:

> The enemy lost five hundred men, while around another 1,200 laid down their arms. Among these prisoners there are ten to twelve chiefs. The treasonous Elbée, the generalissimo of the royal and Catholic armies, who had been wounded at Cholet and whom we thought dead, is in our hands... A military commission that we have just created will issue swift justice to these traitors.[16]

While Elbée was shot by a firing squad alongside three others (while seated in a chair, due to the numerous wounds he had sustained at Cholet in October 1793), the other captured prisoners were shot in groups of several dozen at a time – despite their having laid down their arms and surrendered. Another example comes from the Parein-Félix commission, in Angers, which also pronounced around 1,000 death sentences.[17] While military commissions were, in principle, meant to be merciless, that was not universally true. Those instituted just after the conclusion of hostilities, like the one in Noirmoutier, tended to display a victor's justice that was closer to vengeance than justice.[18] But other military commissions issued a great number of acquittals. The Lenoir commission in Nantes pronounced twice as many acquittals as capital sentences.[19] Out of the 591 judgements issued by the military commission in La Rochelle from October 1793 to the end of Nivôse Year II (mid-January 1794), there were 60 capital sentences while one-third of the cases resulted in deferrals.[20]

Even if the horror of the sheer number of capital sentences issued by tribunals and commissions remains undiminished, these nuances are a necessary consequence of the illuminating work of Eric de Mari on extra-legal punishments and the decree of 19 March 1793 (on the decree, see chapter 5). Out of 21,799 individuals judged to be 'outlawed' (and therefore legally subject to execution without appeal), only 13,048 were executed (around 60 per cent).[21] There were acquittals for dementia, drunkenness or because the condemned was recognized to have been 'mistaken' or to have been forced by counter-revolutionaries to rebel. These mitigating circumstances could have gone unheeded by judges who operated within a framework of unforgiving and merciless laws.

Comparing the map of executions with that of those judged outside the law (maps 7 and 9) highlights the very diverse conditions from one department to another. It is easy to see that certain departments judged a large number of individuals as 'outlawed' but did so with a relative clemency: in Doubs, 673 were judged 'outlawed' but only 63 sentenced to death (9.4 per cent); in Puy-de-Dôme, 28 of the 162 individuals judged 'outlawed' were condemned to death (17.3 per cent); and in the Haute-Marne there were two capital sentences out of 76 cases judged 'outlawed' (2.6 per cent).[22]

These purely numerical elements do not tell the whole story. It is necessary to understand the psychological and medical effects of imprisonment for those who escaped the guillotine or firing squad but continued to wonder when their final day would come. But making such judgements over two centuries later is complicated when testimony about captivity was often written after Thermidor, like Antoine François Delandine's *Depiction of the Lyon Prisons, to Add to the History of Tyranny in 1793 and 1793*, which was published under the Directory.[23] Delandine's text – which included a poem entitled 'The reign of terror' – describes the prison as a kind of waiting-room where 'quiet victims await the day when they will be led to be butchered by the government.'[24] He paints a grim picture that could serve for many other regimes in different countries or historical periods: lack of privacy, small activities to pass the time during interminable days that seem to stretch way beyond twenty-four hours, meetings and conversations, the continual dread of hearing one's name called by a jailor, the dreams and attempts at escape, etc.

Another interesting document testifying to the prison experience, though full of exaggerations and a pronounced political stance, is *Memoirs of a Prisoner to Add to the History of Robespierre's Tyranny*, by Honoré Riouffe, a relatively unknown writer who was close to the Girondins.[25] Arrested in Bordeaux in early October 1793 and then transferred to Paris, he remained incarcerated until just after 9–10 Thermidor, without ever appearing before the Revolutionary Tribunal. He wrote his account in winter 1794. *Memoirs of a Prisoner* was a publishing success, with at least two editions appearing in Paris and a greater number in the provinces – and a new edition appeared during the Restoration in 1823. While the text is full of valuable details on the conditions of detention at the Conciergerie prison next to the Revolutionary Tribunal, Riouffe's imagination seems to have filled in the rest. It is also clear that the writing was heavily influenced by pamphlets and newspapers that he collected after Thermidor. If one believes Riouffe's pages, he had personally witnessed almost all of the most famous prisoners, from the Girondins in October 1793 to the Hébertists and the Dantonists (or Indulgents) of spring 1794, to say nothing of Bailly, Madame Roland, Lavoisier and countless other main players in the Revolution. A study of the prison registries from Paris (which survived the conflagration that ended the Paris Commune of 1871 and are now conserved at the Archives de la Préfecture de Police de Paris) throws light on passages where Riouffe either invented, lied or exaggerated his account. Yet the key purpose of Riouffe's account was not to bear witness to historical accuracy but, as its title makes clear, to stigmatize the 'tyranny of Robespierre'. The text seeks to move the sympathies of its readers to the fate of some of those put to death and to find an outlet for their indignation towards 'the rabble (*canaille*) of bailiffs, clerks and all the subalterns' of the Revolutionary Tribunal (all of whom were, of course, functionally illiterate) and figures like Hébert (who 'died like the most unmanly coward' (*mort comme la femmelette la plus faible*), Danton ('a sub-mediocre man'), without forgetting Robespierre ('a blood-thirsty madman').

The summary executions of armed insurgents tended to be concentrated in domestic fronts, alongside pitched battles between 'rebels' and troops sent to fight them, or followed in the days after a city was reconquered. Massacres of civilians and punitive retribution (rape, seizures) accompanied the repression in the Vendée after the Republican victories in December 1793. These acts, as the recent work of Anne Rolland-Boulestreau tells us, came from the 'infernal columns' which crisscrossed the insurgent territory between January and July 1794 under the orders of generals like Turreau and Huché.[26] Nearly 60 per cent of the massacres by these eleven columns occurred between January and April, with more than 11,000 Vendéens killed. This was a true climax of violence against civilians, if one reads the reports by generals that count the victims (but only a small minority of which give figures): around 1,500 dead in 10 days between 21 and 31 January (2–12 Pluviôse Year II), over 7,000 in February (Pluviôse–Ventôse) – a total of over 19,000 between January 1794 and the first months of 1795.

The writings of the officers leave little doubt that the aim was to frighten civilians and annihilate whatever remained of the Vendéen insurgents. The vocabulary shows a desire to 'dehumanize the enemy.'[27] The soldiers themselves fell prey to fear in the face of these 'enraged Vendéens', transforming the towns they crossed into hunting grounds to flush out the enemy, as if they were setting a trap to track a wild animal, but also to deprive the Vendéens of support from the civilian populations. The situation changed in Floréal Year II with the dismissal of head general Turreau on the 29th (18 May 1794), and from that time onwards, actual combatants – rather than civilians – once again made up the great majority of those killed in the 'Vendée'.[28] But these first few months of 1794 indelibly marked the history of the 'war of the Vendée', inscribing this territory into the annals of the harshest repression.

Whatever the differences in nature there would be between the 'terror' and the 'Vendée', they both came together to give France in 1793 and Year II the durable image of a fratricidal Republic, soiled by violence and spilt blood. The fact that France today does not celebrate the birth of the First Republic says much. There is no celebration on 21 September, when the monarchy was abolished, nor on 22 September – the date on which the Convention decided for its official acts as the first day of the new political regime. France does celebrate 14 July, which became a national holiday in 1880, but 14 July commemorates the federation, in which the constitutionalized monarchy took centre stage.[29] But if we apprehend only this repressive aspect, we may fail to understand the complexity of a revolutionary government that was put in place in order to set up new policies to usher in an ideal city.

2. Fraternal France and fratricidal France

It is easy to see how far this ideal city was from the political realities of 1793 and Year II. The Constitution of 1793 was put on hold until peace was restored. The Republic's government concentrated power in a small band and certain political methods were far removed from ideals set out in the Declaration of the Rights of Man and of the Citizen. The powers entrusted to the members of the Committee of Public Safety between summer 1793 and summer 1794 seem incompatible with the exercise of democracy, even if theoretically these powers could be removed through a simple decision by the Convention (and every single member of the Committee belonged to the Assembly, which thus remained the central political power).

Note too, that the Convention itself extended its powers once the new Constitution was adopted, when it should have separated to make way for a new Assembly. While understandable given the context of summer 1793, this set-up nonetheless violated the normal functioning of institutions on the grounds of the state of exception.

Purges of local authorities by deputies broke down the legitimacy of elections, in direct opposition to the major role given since 1789 to the acts of voting and elections. The institutionalization of the system of sending 'deputies on mission' in spring 1793 led to a large number of deputies using their missions in this or that area to disinvest local officials they considered to be suspect. Then, in August 1793, a decree explicitly recognized the power of deputies to temporarily 'replace, either entirely or in part, the members of constituted authorities or diverse public offices ... with citizens of an unquestionable patriotism.'[30] Even if the replacement was temporary, this procedure boiled down to an elected official disinvesting other elected officials and replacing them with citizens he personally named. In that summer of so-called 'Federalist' revolts, the motivation for disinvesting local elected officials who had shown sympathy for the Girondins, especially those who had called for or participated in the revolts, was overtly political. Running parallel to these politically motivated purges was a desire to modify the social composition of local authorities – which had consisted mainly of lawyers and different strata of the bourgeoisie – by promoting what Albert Soboul has called 'the world of the stall and the shop'.[31]

The decree of 14 Frimaire Year II (4 December 1793) on the 'mode of provisional and revolutionary government', which entrusted this task at the departmental level to deputies 'on mission', included a section on the 'Reorganization and purge of constituted authorities'.[32] The administrative hierarchy arising out of the decisions taken in 1789–90 was partly modified, with a clear weakening of the powers of departmental authorities. The deputies were to purge all the local authorities with the aid of citizen councils: 'A simple measure can bring about this purge. Convene the people into popular societies. Bring the public officials there too. Ask the people their views of the behaviour of those officials. Let the people's judgement dictate yours.'[33] These popular societies or clubs became the embodiment of the sovereign, de facto substituting for elections in which assemblies of citizens came to vote and elect officials. This practice also raises questions about democracy. These popular societies constituted a national network capable of diffusing political orders throughout the Republic. Yet if one considers them more closely, these popular societies, just like the surveillance committees, were far from making up a homogeneous body. They certainly could not be assimilated to the Jacobin 'machine' that Augustin Chopin famously denounced.[34]

A great body of specialized scholarship on the deputies and local purges brings more nuance to the story. Far from becoming victims of a massive political purge, in many cases a great number of local officials were re-assigned offices, if not simply confirming them in office once their political 'purity' was acknowledged. One case shows this. In a long public meeting held in a church converted into a temple of Reason, on 21 Pluviôse Year II (9 February 1794), the deputy Mallarmé proceeded to 'purge' the municipality and the administration of the Gondrecourt district (Meuse), as well as the surveillance committee, the justice of the peace, the director of the post office, gendarmes, the national guard and the popular society. No replacements were ordered, Mallarmé's conclusion amounting to a statement of confidence in the current officials:

> I pronounced in the name of the Law that they had been cleansed [*épurés*]; I ordered them to stay firmly in their office and to continue to carry out their functions in such a way as to keep the Revolution going and to contribute to the strengthening of the reign of liberty.[35]

The undoubted apogee of the revolutionary political societies occurred in 1793 and Year II, contributing to a strong moment of 'pure' democracy (or, as we would put it today, 'direct' democracy). The archives of these societies and of section assemblies in major cities shows that the meetings were not dominated by a small minority adept at empty political talk; rather, these meetings were a central site for debates that were often contentious, if not vituperative.[36] These meetings were also forums in which the acts of voting and electing continued to be exercised. This was true even during the time of political exception when elections were suspended at the national level. In these meetings members elected the officers of the society (the president and secretaries) and other posts (archivist, treasurer); they voted to designate commissairs charged with representing them through addresses or petitions to local authorities, or even to Paris; they also voted to elect new members. The frequent communications, at times daily, between societies, surveillance committees (whose members were, at first, elected), and the municipality show that politics continued at the municipal level, which was considered the primary territorial level for politics.

The Jacobin Club in Paris wanted to create an extremely hierarchical national political network so as to circulate its political orders through devoted, orthodox militants. Yet this plan was far from successful. Of the 6,000 popular societies in existence in Year II in around 5,500 communes, only about 800 (less than 15 per cent) were directly affiliated with the Jacobins in Paris. With the Republic containing around 44,000 communes, the network of societies affiliated to the Jacobs covered only 2 per cent of the communes in France at that time, which hardly amounted to a stranglehold over the territory. The importance of these popular societies also varied considerably across geographic regions, and between cities and the countryside. At the national level, every departmental capital had at least one political society in Year II; 98 per cent of district capitals, but only 60 per cent of cantonal capitals, had at least one political society at the time. At the communal level, though, 86 per cent of communes never had a political society (if one excludes capitals at the cantonal, district or departmental level, that figure goes up to 93 per cent). Taking into account the demographic size of communes is also telling. In Seine-Inférieure, 96 per cent of communes with over 2,000 inhabitants possessed at least one society, but only 12 per cent of communes of 200–500 inhabitants had one, a figure that fell to 2 per cent for communes with less than 200 inhabitants. In the district of Rouen (a city that was also the departmental capital), nearly 30 per cent of communes with less than 200 inhabitants had at least one political society – but not a single commune at that level in the six other districts of the department had one.

These figures raise some questions about the depth of politicization in the countryside, especially considering that France was then a primarily rural nation. It also raises the prospect that democratic practices passed through other channels than political societies. The dynamism of municipal life in the countryside bears witness to this; the evidence is there to find for historians who are prepared to immerse themselves in local archive collections. Regardless of official 'Terror' policies, the general village assembly continued electing rural wardens or shepherds, debating local affairs, and negotiating exterior pressures, especially those coming from the State, in a sort of 'perpetuation of a culture of compromise'.[37]

In the midst of a period that some historians call the era of 'Jacobin centralization', the Bouquier law on schools (29 Frimaire Year II [19 December 1793]) – which was applied in less than half of the communes in the country before being replaced eleven months later by the Lakanal law – placed schools entirely under the authority of municipalities. Schools were made public, free and obligatory (for three years) in what constituted a 'golden age of educational decentralization and the revolutionary public school'.[38] Any citizen could become a teacher; teachers had a total pedagogical freedom – all of which is very far from constituting another 'machine' to forge public beliefs. Local democracy and the right to vote could also be seen in the decree of 10 June 1793. This decree ordered the distribution of communal goods between inhabitants of a commune if at least one-third of them demanded so through a vote. This decree also granted, for the first time, the right to vote to women. This not only responded to women's demands (by the Society of Revolutionary Republican Citizenesses, for instance) but also to the various concrete advantages that females received in 1792–3 rather than full and complete rights to citizenship.[39] The public voice of citizens was also channelled through the right to petition and the right to present claims, a practice that was most used during the government of exception.

The so-called 'Thermidorian' Convention sensed the tremendous political clout of such measures when it forbade, on 25 Vendémiaire Year II (16 October 1794), political societies from allying to each other or presenting collective petitions. This was instituted so as to break down the national, vertical network linked to the Jacobins in Paris as well as the horizontal networks established among societies in the provinces. The same spirit animated the decision on 7 Fructidor Year II (24 August 1794) when the Convention suppressed the forty-eight sections in Paris and regrouped them into twelve arrondissements. This broke down the activist solidarities central to the practice of democracy in the eyes of the *sans-culottes*, namely the right to assemble in order to demonstrate, or, in the other words, popular intervention in the public space.

Organizing political life around the assemblies of inhabitants, political societies and sections in major cities was combined with the desire of the revolutionary government to develop a war economy to fund the army while also instituting social policies to help the most disadvantaged. The state of exception and the state of war were intertwined, which meant bringing together citizens behind a common desire to defend the Republic. The government and local authorities set up multiple measures to help workshops, factories and manufacturing sites, especially for those producing weapons (from simple knives to canons). At the same time, dozens of deputies travelled through the departments to stimulate production or even, *ex nihilo*, create centres to do so.

Certain deputies, such as the Montagnard Pointe, became specialists in that sort of mission.[40] A gunsmith like his father, Pointe first oversaw the manufacture of weapons in his hometown of Saint-Etienne in summer 1793. Captured by the 'Federalists' of Lyon, he returned to Paris, only to leave on a further mission that autumn. He spent many months in the departments of Nièvre and Allier.

Between Pluviôse and Thermidor Year II (February–August 1794), Pointe mainly worked on overseeing and developing the production of canons for the navy. As Pointe was totally immersed in these activities for the war effort and was away from Paris from November 1793 to summer 1794, he was far removed from the political fights playing out in the capital. Pointe was one of the de facto Montagnards sent on a mission after Thermidor. From Pluviôse–Prairal Year III (February–June 1795), Pointe was first in Le Creusot, and then several nearby departments, overseeing foundries.

Other deputies could be mentioned, such as the Montagnards Roux-Fazillac and Brival, who nearly tripled the number of workers in arms manufacturing in Tulle (from 237 in 1792 to 663 in Year III) and doubled the monthly production of rifles. The Montagnard Lakanal created a new arms manufacturing site in Bergerac where 150 workers produced around 4,000 rifles in Year II.[41] These measures were accompanied by worker-friendly social policies, as the decisions taken by another Montagnard, Romme, showed. On a mission to Dordogne and neighbouring departments, Romme was tasked with overseeing arms manufacturing centres. His decisions show to what point the war effort was married to the necessities of disciplined collective action and social matters. While Romme reinforced the power of forge masters over their workers, calling on them to supervise and denounce 'those who are enemies of work, drunks and bad citizens', he also organized the distribution of bread, meat, vegetables and wine in the form of rations that worked as advances on salaries. This payment in kind allowed workers to avoid rising prices and thus worked as a kind of 'subsistence salary' – something that had been a major demand of workers (in the same way that certain agricultural laborers fought to be partly paid in foodstuffs).[42] In addition to payment in kind for work, there was also recourse to a work in kind when citizens were mobilized for a designated task when, for instance, they took time off from their professional activity and contributed to the war effort.

The contribution to the war effort led to civic gifts, at the individual or collective level, throughout the country, as well as subscription campaigns (in Year II, for instance, to construct a ship line per department).[43] The saltpetre (potassium nitrate) harvest is the clearest example of the collective mobilization of citizens. This mineral salt appearing on humid walls (in caves, stables and barns) was part of the composition of the black powder (which mixed up saltpetre, sulphur and coal) used in firearms. Citizens mobilized to harvest saltpetre, 'ateliers for the production of revolutionary saltpetre' appeared, while the Committee of Public Safety ordered in

Year II the establishment of public workshops in the production of the powder.

All of these links between nature, work and wages were also present in the legislation that was adopted in establishing the famous Maximum. The Maximum has at times been presented as the key to a kind of 'economic terror', with even Albert Mathiez, who otherwise could hardly be suspected of hostility to the French Revolution, devoting long pages to what he called 'the economic dictatorship of the Committee of Public Safety'.[44] Yet the debates around the Maximum began well before the first decree was voted in during May 1793 and thus preceded the creation of the committee. These debates show that an overwhelming majority of members in the Convention – even the Montagnards – defended the right to property and had no interest in undermining that right or 'terrorizing' property owners. What was important, in fact, was preserving that right to property by making sure that the natural right to life was not undermined by the right to commerce. All this took up popular calls for the 'taxation' of high prices well before the birth of the Republic. The 'tax' in question was conceived as creating a just price, a threshold that could not be broken.[45] In this way, the Convention and its Committee of Public Safety intended above all to fight against speculation and monopolistic behaviour. At first there was no desire to undermine the right to trade or the right to property, to say nothing of putting in place an 'economic dictatorship'. The aim was simply to guarantee, through state intervention, a minimum of transparency in the market and a relative equality between producers and consumers, as well as between producers. This search for equality did not imply a social equality between buyers and sellers; rather, it was an equality concerning equal access to information about the factors that went into setting prices so that natural competition would not be undermined by speculators. This makes it possible, in a way, to speak of the Maximum as representing an egalitarian conception of liberalism rather than a strike against it.[46] It remains the case that in the dire economic straits of 1793, alongside other forms of crisis, the idea of a smoothly functioning market was a pipedream, especially since the need for access to basic necessities for civilians had to compete with the imperative of provisioning soldiers and armies.

The Convention's first Maximum, passed through a decree dated 4 May 1793, fixed the price of grains.[47] It is telling that the bill placed on the same level tax revolts and speculation – those who sought to arbitrarily tax necessities and those who tried to raise their prices – which were in both cases punished with five years in prison (while recognizably monopolistic behaviour or hoarding was punished with ten years). Prices had to be fixed by local authorities based on inventories declared by owners and with regard to the wage of a day's labour. One major problem was that while the decree mentioned 'different species of grains', it did not provide any clarification as to what these were and did not place each one under the Maximum's reach. With the Maximum having a variable effect from one market to another, speculative behaviour continued, especially since local authorities tended to only tax grains used in bread. Thus oats, which were not taxed, rose to double the price of wheat, whereas normally they would have been half the price. A further problem was that buyers would pay the price required by the Maximum but, to secure desired quantities, would bend the law by more or less discreetly adding various top-ups (free transport, for example). While not breaking the law, such acts went against its spirit and also undermined the efforts to regulate the market.

Another example of the progressive hardening of legislation came on 27 July when a second decree indicated that the death penalty would be applied against individuals judged guilty of monopolistic behaviour. Article 1 was remarkably concise on that score: 'Cornering the market is a capital crime.'[48] Anyone making a false declaration would also be sentenced to death, and the judgements of criminal tribunals of the departments could not be appealed. The severity that was sought after, though, was more difficult to put into practice because a strict implementation of the law would have banned wholesale trading.[49] The decree nonetheless established, for the first time, a list of 'vital foodstuffs and goods' that went well beyond grains (to include meat, wine, fruits and vegetables, butter, etc.). Added to that were several goods that were military necessities (leather, iron and steel, cloth, etc.).

About six weeks later, the revolutionary days of 4 and 5 September led the Convention to place taxation, and not 'terror', on the top of its agenda. On 23 September, a report on the subject was presented, and on 29 September, the Convention decreed a new Maximum. This Maximum concerned 'vital foodstuffs and goods', with a list that was slightly modified from the one that appeared in July, but also 'the wages ... for employees, domestic workers, manual labourers and day labourers'.[50] The maximum price of vital foodstuffs and goods was to be fixed by the administration of each district, calculated on the average price in 1790, increased by about one-third (with some exceptions). Wages and other forms of payment for labour would be handled by municipalities with a similar logic, although the figure for 1790 was increased by 50 per cent (to take into account rising wages since the labour force had shrunk because of enlistment in the army, as decreed by the mobilization in August; in many cases wages were already 50 per cent higher than the 1790 figure). On 2 Ventôse Year II (20 February 1794), a 'general table of the Maximum' was presented before the Convention. This time the Maximum was made uniform across the national territory – this was, in a way, the apogee of economic control in the state of exception. The Maximum undoubtedly played a major role in the arsenal of measures of the 'economic terror', alongside requisitions from the countryside that brought in, against payment in *assignats*, foodstuffs and animals (especially horses). These measures did not manage to durably modify the underlying structures of trade, especially when it came to the practices of buyers and sellers. Yet until it was abolished by the Convention on 4 Nivôse Year III (24 December 1794), the Maximum ensured the preservation of some minimal access to food for the poorest and played an essential role in setting out what was paid for requisitioned food or goods for the war effort.

On top of these state-led economic measures were other decisions aiming at reducing social inequalities, tapping into the demands made in early spring 1793 by the Montagnards Jeanbon Saint-André and Ellie Lacoste, then deputies in the Dordogne and the Lot: 'It is absolutely necessary to aid the poor if you want their help to complete the Revolution. In these extraordinary cases we should only see the great law of the public good.'[51] A whole policy of public aid was in fact born, in the name of national welfare (*bienfaisance*), which did not forget the colonial territories (abolition of slavery on 16 Pluviôse Year II [4 February 1794]). There were also measures to help soldiers and their families, which were necessary to encourage citizen-soldiers to spill blood at the borders or against 'rebels'.[52] A major concern for the Convention in 1793 was ensuring the access of the poorest in the countryside to land, even if a genuine land reform was never contemplated due to strictures about property rights. One decree passed on 13 September (shortly after the revolutionary days of 4 and 5 September when the Convention resisted calls to decree 'terror the order of the day', and just before voting in of the Law of Suspects) gave a loan of 500 *livres* to all untaxed non-property, to be paid back in twenty annuities and without interest, in order to purchase the lands of *émigrés* that had been seized as national property.[53] While the law was applied in very unequal ways across the communes, the Convention nonetheless showed its desire to link the extraordinary measures taken against enemies of the Republic to aid for the needy.[54] The decree also specified that 'defenders of the nation' – citizens who had joined the army – could also take part by allowing them to specify a proxy to act on their behalf.

The famous decrees of Ventôse presented by Saint-Just on 8 and 13 Ventôse Year II (26 February and 3 March 1794) adopted similar principles, but took them further by ordering the confiscation of the property and goods of suspects and 'enemies of the Republic' for the benefit of the needy.[55] While these measures had barely started being implemented before the Convention annulled the laws in autumn 1794, following Saint-Just's execution alongside Robespierre, the laws nonetheless show the ideals of a society that associated the links between property, happiness and the nation. The desire to finish with the 'terror' can also be seen in the effort to distinguish among suspects so that the innocent could be released from an unjust imprisonment so that only the guilty would be punished.

At a time when military efforts seemed to promise the triumph of the Republic over its enemies, peace seemed to be coming soon, and with that it would finally be possible to move from a revolutionary to a constitutional government. The Ventôse decrees were inscribed within the notion of political exception, indirectly suggesting another interpretation of the Law of Prairial (10 June) that accelerated the judgements of the Revolutionary Tribunal.[56] As such, these decrees can be linked to the idea of a *foundation* of the Republic on *civil institutions* in the sense that Saint-Just gave to them. The 'friends of the nation' would be rewarded and the 'conspirators' imprisoned until peace returned and then banished (the Ventôse decrees do not mention capital punishment) – and then repression would no longer be needed in a country that had become once again fraternal without being fratricidal thanks to the success of the Republic's arms. The American historian, Carla Hesse, takes a similar view, arguing that one of the primary aims of the Ventôse decrees was – where possible – to save lives and liberate prisoners.[57]

The military victories of 1794, culminating in Fleurus on 26 June, would not have been possible without the military recovery that began in autumn 1793, which itself was intimately linked to the 'terror in the armies'. The role of deputies was fundamental here, just as it had been in the suppression of different revolts in departments. The institutionalization of the system of 'deputies on mission' in spring 1793 was driven principally by military necessity. The first great collective mission, on 9 March, concerned the mobilization of 300,000 'volunteers' for the armies. In April, several decrees systematized the presence of deputies within the Republic's armies.[58] At first the method chosen by the Convention and the Committee of Public Safety was, if not confused, at least poorly defined, as it depended on constantly changing circumstances and had to deal with the particularities of different fronts. Around sixty representatives left Paris for the armies in April. In most cases there were four deputies per army, but to the two major fronts, the North and the Rhine, twelve and ten deputies, respectively, were sent. At the start of the 'Vendéen' revolt, the number of deputies grew exponentially: six representatives sent on 30 April, followed quickly by twenty more to the coastal army of La Rochelle. This sudden rise explains the exceptionally high number of deputies in 1793 in the coastal army of La Rochelle and then in the Western army – only the army of the North exceeded their numbers (see map 3). On 19 July, the number of deputies to the armies was limited to forty-eight, or four for each army. The Convention and the Committee of Public Safety then gave deputies more precisely defined missions, evidence of the transformation of a measure initially designed to meet the challenges of an emergency. The deputies embedded with the armies were asked to take over all aspects of the army – military operations, provisioning, fortifications, the diffusion or even creation of military newspapers, etc. They were there, not just to assist, but also to exercise surveillance over the generals, though without taking over from them in conducting the war. This created a delicate coexistence when certain deputies took on roles outside their supposed areas of competence.

The Committee of Public Safety, working closely with the Committee of War, intervened more and more in military operations. A number of members of the Committee of Public Safety, most prominently Carnot and Saint-Just, became de facto army leaders. And starting in summer 1793, the arrest or execution of a number of generals (Custine on 27 August, Houchard on 16 November [26 Brumaire Year II], etc.) showed the subordination of the sword to the toga, of military leaders to civilian ones. In the field, a number of deputies began to apply, starting in autumn and winter 1793, a 'terror in the armies' in order to reinforce discipline so as to strengthen France's military might.

The story of the actions of Saint-Just and Le Bas in the armies of the Rhine and the North is well known. They did not hold back from dismissing superior officers where they judged it necessary. In Brumaire Year II (October–November 1793), eleven condemned officers, among them a general and two colonels, were executed by firing squad in front of assembled troops.[59] As Le Bas candidly noted to his wife: 'At the moment when he least expects it, this or that general sees us arrive, requiring him to account for his conduct.'[60] It is difficult to imagine a clearer expression of how the deputies saw their role.

At the other end of the country, two new deputies were sent to the army of the Pyrénées Orientales in early Nivôse Year II (late December 1793). The two deputies were both Montagnards who had experience with military missions, seeing as both had been serving officers before the Revolution. Milhaud graduated as a military engineer in 1788 and was a second lieutenant in 1790; he was a deputy to the Army in the Ardennes in spring 1793 and then to the army of the Rhine that summer before being sent to the front in the Pyrenees – he had, in other words, been continuously active in the army from May 1793 until mid-Fructidor Year II (early September 1794). The other Montagnard deputy, Soubrany, who had been made a second lieutenant in 1780, was designated to join the army of Moselle in spring 1793 and was then sent, with only a brief trip to Paris, to the Pyrénées Orientales. Like his fellow deputy, Soubrany had been with armies for a relatively long period of time. When the two deputies arrived, they were faced with an army that had become completely disorganized and on a front that had seen the only deputy killed in combat (Fabre de l'Herault, killed during a battle to repulse a Spanish incursion on French territory on 30 Frimaire Year II [20 December 1793]). Before Milhaud and Sobrany's mission, 113 individuals had been brought before military justice at the front (from June 1793 to January 1794), mostly on charges of desertion during battle. Surprisingly enough, given that in principle the charge did not lend itself to clemency in any army, only three soldiers were executed. After the two deputies reorganized the military justice at the front, around 200 soldiers were judged between January and May 1793 (Nivôse–Prairial Year II). About one-third of these trials took place in the first month, no doubt to set an example, and in the end about 25 per cent of the cases resulted in a capital sentence. In a shorter period of time a little less than double the number of cases came before the military courts but the number of executions had been multiplied by a factor of 17. What's more, many more executions followed until the summer. Twenty officers were among those condemned to death, among them three generals: Ramel was executed on 13 Germinal year II (2 April 1794), and then Aoust and Delattre were both executed on 14 Messidor (2 July).[61] The re-establishment of discipline played a key role in the changed military situation (for the better) of the French army on this front in early 1794, showing how the 'terror in the armies' played a decisive part in the Republic's military fortunes.

Michelet's lyrical flights, and the entire republican strain of historiography after him, saw the deputies as saviours of the Republic. In Michelet's words, these 'terrible voyagers of the Revolution' were:

> men of fate that it [the Revolution] launched one morning beyond all customs, beyond all familiar realities, far from the centre and the rule.

They were forced by unforeseen circumstances that took them by the throat, to trample on the law to save the law, to commit crimes so as to stamp out crime, to extinguish the light of the world by allowing the only people in whom it still appeared to perish.[62]

While the reality was much more complicated, by highlighting the role played by several deputies to the armies, Michelet was one of the first historians to show how everything was linked together and that the political state of exception gave rise to a number of fatal contradictions. The law was violated in order to be saved; a number of elementary judicial principles born in 1789 were violated by instituting extraordinary justice in their stead; the Declaration of Rights and constitutional operations were violated when the 1793 Constitution was suspended until the return of peace; democratic practices were violated in order to preserve them; and as friend was separated from enemy, something had to be done with the latter.

Better than anyone else, Camille Desmoulins expressed in just a few words the whole infernal spiral of the 'terror': 'You want to exterminate your enemies by the guillotine. Could anything be madder than that? Is it possible to kill one person on the scaffold without creating ten enemies from his family or friends?'[63] In winter 1793, at a time when the Girondins were imprisoned, on the run or already guillotined, and as the two factions of the 'ultra-revolutionaries' (Hébertists) and the 'Indulgents' (or Dantonists) were at each other's throats, Desmoulins seized on recent victories in Lyon and Le Mans, and implicitly those to come, to affirm that: 'Of your enemies, all that remain are cowards and the sick. The courageous and the strong have already emigrated. They have perished in Lyon or in the Vendée; the others do not deserve your rage.'[64] To escape from the contradictions of the 'terror', Desmoulins called for the formation of a 'committee of clemency'.

A few months later, during Germinal Year II (March–April 1794), the elimination of the two rival factions resulted in eleven Montagnards, among them Danton and Desmoulins, facing the guillotine. Condorcet, the last great philosopher of the eighteenth century and a member of the Convention, had been hunted down as a supporter of the Girondins from autumn 1793 – and now found himself arrested in Clamart carrying false papers. He chose to commit suicide by poisoning himself in the room where he was detained.[65] In one way this can be seen as a confirmation of Vergniaud's bleak premonition in March 1793: 'Thus, citizens, it is to be feared that the Revolution, just as Saturn devoured his children, will lead to despotism and all the calamities accompanying it.'[66] From another point of view, this can be seen as a climax, in that month of Germinal, of the inherent political contradictions of the 'terror', of a France that was both fraternal and fratricidal. These contradictions led to 9 and 10 Thermidor; they also led to the invention of a 'system of terror' that allowed those who vanquished Robespierre to conserve the revolutionary government by retrospectively making 'the Terror' into an autonomous entity, a kind of bloody machine that the 'tyrant' had wanted but which now had been killed along with him.

By pretending to have annihilated a 'system of terror', the Convention covered up past violence, chose to rehabilitate certain victims (the Girondins, Desmoulins, but not Danton), and above all gave itself an amnesty for the role it itself played while continuing to benefit from the workings of the revolutionary government in order to complete the task of defeating the Republic's enemies. This act also dismissed those nostalgic for Year II as 'terrorists' or 'Robespierrists' – 1795 saw peace brokered with the major Vendéen leaders, harsh repression of the *émigrés* who arrived in Quiberon, the signing of several peace treaties with a number of the coalition powers fighting France, as well as the repression of the last major demonstrations of the Parisian *sans-culottes* and the tracking down of the final followers of the Montagnards.

In little more than a year (from summer 1794 to autumn 1795), the 'Thermidorian' Convention profoundly changed the political course of the Revolution and gave birth to a directorial republic that was far removed from its 1792–4 predecessor. The Consular Republic marked a new page when, in 1804, a new Constitution opened with these words: 'The Government of the Republic is confined to the Emperor, who takes the title Emperor of the French.' Despotism engendered by the Revolution?

Conclusion:
How the Convention Reconstructed Itself After Thermidor

If the political exception experienced by the First Republic was thus able to bring together in association a France that was both fratricidal and fraternal, it is also due to the fact that the so-called Montagnard Convention had been very concerned with social issues, particularly through the public relief policies that it implemented.[1] How could it have been otherwise when this Assembly had heard more than one speech inviting it to 'make the poor live', while Saint-Just summed it up with a sentence full of meaning inserted in one of the reports he wrote to present the Ventôse decrees: 'The unfortunate are the powers of the earth; they have the right to speak as masters to governments that neglect them'.[2] Hannah Arendt interpreted this as 'a new notion of freedom, based on liberation from poverty [and] changing both the course and purpose of the revolution'.[3] Did this desire to establish the 'freedom to be free', to use her words, mark a 'turning point' and, above all, explain that, following it, 'the French Revolution ended in disaster'?[4] While such a reflection is not without interest, it is nevertheless once again part of a very generalized vision of the French Revolution and the revolutions that followed it, one which has much in common with statements about the alleged origins of twentieth-century totalitarianism being rooted in the 1790s.

Comparing revolutions is certainly a stimulating intellectual exercise, but too often it leads to errors of perspective due to a certain decontextualization of historical analyses. Moreover, the Thermidorian invention of *the Terror* as a 'system' has completely distorted these analyses by focusing on the repressive aspects of the first years of the Republic. From then on, the historiographical quarrels between historians who put forward the so-called thesis of circumstances to justify terror and those who saw *the Terror* as a stage in the origins of twentieth-century totalitarianism have helped to confuse the picture. These historiographical disputes, despite their various nuances, have been based on the common assumptions both that 'terror' was a reified entity, a 'system' separate from the revolutionary government, and that this so-called 'system' ended in the aftermath of the death of Robespierre and his co-accused.

But whilst the Law of 22 Prairial was very quickly suppressed (14 Thermidor, Year II [1 August 1794]) and, in a few weeks or months, the events of Thermidor did indeed lead to the release of the great majority of the suspects imprisoned in 1793 or in the Year II, does it follow that the Convention decided to implement a process of reconciliation and what jurists today call transitional justice? The evidence suggests otherwise, for whilst 'transitional justice' aims to re-establish the rule of law after the end of an authoritarian regime and/or armed conflict, in the case of the French Revolution, it took more than a year after the summer of 1794 before a new Constitution was adopted and the Convention broke up to make way for the Directory. Moreover, re-establishing the rule of law would presuppose that it no longer existed, and yet ordinary laws never disappeared in favour of the so-called revolutionary laws in 1793 and in the Year II, since the state of political exception did not imply a denial of the legitimacy of the Convention and an abolition of the rule of law. As for the idea of promoting national reconciliation, based among other things on reparations granted to the victims and their families, but also on measures designed to pay tribute to the dead through commemorations and above all to aim for a non-recurrence of human rights violations, here again the realities of the so-called Thermidorian Convention do not fit readily into this format; nor can the regime which succeeded it, the Directory, be easily identified as a society that functioned as democratically or as peacefully.

Certainly, the Carrier trial in December 1794 can be seen as a precursor in embryo form of the so-called 'truth' commissions that were set up at various points in the twentieth century after the end of certain authoritarian regimes; and one author recently referred to the Year III as the time of 'Terror on Trial'.[5] But isn't Carrier the tree that hides the forest? Was he not almost the only former representative of the people on mission to be prosecuted, tried and sentenced for executions covered by his authority? Several other Montagnard 'missionaries' were also denounced for their actions whilst on mission, as evidenced today by the hundreds of denunciatory letters preserved in the National Archives.[6] However, none of them were subsequently brought before a court of justice to answer for such executions. The only other exception was Lebon, who was also imprisoned, tried and then belatedly sentenced to death (24 Vendémiaire Year IV [16 October 1795], a few days before the end of the Convention). Whilst Lebon was arrested immediately after 9–10 Thermidor, his initial arrest was due to the accusation that he had been close to Robespierre, rather than for his activities as a deputy on mission. It was only in a second phase that the repression carried out under his authority in Arras and Cambrai featured in the pamphlet literature by then being published as part of a campaign attacking former Montagnards and Jacobins.

A print published on 24 Floréal Year III (13 May 1795), under the title *Les Formes acerbes* (The Acerbic Forms), provides an enlightening testimony to this. One of the pamphleteers who were relentless in their attacks on Lebon, Louis-Eugène Poirier, a lawyer, also called Poirier of Dunkirk, claimed authorship with these words addressed to the imprisoned 'terrorist': 'an object of horror, of eternal horror, such as Hell has vomited from its breast, had to remain before your eyes forever, frightening posterity forever, which will retreat in terror'.[7] The author of the original drawing, Louis Lafitte, composed his work along two axes.[8] The first axis separates the lower level, strewn with decapitated corpses on which stands a Lebon transformed into a monster who drinks steaming blood from two cups replenished by two guillotines (representing Arras and Cambrai), whilst the top of the composition is reserved for clouds where a female allegory of the Convention watches Justice unveil the Truth while a winged genius blows a trumpet over freed prisoners placed on the edge of a precipice. The second axis divides with a river of water and blood, fed by the two guillotines, on the left the liberated prisoners stretch their arms out to the clouds as a sign of gratitude to the Convention, on the right furies and the beasts feed on the flesh of corpses. Across the trumpet's pennant are written the words: '9 Thermidor. Humanity Justice Virtue to the order of the day'.

Can we argue that this personification of the Convention (which, placed under the eye of Surveillance, orders the release of detainees and sends the 'terrorists' back to the hells that had spewed them out onto the earth[9]) represents an unmistakable and unequivocal symbol of transitional justice? Some might conclude that it does.[10] There is a major problem, however, with an image that seeks to depict the Convention as a single unified entity, as if this Assembly had truly been as one and indivisible as the Republic, had not been traversed by conflicts and had not been even more hesitant in the face of its own contradictions when it came to staging the 'exit' from *the Terror*.

However, among the ghosts haunting the Convention hall in the months following Robespierre's elimination, both the deputies who died violent deaths and those imprisoned or reduced to the state of outcasts on the run since 1793, not all of them were deemed to have the right to the same treatment and a supposed desire for national reconciliation; far from it.[11] Indeed, the Convention could not rehabilitate the memory of all its members who had died a violent death without engaging in a collective reflection on shared responsibilities, on the one hand, in the successive purges that struck it from 1793 to 1795, and on the other hand and above all, in the repressive violence of 'terror'. The famous phrase attributed to Carrier at the time of his trial, no doubt in reality invented later by another member of the Assembly, sums it up well: 'everyone is guilty, right down to the President's bell'.[12]

Unless one imagines, in a way that is fanciful to say the least, an Assembly reduced to a few dozen Montagnards, each one more 'terrorist' than the next, and deliberating in the Year II in an obsessive climate of fear for their own lives, which belies a scrupulous examination of the minutes of the debates, even at the height of what is usually presented as the culmination of *the Terror*, it must be noted that few representatives of the people took the floor to oppose the radicalization of repressive legislation. As we have seen, several major repressive provisions were voted by the Convention in March and April 1793, when the Girondins were still supposed to be in the majority. As for the deputies who chose to sit cautiously in the political centre (the Plain), they, too, supported with their votes these decrees which aimed at repressing refractory priests, *émigrés*, 'Vendéens' and other suspects of all kinds.

How in these conditions was it possible for the Convention to 'get out' of *the Terror* without setting in motion a process likely to lead to a reflection on the collective responsibility of the Convention's membership? Worse still, while it was relatively straightforward to recall into the Assembly those deputies who had been detained for many months by virtue of an arrest decree, could the same be done for those who had been declared 'outlawed' without calling into question the very notion of outlawing? Lastly, if no one then thought of paying tribute to all the dead of the Convention, given the persistence of political divisions, should the honours of commemoration be limited to Girondins alone, a problem – we should note in passing – which also had material consequences for the aid granted to families of the victims?

Conclusion 161

On 18 Frimaire Year III (8 December 1794), on behalf of the Committees of Public Safety, General Security and Legislation, Merlin de Douai presented a draft decree on 'the case of our seventy-three colleagues who have been arrested'; then he listed the names of the 'seventy-three' detainees to be released and the decree was immediately passed amid applause.[13] Various interventions by deputies then came to propose other names, often because of solidarity between elected representatives of the same department, and the list ended up including seventy-six names of Girondins who had been banned from being reintegrated into the Convention.[14] However, two of them, Devérité and Dulaure, were in a different case, since they had been subject to an indictment, had fled and had therefore been outlawed. Recalling them would amount to opening Pandora's box, as it would raise the question of recalling the other fugitives who, between July and October 1793, had also been indicted or declared 'traitors to the *patrie*'. The very next day, after an intervention by Grégoire in favour of a re-examination of the case of Lanjuinais, another Girondin, the Convention decreed that these three committees, meeting together, would submit to it a report on all the representatives outlawed.[15] Finally, on 27 Frimaire (17 December), after a new report presented by Merlin de Douai, the Convention opted for a kind of compromise by decreeing that these outlawed representatives would not be recalled, but that it would undertake not to further any legal action against them.[16]

During the debates, Pénières-Delzors, a Girondin who had escaped the various repressive decrees of 1793, demanded that the outcasts be allowed to appear before the court to be cleared and added: 'The day Philippeaux and Camille Desmoulins were sent to the scaffold, it was decided not to open the discussion that would have saved them, that would have made their innocence known. I ask that our colleagues be brought before the Revolutionary Tribunal'.[17] As this decree did not order the reinstatement of the outlawed representatives, the Convention decided to recall them only on 18 Ventôse Year III (8 March 1795),[18] in a political context increasingly openly hostile to the last Montagnards and the Jacobins with the first violence of the 'white terror'. Twenty-four other outcasts were then allowed to return to the benches of the Assembly. Then, on the 22 Germinal (11 April), ten days after the failure of the 'revolutionary day' (popular insurrection) of the 12th (1st April) in Paris, the Assembly went much further and annulled all the outlaw decrees issued 'as a result of or on the occasion of' 31 May and 2 June 1793, which authorized the return of the fugitives concerned. Despite several protests against the fact that the decree would exonerate those who had taken up arms, including Précy, the royalist military leader of the Lyon revolt, the decree was passed.[19]

Only two things remained to be resolved: the question of reparations to the families of the victims and the organization of a commemorative ceremony. In the first case, the widows, children and other relatives of representatives who died under the 'reign' of the so-called 'Decemviral tyranny', had been sending numerous letters and petitions to the Convention calling first for the unsealing of the seals and the restitution of property, and then for public relief.[20] In each case the Assembly first ordered the payment of the compensation due to the deceased as legislator, then granted public assistance (according to modalities which were still under discussion under the Executive Board), the amounts of which were quickly reduced by monetary depreciation. Moreover, such balsam applied to wounds could in no way replace all losses, which, as Gorsas's widow wrote, 'it is impossible to mend, that of a dear husband, that of a tender father'.[21]

In the same way, no national tribute could bring a dead person back to life. However, the living could stage the past to validate the thesis of a horrible 'system', now happily ended by the Convention, attributed to the scapegoats of Thermidor (Robespierre and his 'accomplices') and the following months (Carrier, Lebon, the four 'great culprits' and all those then supposed to be part of the 'tail of Robespierre'). On 14 Prairial (2 June), in an even more tense context after the 'revolutionary day' or popular uprising of the 1st Prairial (20 May), marked by the assassination of the deputy Féraud in the Convention hall itself, the Assembly decreed the principle of a funeral ceremony in honour of the 'friends of liberty', the date of which (given in the Gregorian calendar) was set for 3 October in memory of the decrees against the Girondins in 1793. On the same day, the Convention immediately paid fitting homage to Féraud, who was added to the list of 'martyrs'.[22] Then, on 11 Vendémiaire Year IV (3 October 1795), all the members of the Convention, in official costume and with bands of black crepe on their arms, attended the ceremony where 'tunes and funeral songs were sung in honour of the victims of Decemviral tyranny'.[23] A funerary urn covered with black crepe and wreaths, shaded with oak and cypress foliage and surmounted by a palm tree, rested on a base with this inscription as an epitaph: 'They commended their fathers, wives and children to the *patrie*. To the magnanimous defenders of freedom, who died in prisons or on the scaffolds during the tyranny'.

In the midst of royalist unrest and just as the Convention was about to break up, having ensured that two-thirds of the seats on the Council of Five Hundred and the Council of Elders (the two Assemblies under the new regime, the Directory) would be reserved for former members of the Convention, the political sleight of hand begun in the aftermath of Thermidor was completed. By maintaining most of the workings of the revolutionary government, the so-called Thermidorian Convention was able to continue to repress opposition, whether it came from those nostalgic for the monarchy, from Jacobin and Montagnard circles, or from the *sans-culottes*. In Prairial Year III, the deputies did not hesitate to strike very hard, by creating a military commission in charge of the repression and by sending eight of its Montagnard members to their deaths (the six 'martyrs of Prairial' on 29 Prairial [17 June], preceded by two other suicides, Rühl on 10 Prairial [29 May] and Maure on 15 Prairial [3 June]. In the summer of 1795, one year after Thermidor, three quarters of the last Montagnards, those representatives who remained faithful to their ideals, were banned, some of them condemned to death or deportation to French Guyana.[24]

In a political flip-flop, the Convention recalled a hundred or so Girondins and celebrated their deceased colleagues, while once again using arrest decrees or indictments against several of its members without concern for the blatant contradiction. At the moment the Convention disbanded, on 4 Brumaire Year IV (26 October 1795), it voted an amnesty for the 'facts' linked to the Revolution, infinitely too late to enter into the framework of a true transitional justice, except to consider that national reconciliation was to take place in spite of a legion of excluded people. Moreover, as a perfect symbol of the many political changes that took place in the Year III, the ceremony to celebrate the anniversary of 3 October 1793 was accompanied by a list of 'forty-seven [representatives of the people] fallen under the *décemvirale* axe'.[25] The list ended with the names of Desmoulins and Philippeaux, the first presented as a man who fought against *the Terror*, the second as the one who would have had the courage to publicly equate what was happening in the 'Vendée' with a desire on the part of the Montagnards to not put an end to this civil war in order to better establish their power and maintain *the Terror*. Who better than these two Montagnards to be associated with the dead Girondins, since the objective was still and always would be to denounce the so-called 'system' set up by apprentice dictators, while absolving a Convention that had purged itself of the majority of the last Montagnards?

More than two centuries later, we are still living under the influence of what was invented in those years, we still speak of a period called *the Terror*, whose paternity is most often attributed to Robespierre and his 'henchmen'. To try to understand 'terror' not by considering it as one of the levers wielded by the revolutionary government in a time of political exception, but by reducing it to the 'system' presented by Tallien and the Thermidorians, is to deprive ourselves of the means to better apprehend the contradictions of this Revolution of Human Rights, and how it came to be confronted with demons whose very existence the deputies of the Constituent Assembly of 1789, in their initial enthusiasm, could never have envisaged.

Chronology for the Years of the National Convention

1792	
August	9 – Formation in Paris of an insurrectional commune. 10 – Assault on the Tuileries; the King's powers are suspended by the Legislative Assembly. 13 – The king and his family are imprisoned in the Temple. 17 – Creation of an extraordinary court in Paris. 19 – La Fayette surrenders to the Austrians after trying in vain to direct his troops against Paris. 23 – The Prussians take Longwy. 30 – The Prussians lay siege to Verdun.
September	2 – Verdun falls. 2–5 – Massacres in Parisian prisons; several similar massacres take place in the provinces; election of representatives to the National Convention. 20 – Victory of the French troops at Valmy. 21 – First session of the Convention that decides the abolition of royalty; French troops enter Savoy. 22 – First day of the Republic; the Convention sends on mission six of its members, the first of the 'missionaries of the Republic'. 24–29 – Start of the siege of Lille by the Austrians. 29 – French troops enter the country of Nice.
October	5 – French troops enter Worms. 7 – The Austrians lift the siege of Lille. 8 – At the Convention, the Girondin deputy, Buzot accuses the Paris Commune of causing trouble and calls for the creation of a guard drawn from the departments to protect the Convention.

	9 – Decree ordering that any *émigré* who has taken up 'arms by hand' or who has already served against France be judged by a military commission and executed within twenty-four hours. 10 – Brissot, Girondin deputy, is excluded from the Jacobin Club. 14–19 – The Prussians evacuate Verdun and Longwy. 21 – French troops enter Mainz. 23 – Decree banning *émigrés* for life and punishing them with death if they return to France, including 'without weapons'. 27 – General Dumouriez, at the head of French troops, enters Belgium. 29 – Violent speech at the Convention by the Girondin deputy Louvet against Maximilien Robespierre.
November	6 – French victory at Jemappes. 10 – New decree on émigrés, modifying that of 23 October, which gives any *émigré* who has returned fifteen days to leave France on pain of death. 13 – Beginning of the debates at the Convention on the King's trial; speech by the Montagnard deputy Saint-Just, arguing that the King should 'be tried as an enemy' and executed. 14 – French troops enter Brussels. 20 – Discovery of the 'armoire de fer' at the Tuileries. 27 – Savoy is attached to France. 28–30 – French troops enter Liege and Antwerp.
December	5 – Decree carrying the death penalty against anyone exporting grain out of France. 11 – Louis XVI's first appearance before the Convention which judges him. 17 – Lively exchanges at the Convention between Girondins and Montagnards on a project of the former aiming to force into exile the members of the 'Bourbons-Capet family', except those prisoners at the Temple. Philippe d'Orléans, sitting with the Mountain, is the target of this project, so the Montagnards plead for the inviolability of national representation and obtain the abandonment of the project. This question of the inviolability of representatives will resurface the following 1 April.

Chronology for the National Convention 1793

	1793
January	1 – The Convention creates a General Defence Committee, a forerunner of the Committee of Public Safety, with members drawn from seven other committees. 15–20 – Votes at the Convention on the Fate of the King. 20 – Assassination of Le Peletier de Saint-Fargeau, a Montagnard deputy, who voted for the death of the king. 21 – Execution of Louis XVI on the Place de la Révolution. 24 – Pantheonization of Le Peletier. 28 – In Westphalia, the Count of Provence declares himself regent in the name of Louis XVII, prisoner in the Temple. 31 – The country of Nice is attached to France.
February	Tax riots in Paris supported by the Enragés. 1 – France declares war on England and Holland. 17 – Dumouriez's army enters Holland. 24 – The Convention decrees the raising of 300,000 'volunteers' for the armies.
March	1 – Start of the Austrian counter-offensive. 7 – France declares war on Spain. 9 – Decree that sends members of the Convention to all departments to speed up the raising of the 300,000 troops. This text marks the transformation of these 'missionaries' into a true revolutionary institution (the adjective here being synonymous with extraordinary). Beginning of uprisings in several western departments, including the Vendée. 9–10 – Several printing works of the Girondin newspapers are ransacked in Paris by *sans-culottes*. 10 – Creation in Paris of an extraordinary criminal court (later called the Revolutionary Tribunal). 11 – Taking of Machecoul by the 'Vendéens' who massacre the republicans there. 14 – Taking of Cholet by the 'Vendéens'. 18 – French are defeated at Neerwinden. 19 – Decree outlawing (placing '*hors la loi*') armed insurgents: which orders the condemnation to death within twenty-four of insurgents taking up arms, with no appeal; in the Vendée, a column of 3,000 soldiers is defeated by the insurgents (Battle of Pont-Charrault). 21 – Creation of surveillance committees. 28 – Decree ordering that *émigrés* who have returned, but who are not affected by the decree of 9 October, be tried by a departmental criminal court to be sentenced to deportation or capital punishment.

April	Loss of the left bank of the Rhine. 1 – On the proposal of Girondin Birotteau, a decree orders that the Convention may, 'without regard to the inviolability of a representative', indict one of its members suspected of collusion with 'enemies of liberty, equality and the republican government'. 4 – For the first time, commissioners drawn from the Convention are referred to as representatives (deputies) on mission. 4–5 – General Dumouriez passes to the enemy after trying to lead his army on Paris; emigration of the Duke of Chartres (son of the Duke of Orléans and future Louis-Philippe). 6 – Start of siege of Mainz, where French troops are imprisoned; creation of the Committee of Public Safety. 9 – First decree systematically organizing the missions of representatives to the armies. 13 – Pursuant to the decree of 1 April and at the proposal of Girondin Boyer-Fonfrède, on 12 April, the Convention decrees the indictment of Marat. 15 – A deputy from the Parisian sections, accompanied by the mayor, asks the Convention to exclude twenty-two Girondin deputies. 24 – Marat is acquitted by the Revolutionary Tribunal. 30 – Decree sending sixty-three deputies on mission to the eleven armies of the Republic (and to Corsica), including twelve to the army of the North and ten to that of the Rhine, the fronts most exposed at the time.
May	4 – The Convention decrees a maximum grain price. 5 – The 'Vendéens' take Thouars. 7 – A 'work, monitoring and correspondence plan', adopted by the Committee of Public Safety and confirmed by the Convention, specifies the powers of deputies on mission. 8 – Austrian troops advance in the north. 10 – Creation of the Society of Revolutionary Republican Citizenesses, a women's club close to the *Enragés*. 18 – Creation of a Commission of Twelve (Girondin) to investigate the Paris Commune. 24 – This commission puts Hébert and Varlet under arrest. 25 – The 'Vendéens' take Fontenay-le-Comte. 26 – Beginning of the siege of Valenciennes by the English and the Dutch. 29 – Beginning of the Lyon uprising against the Jacobin municipality controlled by Chalier's supporters.

		31 – First demonstration in front of the Convention to demand the arrest of the Girondin leaders.
June		2 – Under pressure from *sans-culottes* who encircle the place of its meetings, the Convention decrees the arrest of twenty-nine Girondin representatives and two ministers of the same political movement (end of the so-called 'Girondin' Convention). In the days and weeks that follow, the 'federalist' movement begins in the provinces to protest against this coup de force. 9 – The 'Vendéens' take Saumur. 10 – Brissot, Girondin deputy on the run, is arrested in Moulins (Allier); he is then brought back to Paris. 18 – The 'Vendéens' take Angers. 21 – The Convention decrees that the Lyon rebel authorities are responsible for the life of Chalier and the other Jacobins arrested in the city. 24 – Adoption of the Constitution and Bill of Rights of 1793. 25 – Jacques Roux reads his 'Manifesto of the *Enragés*' before the Convention; by this date, out of twenty-nine Girondin representatives arrested on the 2nd, twenty have chosen to flee; only Brissot has as yet been recaptured (on the 10th). 29 – The 'Vendéens' are pushed back before Nantes.
July		4 – Speech in Lyon by Birotteau, Girondin deputy on the run, who fuels the 'federalist' revolt by describing the Convention as an Assembly reduced to a handful of Montagnards and defended by only 2,000 *sans-culottes*. 12 – Uprising in Toulon. 13 – Marat murdered by Charlotte Corday. 16 – Execution of Chalier in Lyon; funeral ceremony in the streets of Paris in homage to Marat, whose body is buried in the Jardin des Cordeliers. 17 – Execution of Charlotte Corday. 23 – Mainz surrenders. The French garrison obtains the right to return to France with its weapons; it is sent to the 'Vendée' under the name of the Army of Mainz. 26–27 – Decree carrying the death penalty against hoarders. 28 – Fall of Valenciennes; on a proposal by Saint-Just on the 8th (but with modified lists), a decree of the Convention classifies the fugitive Girondin deputies (thus in addition to those already imprisoned) into two categories: eighteen 'traitors to the *patrie*' (de facto placed outside the law) and eleven other decrees of indictment.

August	1 – Decree ordering ruthless repression in the 'Vendée'. 7 – Beginning of the siege of Lyon, a city declared in a 'state of rebellion', by troops sent by the Convention. 10 – Celebration of the 'Republican Meeting' in Paris, organized by David, to celebrate the anniversary of 10 August 1792 and to make public the acceptance of the new Constitution which was submitted to the citizens' vote by referendum. 18–21 – English troops march on Dunkirk to lay siege to this city, a traditional issue in Anglo-French struggles. 19 – First artillery fire against the city of Lyon. 22–23 – In the night, the besieging troops bombard Lyon with red cannonballs and other incendiary projectiles. 23 – The Convention decrees a mass raising of troops for the armies of the Republic. 25 – Takeover of Marseille, a 'federalist' city, by troops of the Convention. 27 – The insurgents in Toulon hand the city over to the British.
September	2 – Baille, one of two deputies on mission captured by the English in Toulon, hangs himself in prison. The second, Beauvais, would not be released, more dead than alive, until the city was retaken. 4–5 – Popular demonstrations in Paris; demand for 'making terror the order of the day', not followed by the Convention; creation of an *armée révolutionnaire*. 8 – French victory at Hondschoote; lifting of the siege of Dunkirk by the English. 11 – Adoption of a uniform Maximum Grain Level across the country. 17 – The Law of Suspects is voted for. 18 – Takeover of Bordeaux, a 'federalist' city. 19 – Victory of the 'Vendéens' in Torfou. 22 – Spanish troops enter the Pyrénées Orientales. 29 – Decree establishing a General Maximum of prices and wages; the besiegers launch the final assault on Lyon. 30 – Siege of Maubeuge by Austrian troops.
October	3 – Decree establishing two lists of Girondin deputies, one of forty-one indicted detainees (to which is added Philippe Égalité [Orléans]) and the other of twenty fugitives declared 'traitors to the *patrie*', thus threatened with execution within twenty-four hours of their capture. More than seventy others are arrested and imprisoned, which makes the Girondin presence within the Convention disappear.

Chronology for the National Convention 1793 171

	7 – Gorsas, the first Girondin deputy sentenced to death, is guillotined. 9 – Takeover of Lyon after two months of siege. 10 – The government is declared 'revolutionary until peace'. 12 – Decree on the annihilation of Lyon, which becomes 'Ville-Affranchie'. 16 – Execution of Marie-Antoinette. French victory at Wattignies; the siege of Maubeuge is lifted. 15–18 – Republican victory over 'Vendéens' in Cholet; the latter cross the Loire, marking the beginning of the 'virée de Galerne'. 24 – In Bordeaux, a second Girondin representative, Birotteau, is guillotined. 30 – Twenty-one Girondin deputies (Brissot, Vergniaud, Carra, Fauchet, etc.) are condemned to death as 'traitors'; one, Valazé, commits suicide in the courtroom. 31 – Execution of the twenty Girondins.
November	2 – The Girondin deputy Lidon, on the run and about to be arrested in Corrèze, commits suicide. 3 – Execution of Olympe de Gouges. 6 – Execution of the Duke of Orléans (who sat on the Convention as a Montagnard representative under the name Philippe Égalité), as well as the Girondin deputy Coustard de Massy. 8 – Execution of Madame Roland, wife of the former outlawed Girondin minister, and 'muse' of the Girondins. 10 – A decree specifies that a people's representative (deputy) may be arrested on the basis of the report of one of the committees, but may not be indicted without having been heard by the Convention (unless he refuses to submit to arrest, in which case an indictment is issued within eight days). 12 – Execution of Bailly, first mayor of Paris in 1789. 12–15 – At the end of the 'virée de Galerne', the 'Vendéens' are pushed back in front of Granville. 14 – Execution of the Girondin deputy Manuel. 15 – Suicide of former Girondin minister Roland; execution of Girondin deputy Cussy. 20 – The Girondin deputy Chambon is shot during an attempted arrest in Corrèze. 24 – Doublet, Girondin deputy, dies in prison. 29 – Execution of Barnave.

December		3 – The 'Vendéens' are pushed back in front of Angers. 4 – Decree of 14 Frimaire Year II organizing the 'revolutionary government'. 4–5 – Two hundred and sixty-nine convicted insurgents are shot in Lyon. 5 – Publication of *Le Vieux Cordelier*, the newspaper of Camille Desmoulins, who becomes the spokesperson for the Indulgents; execution of two Girondin deputies, Kersaint and Rabaut Saint-Étienne. 6 – Yzarn de Valady, Girondin deputy, is captured and guillotined in Périgueux. 8 – Another Girondin deputy, Noël, arrested near the Swiss border and brought back to Paris, is guillotined there, along with Madame du Barry, Louis XV's last favourite. 12–13 – The 'Vendéens' are crushed in Le Mans. 19 – French forces recapture Toulon. 20 – Fabre de l'Hérault, Montagnard deputy on mission, is killed by the Spaniards on the Pyrenean front. 21 – Grangeneuve, Girondin deputy, is arrested and guillotined in Bordeaux. 23 – The remnants of the 'Vendée' army are annihilated in Savenay. 26–29 – French victory of the Geisberg which allows the takeover of Wissembourg and the end of the siege of Landau; the threats to Alsace are lifted.
1794		
January		7 – Fraught verbal exchange between Robespierre and Camille Desmoulins at the Jacobins. 17 – Dechézeaux, a deputy based in 'the Plain' but considered a Girondin, is guillotined in La Rochelle. 22 – Bernard, Girondin deputy, is guillotined. General Turreau launches his 'infernal columns' on the 'Vendée'.
February		4 – Decree of 16 Pluviôse Year II which abolishes slavery in the French colonies. 5 – Robespierre's speech on 'virtue' and 'terror'. 8 – The 'Vendéens' take Cholet again, but have to retreat after a few hours. 10 – Leader of the *Enragés*, Jacques Roux, commits suicide in prison. 26 (and 3 March) – Ventôse decrees, presented by Saint-Just, which provide for the confiscation of suspects' properties and their distribution to the poor.

Chronology for the National Convention 1794

March	13 – Arrest of the 'Hébertists'; decree ordering the outlawing of any defendant who evades justice (whereas, in March 1793, at the creation of the Revolutionary Tribunal, a fugitive was given three months to finally surrender on pain of being 'treated as an *émigré*'). 24 – Execution of the 'Hebertists'; the Montagnard Anacharsis Cloots, a member of the Convention, is executed with them. 28 – Beauvais, Montagnard deputy, captured and imprisoned for several months by the English in Toulon, freed when the city was retaken, dies as a result of this captivity. 29 – The philosopher Condorcet, a deputy close to the Girondins, outlawed since July 1793, is arrested and commits suicide in prison by swallowing poison. 31 – Arrest of the 'Dantonists' ('Indulgents') during night.
April	1 – The Executive Council is replaced by twelve executive commissions, eliminating ministers and strengthening the Committee of Public Safety 's control over executive power. 5 – Execution of the 'Dantonists', among them nine Montagnard deputies (Danton, Desmoulins, Basire, Chabot, Delacroix, Delaunay, Fabre d'Églantine, Hérault de Séchelles and Philippeaux). 13 – Execution of Chaumette and the deputy Simond, a Montagnard, as well as the widows of Camille Desmoulins and Hébert. 15 – Decree ordering the transfer to the Revolutionary Tribunal in Paris of all 'conspiracy defendants' arrested throughout the national territory. 30 – Takeover of Landrecies by the Austrians.
May	1 – The Girondin representative Rebecqui, pursued for many months, commits suicide by drowning in the port of Marseille. 8 – Abolition of most of the exceptional courts in the provinces; execution of several former tax *fermiers-généraux*, including Lavoisier. 10 – Execution of Madame Elisabeth, sister of Louis XVI; decree of the Committee of Public Safety creating the Orange Commission in the Vaucluse. 18 – General Turreau is removed from his command of the Western Army. 23–24 – Assassination attempt against Collot d'Herbois and arrest of a young woman (Cécile Renault) accused of trying to kill Robespierre.

		26 – The Girondin Masuyer is guillotined; decree prohibiting henceforth the taking of prisoners among the English and Hanoverians.
June		8 – Festival of the Supreme Being. 10 – Decree of 22 Prairial Year II 'Law of Prairial', inaugurates 'Great Terror' in Paris. 17 – Execution of Cécile Renault, Admirat (who tried to kill Collot d'Herbois) and fifty-two other convicts, all dressed in the red shirt reserved for assassins (under the 1791 Penal Code). 19–25 – Five Girondin deputies, who had been hunted for about a year, are guillotined (Guadet and Salle on the 19th, Barbaroux on the 25th) or commit suicide (Buzot and Pétion on the 24th) in the Gironde department where they had taken refuge. 25 – French take Charleroi. 26 – Osselin, a deputy sitting in the Plain, imprisoned since 1793, is guillotined. 26 – French victory in Fleurus – turns tide for French armies.
July		8 – French troops enter Brussels. 25 – French troops enter Saint Sébastien. 26 – Robespierre's last major speech at the Convention. 27 – Parliamentary coup against Robespierre and his friends (9 Thermidor, Year II). The French troops of Pichegru and Jourdan enter Antwerp and Liege. 28 – Execution of Robespierre and his 'accomplices'. Among them, five Montagnard members of the Convention perish (Le Bas commits suicide, then the two Robespierre brothers, Saint-Just and Couthon are executed, the guillotine being reinstalled on the Place de la Révolution for this execution). 29 – Execution of seventy-one captives, the Paris Commune is annihilated by repression.
August		1 – Repeal of the Law of 22 Prairial. Wave of release of prisoners. 5 – The English take Corsica. 9–20 – Arrest and release of Bonaparte on suspicion of 'Jacobinism'. 24 – Overhaul of the committee system; the Committee of Public Safety loses some of its prerogatives. 26 – Méhée de la Touche, linked to Tallien, launches the theme of 'Robespierre's tail', which triggers a pamphleteering campaign hostile to the Jacobins and to Robespierre's supposed supporters. 28 – Tallien theorizes the concept of a 'system of terror'.

	29 – Seven former members of the Committees of Public Safety and General Security are denounced before the Convention (Barère, Billaud-Varenne, Collot d'Herbois, Amar, David, Vadier and Voulland). The denunciation is rejected as slanderous; however, it illustrates the first attacks against certain Montagnards presented as former supporters of Robespierre. 30 – Liberation of Condé-sur-l'Escaut by French troops.
September	8–15 – Trial of the citizens of Nantes sent to the Revolutionary Tribunal by the Montagnard deputy on mission Carrier; they are acquitted and Carrier in turn denounced. 11 – Publication of *L'Orateur du peuple*, by Fréron, which becomes the emblematic newspaper of the anti-Jacobin 'reaction'. 17 – French troops enter the United Provinces. 18 – The Convention decrees that it will no longer support the costs of any cult. 21 – Transfer of Marat's remains to the Pantheon. 23 – French troops take Aachen.
October	3 – New denunciation presented to the Convention against former committee members, this time limited to Barère, Billaud-Varenne and Collot d'Herbois. 5 – Publication of *Le Tribun du peuple*, Babeuf's newspaper. 16 – Decree prohibiting political societies from affiliating with each other. 23 – French troops enter Koblenz; almost the entire left bank of the Rhine is in French hands. 29 – The Convention decides to create commissions of twenty-one members to investigate the cases of denounced deputies; a first commission is immediately created for the case of Carrier.
November	1 – General Hoche is appointed Commander-in-Chief of the Western Army. 9 – The Jacobin Club is targeted by the '*Jeunesse dorée*' (Golden Youth) in Paris. 12 – The Convention orders the closure of the Jacobin Club of Paris. 17 – French victory at La Montagne Noire, in the Pyrenees. 23–24 – The Convention votes to impeach Carrier.
December	8 – The Convention authorizes the return of seventy-six Girondin deputies arrested after June 1793. 16 – Execution of Carrier. 24 – Abolition of Maximum.

	27 – Creation of a commission of twenty-one to investigate the cases of Collot d'Herbois, Billaud-Varenne, Barère and Vadier; they are presented to public opinion under the name of the 'principal culprits' (*grands coupables*). 29 – French offensive led by General Pichegru in Holland.
1795	
January	5 – Report by Courtois, a member of the Convention, presented to the Convention on the 'papers found at the homes of Robespierre and his accomplices'. 17 – French troops enter Utrecht. 19–20 – French troops enter Amsterdam.
February	First serious manifestations of 'white terror'. 8 – Decree prohibiting the entry of the remains of a citizen into the Pantheon less than ten years after his death; in application of this text, de-Pantheonization of Marat and Le Peletier. 9 – Beginning of break-up of the coalition against France. Ferdinand III, Grand Duke of Tuscany, nephew of Marie-Antoinette, is the first to sign a separate peace with France. 17 – La Jaunaye Accords, beginning of a pacification of the 'Vendée'. 19 – Abolition of surveillance committees (also known as revolutionary committees) in communes with fewer than 50,000 inhabitants. 23 – Decree placing civil servants dismissed after Thermidor Year II under house arrest.
March	2 – Arrest of Collot d'Herbois, Billaud-Varenne and Barère (Vadier goes underground). 8 – Recall within the Convention of twenty-four Girondin deputies who had been outlawed and for that reason not reintegrated with the seventy-six others on 8 December 1794. 21 – Adoption of the so-called 'grand police' law. 22 – Consideration of the case of the three arrested former members of the Committee of Public Safety begins before the Convention, in their presence.
April	1 – Popular riots repressed in Paris (12 Germinal Year III); Collot d'Herbois, Billaud-Varenne and Barère are condemned to deportation to French Guyana and leave Paris immediately for the island of Oléron (Vadier remains untraceable); other members of the Convention, Montagnards, are arrested. 5 – Treaty of Basel which concludes the peace between France and Prussia.

Chronology for the National Convention 1795

May	10 – Decree obliging former 'terrorists' to surrender their weapons; Barère, Billaud-Varenne and Collot d'Herbois arrive at the fortress of Oléron, a place of detention where they must await deportation to French Guyana. 2 – Treaty of Saint-Florent with Stofflet, 'Vendéen' chief. 4 – Massacre of a hundred former 'terrorists' in the prisons of Lyon. 7 – Execution of Fouquier-Tinville, former public prosecutor at the Revolutionary Tribunal. 16 – Creation of the Batavian Republic following the signing in The Hague of a peace treaty between France and the United Provinces. 20 – Popular riots suppressed in Paris (1 Prairial Year III); assassination of Féraud, a deputy sitting in the Plain, in the very hall of the Convention; several members of the Convention, Montagnards, are arrested. 24 – The Convention reports the deportation decree issued against Barère, Billaud-Varenne, Collot d'Herbois and Vadier, ordering their transfer to the criminal court of Charente-Inférieure. This threat of a probable death sentence cannot be carried out, however, because the new decree arrives in Oléron several days after the ships had sailed to Cayenne. 26 – The flotilla taking Billaud-Varenne and Collot d'Herbois to French Guyana leaves La Rochelle, with only Barère remaining detained on the island of Oléron (before being transferred to prison in Saintes, from where he escaped). 29 – The arrested Montagnard deputy Rühl commits suicide at his home.
June	3 – Another arrested Montagnard, Maure, commits suicide in his home. 5 – Massacre of former 'terrorist' prisoners at Fort Saint-Jean in Marseille. 8 – Death of Louis XVI's son in the Temple; the Count of Provence becomes the potential successor of Louis XVI under the name of Louis XVIII. 10 – Decree of the Convention authorizing the return of *émigrés* who left after 31 May 1793. 17 – Death of the 'Martyrs of Prairial', six members of the Convention, Montagnards, who commit collective suicide at the announcement of their death sentence (Duquesnoy, Goujon and Romme manage to kill themselves, Bourbotte, Du Roy and Soubrany do not succeed in their act and are guillotined).

	24 – Verona Manifesto of Louis XVIII.
	25 – Disembarkation of 4,000 *émigrés* in Brittany who join the Chouans in Quiberon.
July	21 – The Quiberon rally is defeated by General Hoche's troops.
	22 – France and Spain conclude peace in Basel.
August	18–30 – Voting on decrees of two-thirds 'des deux tiers' permits Convention deputies to sit in the new Assemblies.
	22 – The Convention adopts the new Constitution (known as the 'Year III' Constitution) which includes a Declaration of Rights and Duties.
September	23 – Proclamation of the results of the referendum on the Constitution of Year III.
October	1 – Belgium, which has been divided into nine departments since 31 August, is attached to France.
	5 – Royalist riot in Paris (13 Vendémiaire Year IV), suppressed by Barras and General Bonaparte.
	16 – Lebon, Montagnard, the last member of the Convention executed in connection with the 'terror', is guillotined in Amiens.
	26 – Separation of the Convention. It votes an amnesty for the 'facts' of the Revolution.
	27–28 – Beginning of the Directory.

Maps

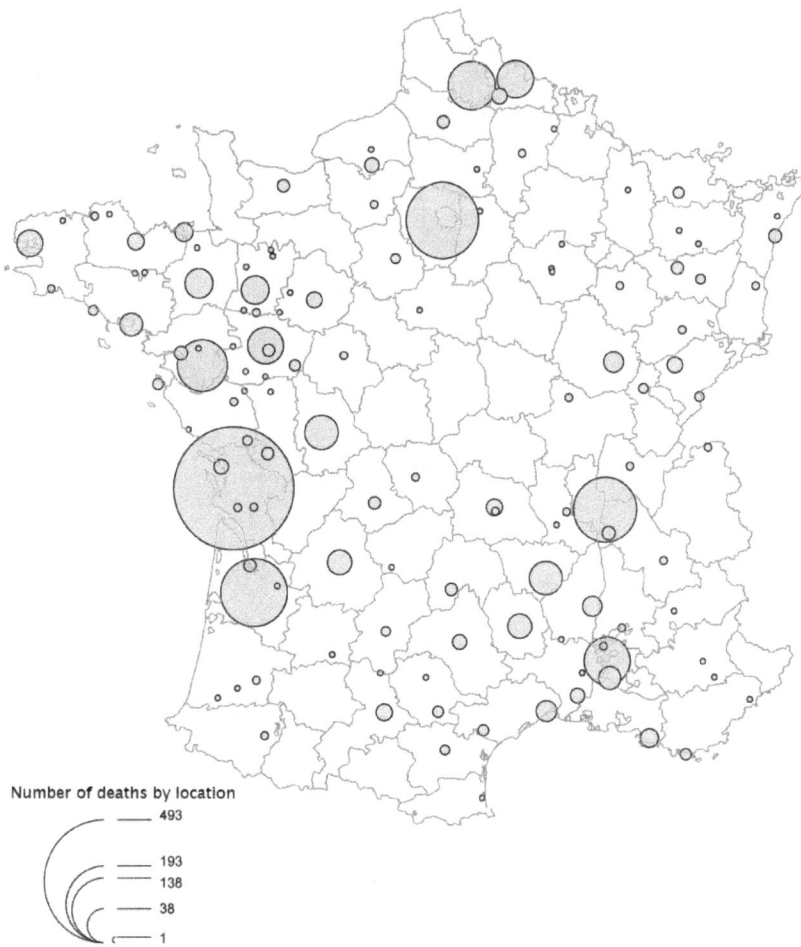

Map 1: The clergy who died in the Year II, 'victims' of the 'terror' according to the martyrology of the abbé Guillon (1821).

Design & mapping: M. Biard & F. Delisle, 2020, after S. Baciocchi & P. Boutry (EHESS/CRH/CARE).

Source: abbé A. Guillon, *Les Martyrs de la Foi pendant la Révolution française* . . ., 1821, vols 2, 3 and 4.

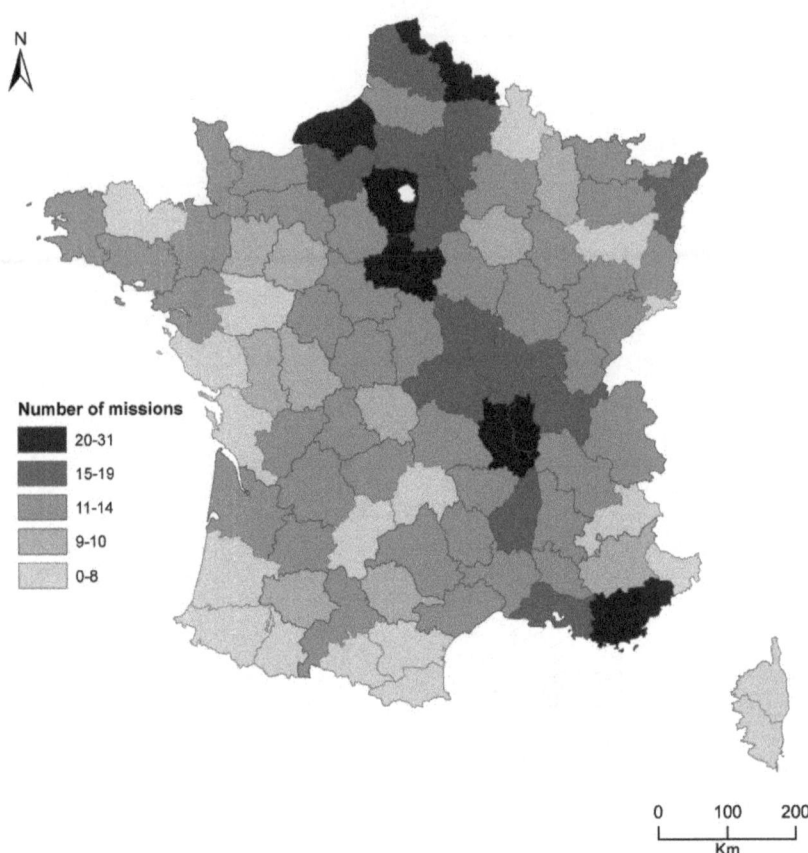

Map 2: The deputies of the Convention sent 'on mission', by department.
Design & mapping: M. Biard & F. Delisle, 2020
Source: M. Biard, *Missionnaires de la République. Les représentants du peuple en mission (1793–1795)*.

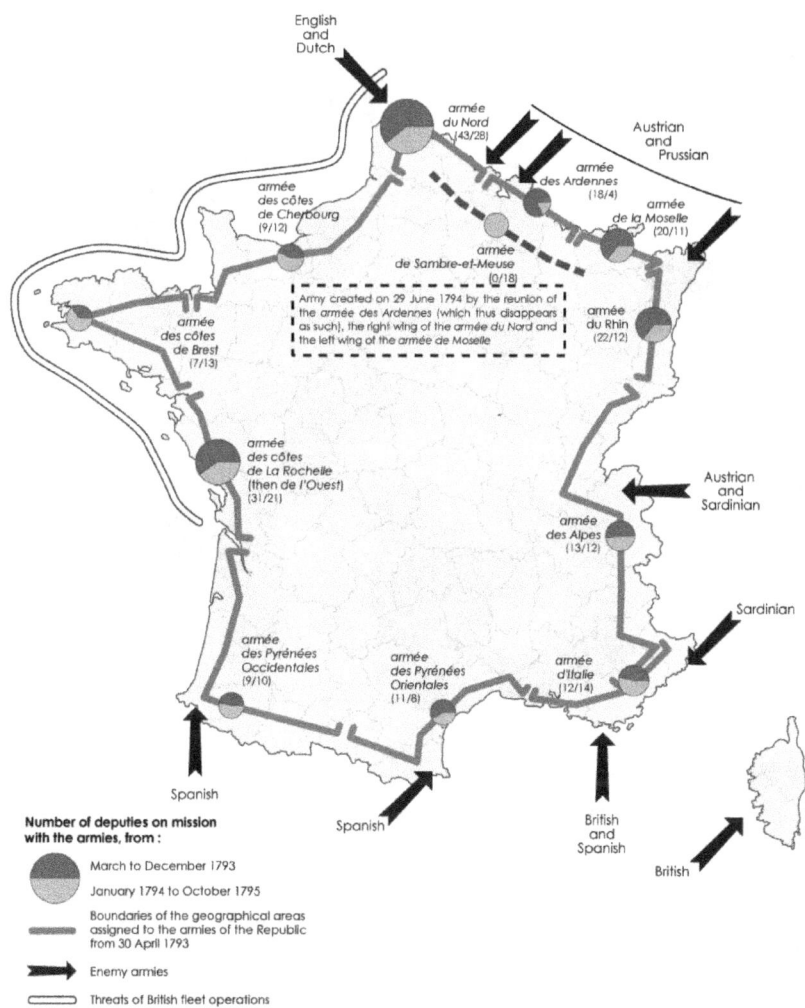

Map 3: The deputies sent 'on mission' with the armies.
Design & mapping: M. Biard & F. Delisle, 2020.

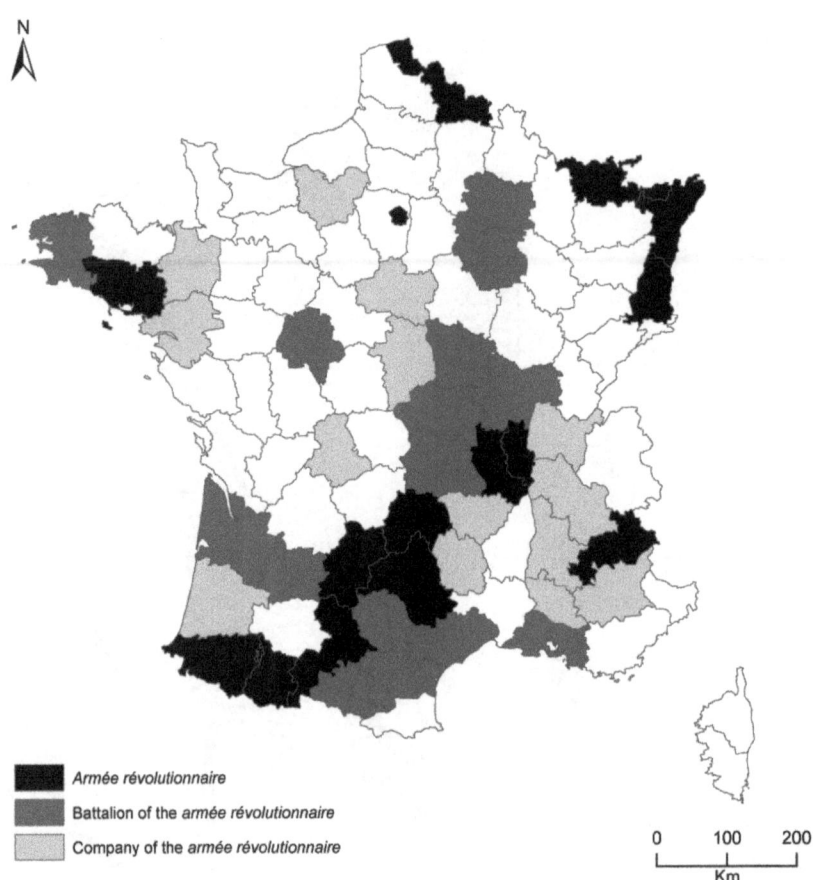

Map 4: The *armées révolutionnaires*. Departments where at least one army, a battalion, or a company was created.

Design & mapping: M. Biard & F. Delisle, 2020.

Maps 183

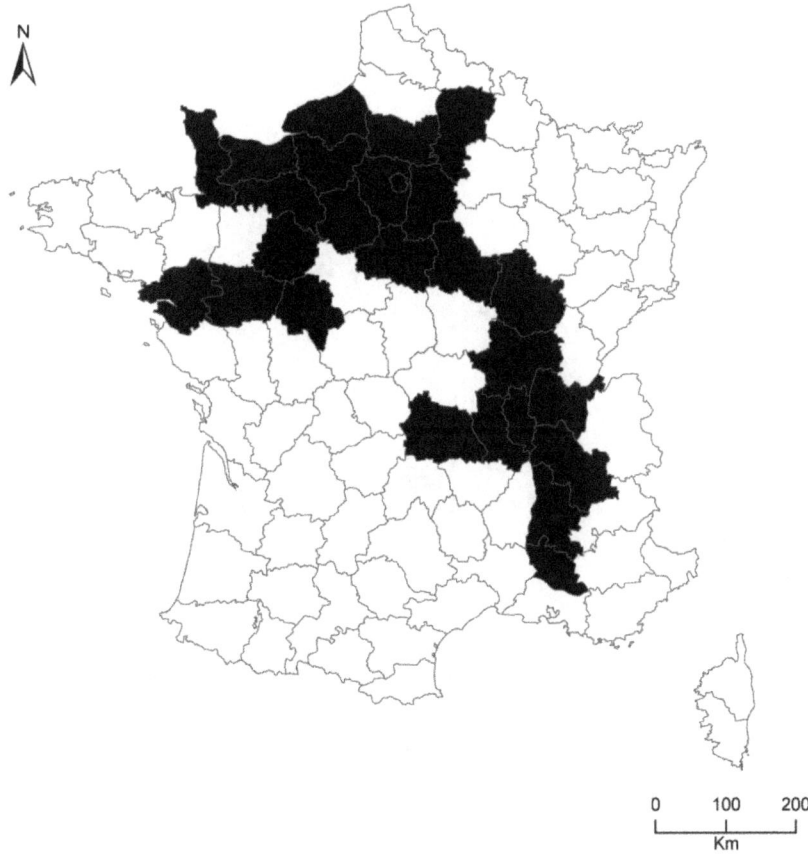

Map 5: Operations of the Parisian *armée révolutionnaire*.
Design & mapping: M. Biard & F. Delisle, 2020, after Richard Cobb.

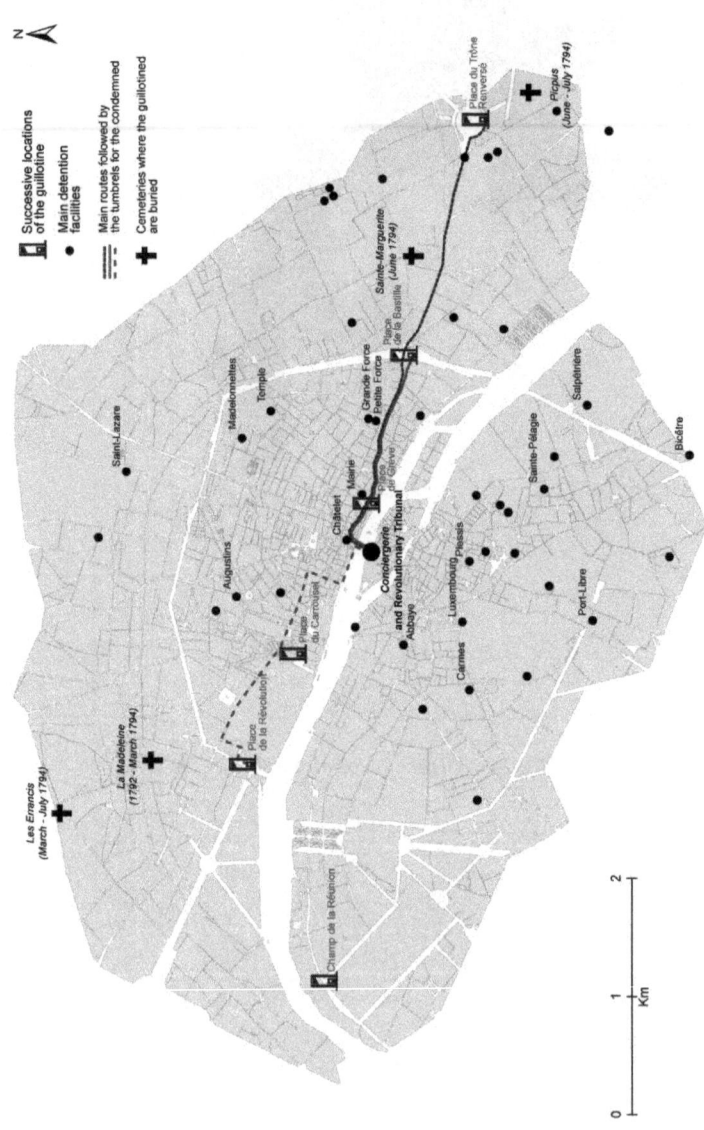

Map 6: Prisons, sites of the guillotine, and cemeteries used for victims in Paris.
Design & mapping: Biard & F. Delisle, 2020.
Sources: © ALPAGE: Paul Rouet, 2015 & *Atlas de la Révolution française*.

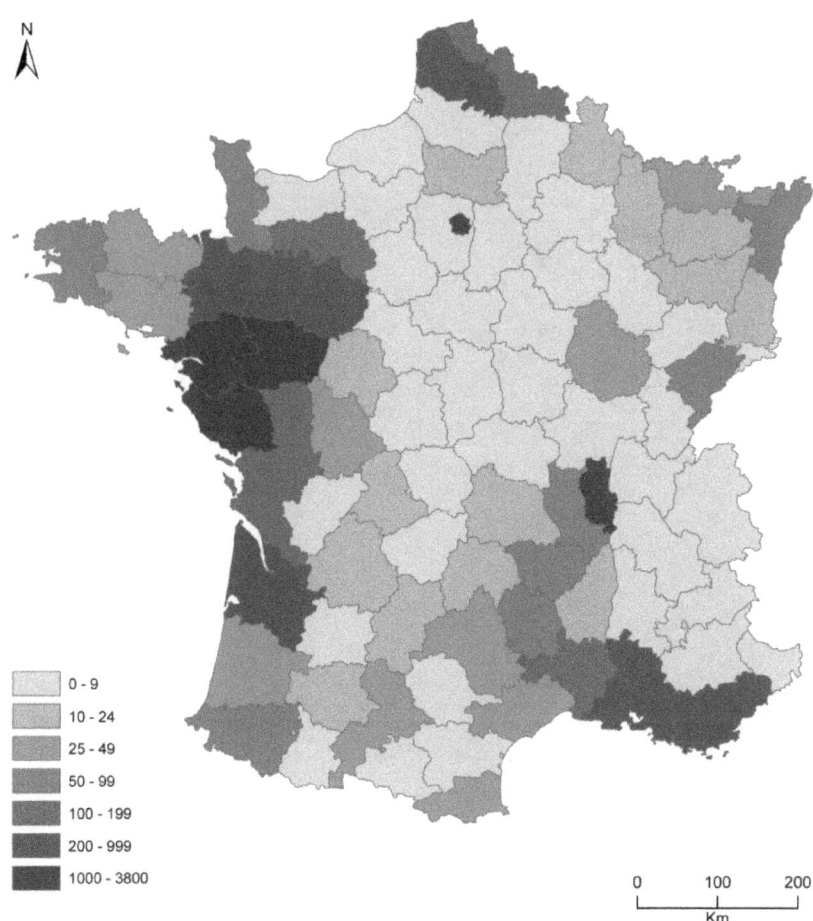

Map 7: Number of people sentenced to death, by department.
Design & mapping: M. Biard & F. Delisle, 2020, after Donald Greer.

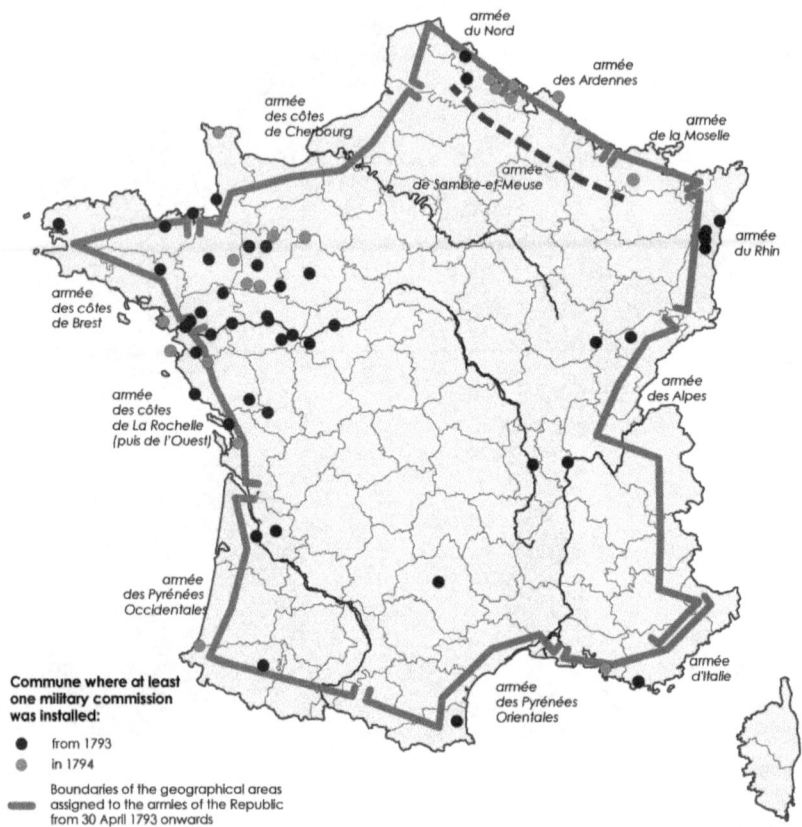

Map 8: The military commissions.
Design & mapping: M. Biard & F. Delisle, 2020.

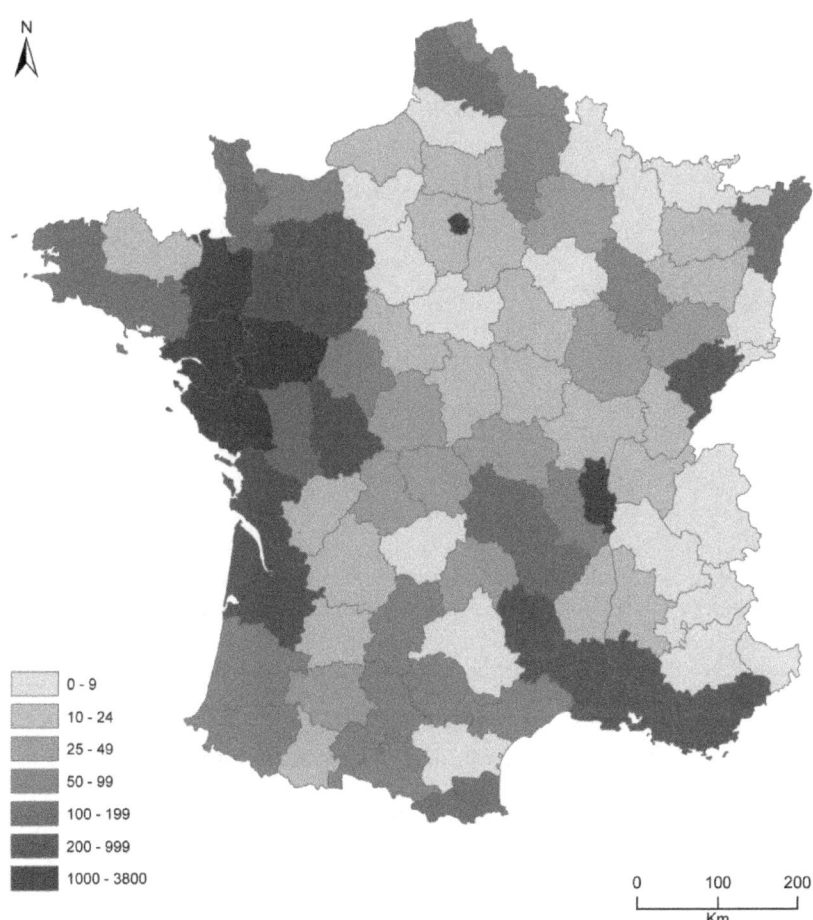

Map 9: Number of individuals judged to be 'outlawed' (*hors la loi*), by department.
Design & mapping: M. Biard & F. Delisle, 2020, after Eric de Mari.

Some Further Reading

A complete list of works consulted (in French and English) appears in the footnotes. A full bibliography is included in the French edition of this book.

David ANDRESS, *The Terror: Civil War in the French Revolution*, London, Little Brown, 2005.
Keith Michael BAKER (ed.), *The French Revolution and the Creation of Modern Political Culture*, vol. 4, *The Terror*, Oxford, Pergamon Press, 1994.
Michel BIARD, *Missionnaires de la République. Les représentants du peuple en mission (1793–1795)*, Paris, CTHS, 2002 (new edition, Vendémiaire, 2015).
Michel BIARD (ed.), *Les politiques de la Terreur, 1793–1794*, Rennes, Presses Universitaires – Société des études robespierristes, 2007.
Michel BIARD, *La Liberté ou la mort. Mourir en député 1792–1795*, Paris, Tallandier, 2015.
Michel BIARD, *Terreur et Révolution française*, Toulouse, UPPR, 2016.
Howard G. BROWN, *Mass Violence and the Self: From the French Wars of Religion to the Paris Commune*, Ithaca, NY, Cornell University Press, 2018.
Dan EDELSTEIN, *The Terror of Natural Right. Republicanism, the Cult of Nature and the French Revolution*, Chicago, IL, University of Chicago Press, 2009.
Hugh GOUGH, *The Terror in the French Revolution*, New York, St. Martin's Press, 1998.
Donald GREER, *The Incidence of the Terror during the French Revolution. A Statistical Interpretation*, Cambridge, MA, Harvard University Press, 1935.
H-France Salon, 'Rethinking the French Revolutionary Terror', in

'230 Years After: What does the French Revolution Mean Today?', *H-France Salon*, vol. 11, Issues 16–21 (2019), at: https://h-france. net/h-france-salon-volume-11-2019/

Jeff HORN, *The Making of a Terrorist: Alexandre Rousselin and the French Revolution*, Oxford, Oxford University Press, 2021.

Annie JOURDAN, *Nouvelle histoire de la Révolution*, Paris, Flammarion, 2018.

Marisa LINTON, *Choosing Terror. Virtue, Friendship and Authenticity in the French Revolution*, Oxford, Oxford University Press, 2013.

Colin LUCAS, *The Structure of the Terror: the Example of Javogues and the Loire*, Oxford, Oxford University Press, 1973.

Jean-Clément MARTIN, *La Terreur. Part maudite de la Révolution*, Paris, Gallimard, coll. Découvertes, 2010.

Jean-Clément MARTIN, *La terreur. Vérités et légendes*, Paris, Perrin, 2017.

Jean-Clément MARTIN, *Les échos de la Terreur. Vérités d'un mensonge d'Etat 1794–2001*, Paris, Belin, 2018.

Peter McPHEE, *Robespierre. A Revolutionary Life*, New Haven, CT, Yale University Press, 2012.

Peter McPHEE, *Liberty or Death. The French Revolution*, New Haven, CT, Yale University Press, 2016.

Arno MEYER, *Violence and Terror in the French and Russian Revolutions*, Princeton, NJ, Princeton University Press, 2000.

Robert Roswell PALMER, *Twelve who Ruled. The Year of the Terror in the French Revolution*, Princeton, NJ, Princeton University Press, 1973 (1941).

Jeremy D. POPKIN, *A New World Begins: The History of the French Revolution,* New York, Basic Books, 2020.

Ronald SCHECHTER, *A Genealogy of Terror in Eighteenth-Century France*, Chicago, IL, University of Chicago Press, 2018.

Ronen STEINBERG, *The Afterlives of the Terror. Facing the Legacies of Mass Violence in Postrevolutionary France, Ithaca, NY*, Cornell University Press, 2019.

Timothy TACKETT, *The Coming of the Terror in the French Revolution*, Cambridge, MA, Harvard University Press, 2015.

Sophie WAHNICH, *In Defence of the Terror: Liberty or Death in the French Revolution*, New York, Verso, 2016 (French edition, 2003).

Notes

Introduction: The Demons of Terror

1 Jules Michelet, *Histoire de la Révolution française*, Paris, Chamerot, 1847, vol. I, p. XI. The definite article and the capital T then reappear many times in his writings, above all in volumes VI and VII, devoted to the years 1793 and 1794, even if there is nothing systematic about their employment. In 1841, a capital letter also features in the *Souvenirs de la Terreur*, but only in the title of the work, which is something else (*Souvenirs de la Terreur de 1788 à 1793, par M. Georges Duval; précédés d'une introduction historique par M. Charles Nodier*, Paris, Werdet, 1841). Moreover, the author himself distinguishes between the use or non-use of capital letters, especially since he systematically underlines the term in italics: 'Now a word about the title of my book. I entitle it *Souvenirs de la Terreur*, although my account begins in the year 1788. It's my opinion that *the terror* began at the same time as the revolution [. . .] up until 9 thermidor of the year 2 of the republic, Paris and the whole of France were under the yoke of *the terror*' (ibid., pp. ix–x). Precedents also exist for the use of capital letters in the title of a work but not in its text (thus *Des Effets de la Terreur* by Benjamin Constant in the Year V, and again the capitalization does not appear clearly until the 'printer's notice' that opens the edition. The title itself is composed entirely in capital letters). On the other hand, in their original editions, the first histories of the French Revolution, by Thiers (1823–1827), Mignet (1824), Buchez and Roux (1834–1838), Blanc (1847–1862) and Lamartine (1847) do not use the word with a capital T. Lamartine sometimes emphasized the word using italics, but not in a systematic way, and without using capitalization. Cabet, for his part, sometimes used it in his own account of the Revolution, but this is hardly signifi-

cant, because this author multiplies his use of capitals erroneously and indiscriminately, for example to write: 'People', 'Virtue', 'Morality', 'Deputy', etc. (Etienne Cabet, *Histoire populaire de la Révolution française de 1789 à 1830*, Paris, Pagnerre, 1839–1840).

2 Louis Blanc, *Histoire de la Révolution française*, Paris, Furnes, Pagnerre, second edition, 1869. Louis Blanc had previously critiqued Quinet's use of the term: 'I would not be one of those whom Edgar Quinet's book has deeply grieved, if the author had not distorted [...] the nature of what he condemns [...] if, by making the Terror a *system*, he had not made the most intelligent and devoted revolutionaries responsible for the fatality they had to endure and the very excesses they fought against [...] No, no, whatever Mr. Quinet says, the Terror was not a *system*; it was, quite otherwise, an immense misfortune, born of prodigious peril' (ibid., vol. I, pp. xvii–xviii. The italicizations are those of Louis Blanc). The work of Edgar Quinet had appeared in 1865 under the title *La Révolution*, Paris, Lacroix, Verboeckhoven.

3 The politics behind this controversy featured in a polemical study by Steven Kaplan, *Farewell Revolution: The Historians' Feud, France, 1789–1989*, Ithaca, NY, Cornell University Press, 1996 (French edition, 1993).

4 Simon Schama, *Citizens: A Chronicle of the French Revolution*, London, Penguin, 1989.

5 For recent approaches to these debates, see the contributions by Michel Biard, Mette Harder, Carla Hesse and Ronen Steinberg, edited and introduced by Marisa Linton, to 'Rethinking the French Revolutionary Terror', part of the H-France Salon, '230 Years After: What does the French Revolution Mean Today?', *H-France Salon*, vol. 11, nos 16–21 (2019), at: https://h-france.net/h-france-salon-volume-11-2019/

6 Timothy Tackett, *Anatomie de la Terreur. Le processus révolutionnaire 1787–1793*, Paris, Le Seuil, 2018 (the English-language edition appeared under the title: *The Coming of the Terror in the French Revolution*, Cambridge, MA, Harvard University Press, 2015). As an indication of a shift in Tackett's own thinking, this sentence does not appear in the original edition, but in a note in the foreword to the French edition (p. 379).

7 See Howard G. Brown, 'The Thermidorians' Terror: Atrocities, Tragedies, Trauma', in David A. Bell and Yair Mintzker (eds), *Rethinking the Age of Revolutions: France and the Birth of the Modern World*, Oxford, Oxford University Press, 2018, pp. 193–235. Brown states that, 'The "Terror" as a distinct period of the French Revolution was largely a construct of lawmakers who took the reins of government after the defeat of Robespierre and his closest allies'.

8 Haim Burstin, *Révolutionnaires. Pour une anthropologie politique de la Révolution française*, Paris, Vendémiaire, 2013. François Furet and Denis Richet, *La Révolution*, Paris, Hachette, 1965–1966.

9 It was Napoleon Bonaparte, some years after the time designated as *the*

Terror, who forcibly reinstated slavery in those colonies that remained to France. Saint-Domingue remained at liberty, though at a terrible cost in lives. The complex issue of slavery in the colonies and within France has generated a formidable historiography, including Jeremy Popkin, *You Are All Free: The Haitian Revolution and the Abolition of Slavery*, Cambridge, Cambridge University Press, 2010; and Laurent Dubois, *Avengers of the New World: The Story of the Haitian Revolution*, Cambridge, MA, Harvard University Press, 2005. For recent thinking on the problematic nature of 'rights', see the contributions by Mita Choudhury, Pernille Røge and Pierre Serna, edited and introduced by Ian Coller to 'Whose Revolution?', part of the *H-France Salon*, '230 Years After'.

10 Carla Hesse, 'Terror and the Revolutionary Tribunals', in 'Rethinking the French Revolutionary Terror'.
11 Ibid. On violence in the American Revolution, see Holger Hoock, *Scars of Independence: America's Violent Birth*, New York, Crown, 2017. See too, Annie Jourdan, *La Révolution, une exception française?*, Paris, Flammarion, 2006; and the contributions by Rafe Blaufarb, Paolo Conte, Anna Karla and Matthijs Lok, edited and introduced by Annie Jourdan to 'The French Revolution Abroad', part of the *H-France Salon*, '230 Years After'.
12 Henry and other founding fathers of the American Revolution were familiar with this political phrase which appeared in Joseph Addison's play, *Cato, a Tragedy*, written in 1712.

Chapter 1: *The Terror* – a Concept Imposed by the Thermidorians

1 Edmund Burke, *Reflections on the Revolution in France, and on the Proceedings in Certain Societies in London Relative to that Event*, London, J. Dodsley, 1790.
2 Ibid., p. 103.
3 Thomas Paine, *Rights of Man: Being an Answer to Mr. Burke's Attack on the French Revolution*, London, Joseph Johnson, 1791; this edition, London, Penguin, 1969, p. 80.
4 Ibid.
5 This text is published in No. 10 of his newspaper, *Le Défenseur de la Constitution* (*Œuvres de Maximilien Robespierre* [henceforth OMR], Paris, Société des études robespierristes, 2011, vol. IV, p. 305).
6 OMR, vol. X, p. 357. On Robespierre's link between virtue and terror, see Marisa Linton, 'Commentary on Maximilien Robespierre, *On the Principles of Political Morality*' (1794), in Rachel Hammersley (ed.), *Textual Moments in the History of Revolutionary Thought*, London, Bloomsbury Academic Press, 2015; and Hervé Leuwers, *Robespierre*, Paris, Fayard, 2014, chap. 21.
7 *Archives Parlementaires de 1787 à 1860. Recueil complet des débats*

législatifs et politiques des chambres françaises [. . .], founded under the direction of M.J. Mavidal and M. E. Laurent, Paris, Dupont, 102 vols, 1879–2012, vol. XCIV, p. 302 [henceforth *AP*].
8 Ibid.
9 *AP*, vol. XCV, p. 297.
10 Ibid.
11 Ibid., p. 298.
12 See Cesare Vetter, '"Système de terreur" et "système de la terreur" dans le lexique de la Révolution française', https://revolution-francaise.net/2014/10/23/594-systeme-de-terreur-et-systeme-de-la-terreur-dans-le-lexique-de-la-revolution-francaise. See too, Cesare Vetter, Marco Marin and Elisabetta Gon, *Dictionnaire Robespierre. Lexicométrie et usages langagiers. Outils pour une histoire du lexique de l'Incorruptible*, Trieste, EUT, 2016, vol. I, pp. 475–89.
13 Barère mentioned a 'system of terror' on 10 November 1792 to describe what, in his eyes, was the overwhelming power of the municipality of Paris. *AP*, vol. LIII, p. 349. See too, Cesare Vetter, 'Système de terreur'. On 8 July 1793, Saint-Just had associated a 'system of terror' with the Girondin deputies, whom he deemed responsible for spreading distrust and hatred against Paris, *AP*, vol. LXVIII, p. 428. Another Montagnard, Mallarmé, used the expression at the Jacobin Club on 22 August, reported in *Le Moniteur*, 10 Fructidor Year II (27 August 1794).
14 *AP*, vol. XCIV, pp. 56–7.
15 Ibid., p. 57.
16 Ibid., p. 58.
17 Michel Biard, *Collot d'Herbois. Légendes noires et Révolution*, Lyon, Presses Universitaires de Lyon, 1995, pp. 182–8.
18 See Ariane Fichtl, *La Radicalisation de l'idéal républicain. Modèles antiques et la Révolution française*, Paris, Classiques Garnier, 2020, pp. 235–52.
19 'One was to dominate in Paris, the other had the mountains of Auvergne, and the Pyrenees, the Alps and the Mediterranean were the present made to the brotherhood; and the one who had the most cunning and apparent *sang-froid* was going to watch over the command of the armies of the North and the Rhine, already prepared by his intrigues. Saint-Just was the plenipotentiary of the North; Couthon and young Robespierre, the pacifying congress of the South; Robespierre the elder reigned in Paris over heaps of corpses; the death of the republicans, the debasement of the Convention and the usurpation of the commune ensured its tyrannical domination' (*AP*, vol. XCIII, p. 635).
20 On the many dimensions of the 'black legend' of Robespierre, see Marc Belissa and Yannick Bosc, *Robespierre. La fabrication d'un mythe*, Paris, Ellipses, 2013; and Bronislaw Baczko, *Ending the Terror: The French Revolution After Robespierre*, Cambridge, Cambridge University Press, 1994, chap. 1.
21 *AP*, vol. XCV, p. 494.

22 See, for example, Address of the general council of the inhabitants of the commune of Donzy (Nièvre) to the National Convention, 7 Brumaire Year III (28 October 1794) (*AP*, vol. CI, pp. 281–2).
23 Michel Biard, 'Après la tête, la queue. La rhétorique antijacobine en fructidor an II et vendémiaire an III', in Michel Vovelle (ed.), *Le tournant de l'an III. Réaction et Terreur blanche dans la France révolutionnaire*, Paris, Éditions du CTHS, 1997, pp. 201–13.
24 Michel Biard, *La Révolution hantée. Enfers fantasmés et Révolution française*, Paris, Vendémiaire, 2017.
25 Filbomets [anonymous], *Grande comète, ou Voyez ma queue*, no place, no date [Fructidor Year II or start of Year III], p. 1. The titles listed here refer to: Fethemésl [Jean-Claude Méhée de la Touche], *La Queue de Robespierre, ou les Dangers de la liberté de la presse*, Paris, Rougyff, Fructidor Year II; Fethemésl [Jean-Claude Méhée de la Touche], *Rendez-moi ma Queue, ou Lettre à Sartine Thuriot sur une violation de la liberté de la presse et des droits de l'homme, par l'auteur de la Queue de Robespierre*, no place, no date [Paris, Fructidor Year II]; Fethemésl [Jean-Claude Méhée de la Touche], *Défends ta Queue, par l'auteur de la Queue de Robespierre*, no place [Paris], Guffroy, no date [Fructidor Year II]; Marie et Prévost, *Réponse à la Queue de Robespierre, par un franc républicain*, Paris, Prévost, no date [Fructidor Year II]; Baralère [Jean-Baptiste Jollivet], *Coupons-lui la queue*, Paris, Imp. des Amis de la Vérité, no date [Fructidor Year II].
26 Anonymous, *La Tête à la Queue, ou Première lettre de Robespierre à ses continuateurs*, no place [Paris], Guffroy, no date [Fructidor Year II or start of Year III], pp. 1 and 6–7.
27 The phrase 'reign of terror' was in use as early as 1795, as in *Le Moniteur* of 14 Pluviôse Year III (2 February 1795), which reported an intervention by Parisian *sectionnaires* before the Convention three days earlier, which concluded: 'No, you swore it with the whole people, the reign of terror is over'. Madame de Staël was one of the first authors to use it – in a text published in Switzerland in 1796, then in Paris the following year: *De l'influence des passions sur le bonheur des individus et des nations, by Mad. la Baronne Staël de Holstein*, Lausanne, Mourer et Hignou, 1796, pp. 6 and 136.
28 *Le Moniteur*, 16 November 1792.
29 Ibid.
30 *AP*, vol. XCII, pp. 391–3.
31 Georges Lefebvre, *The Great Fear of 1789: Rural Panic in Revolutionary France*, Princeton, NJ, Princeton University Press, 1947 (original French edition, 1932); Timothy Tackett, *When the King Took Flight*, Cambridge, MA, Harvard University Press, 2003.
32 *Le Moniteur*, 21 April 1793.
33 *AP*, vol. LXXIV, pp. 315–16.
34 Ibid., vol. LII, p. 109.
35 Ibid., p. 139.

36 Discours à la Convention nationale le 3 décembre 1792 (*OMR*, vol. IX, p. 130).
37 *Le Moniteur*, 20 January 1793.
38 *AP*, vol. LII, p. 563.
39 Ibid., vol. LIII, p. 57.
40 Ibid., p. 349.
41 Ibid., vol. LXI, p. 48. On the 20th, Vergniaud's fellow Girondin Gensonné claimed that 'the majority of the inhabitants of Paris ... does not abandon the exercise of its sovereignty' to a handful of men who dominate 'the sections by fear of proscriptions and by terror': vol. LXIII, p. 18.
42 Marat, speaking after his acquittal by the Revolutionary Tribunal, claimed that policies of terror had brought him there, and could be used against other Montagnards: *Le Moniteur*, 3 May 1793.
43 Ibid., 10 July 1793.
44 An address by the Convention to the French, the day after the death of Le Peletier, was unambiguous on this point: 'there is an attempt to sow terror in the Republic' (*AP*, vol. LVII, p. 605). On the assassination of Le Peletier and Marat, see Michel Biard, *La Liberté ou la mort. Mourir en député (1792–1795)*, Paris, Tallandier, 2015.
45 Convinced like all his fellow Montagnards that Corday was linked to the outlawed Girondins, some of whom had gathered in Calvados, where she came from, Couthon declared on 14 July that the Girondins 'intended, through the assassination of the patriots, to produce a great terror' (*AP*, vol. LXVIII, p. 723). On the impact of Marat's assassination, see Guillaume Mazeau, *Le bain de l'histoire. Charlotte Corday et l'attentat contre Marat 1793–2009*, Seyssel, Champ Vallon, 2009; and Ian Germani, *Jean-Paul Marat: Hero and Anti-Hero of the Revolution*, New York, Edwin Mellen Press, 1992.
46 Jacques Guilhaumou, '"La terreur à l'ordre du jour": un parcours en révolution (1793–1794)', https://revolution-francaise.net/2007/01/06/94-la-terreur-a-lordre-du-jour-un-parcours-en-revolution-juillet-1793-mars-1794.
47 On fear of assassination, see Marisa Linton, 'The Stuff of Nightmares: Plots, Assassinations, and Duplicity in the Mental World of Jacobin Leaders, 1793–1794', in David Andress (ed.), *Experiencing the French Revolution*, Oxford, Studies on Voltaire and the Eighteenth Century, 2013, pp. 201–17.
48 The so-called 'primary' assemblies brought citizens together when they were asked to exercise their right to vote and elect.
49 On 4 July 1793, even before Marat's assassination, Girondin Birotteau had already made this kind of statement – as inflamed as it was unfounded – during his visit to Lyon, a city then in revolt against the Convention: 'There is no longer any Convention; there is only a handful of scoundrels in the temple of laws, who are fattened by your blood, who spend in four days all the income of the public treasury of a whole

year . . . Citizens, let us not deceive ourselves, the deputies who remain at the Convention now present only a faction whose unique and cherished system is oppression . . . do not deliberate any more, but march on Paris; the universality of Paris is animated by the same principles as you' (Michel Biard, *1793. Le siège de Lyon. Entre mythes et réalités*, Clermont-Ferrand, Lemme édit, 2013, pp. 15–17).
50 *AP*, vol. LXX, p. 548.
51 Ibid., vol. LXXII, p. 102.
52 Ibid., p. 103.
53 See Jean-Clément Martin, *Les échos de la Terreur. Vérités d'un mensonge d'Etat, 1794–2001*, Paris, Belin, 2018, pp. 58–62.
54 See the work in particular of: Jean-Clément Martin, *La terreur. Vérités et légendes*, Paris, Perrin, 2017; Jean-Clément Martin, *Les échos*; and Annie Jourdan, *Nouvelle histoire de la Révolution*, Paris, Flammarion, 2018.
55 *AP*, vol. LXXIII, p. 420.
56 Ibid.
57 Michel Biard, *Missionnaires de la République. Les représentants du peuple en mission (1793–1795)*, Paris, Editions du CTHS, 2002 (new edition: Paris, Vendémiaire, 2015).
58 *AP*, vol. LXXVI, p. 596.
59 Ibid., vol. LXXVII, p. 30.
60 Ibid., vol. LXXIX, p. 120.
61 See Guilhaumou, 'La terreur'.
62 Ibid.
63 René Robinet, 'Au Tribunal criminel du Nord: le jugement des "magistrats" municipaux nommés sous l'occupation autrichienne de 1793–1794', *Revue du Nord*, 1989, no. 282–283, pp. 903–18.
64 Peter McPhee, *Liberty or Death: The French Revolution*, New Haven, CT, Yale University Press, 2016, p. 289.
65 Timothy Tackett, *The Coming of the Terror in the French Revolution*; and Marisa Linton, *Choosing Terror. Virtue, Friendship and Authenticity in the French Revolution*, Oxford, Oxford University Press, 2013.

Chapter 2: The Meaning of 'Terror' Before the Revolution

1 P.J.B. Buchez and P.C. Roux (eds), *Histoire parlementaire de la Révolution française depuis 1789 jusqu'à l'Empire*, 40 vols, Paris, Paulin, 1833–1838, vol. 29, p. 41. See, too, the account of the events of 4 and 5 September 1793, in Jourdan, *Nouvelle histoire*, pp. 204–11.
2 Debates between adherents of 'circumstances' versus 'ideology' interpretations of the revolutionary 'terror' have generated intense controversy and an immense historiography. Some of this historiographical debate is summarized in Hugh Gough, *The Terror in the French Revolution*, New York, St. Martin's Press, 1998; and, more recently, Paul R. Hanson,

Contesting the French Revolution, Oxford, Wiley-Blackwell, 2009, chaps 6 'Regeneration and Terror', and 9 'Revolutionary Violence'.
3 François Furet, 'Terror', in François Furet and Mona Ozouf (eds), *Dictionnaire critique de la Révolution française*, Paris, Flammarion, 1988, p. 156.
4 Jack R. Censer, 'Intellectual History and the Causes of the French Revolution', *Journal of Social History*, 2019, vol. 52, pp. 545–54.
5 Keith Michael Baker, *Inventing the French Revolution*, Cambridge, Cambridge University Press, p. 305. Baker has modified his position to some extent, in Baker, 'Enlightenment Idioms, Old Regime Discourses and Revolutionary Improvisation', in Thomas E. Kaiser and Dale K. Van Kley (eds), *From Deficit to Deluge: The Origins of the French Revolution*, Stanford, CA, Stanford University Press, 2011.
6 These approaches are discussed in Marisa Linton, 'The Intellectual Origins of the French Revolution', in Peter Robert Campbell (ed.), *The Origins of the French Revolution*, Houndmills, Palgrave, 2005, pp. 139–59. On the articulation of ideas, see Sophia Rosenfeld, *The Problem of Signs in Late Eighteenth-Century France*, Stanford, CA, Stanford University Press, 2001; and Sophia Rosenfeld, 'Thinking About Feeling, 1789–1799', *French Historical Studies*, 2009, vol. 32 pp. 697–706.
7 Works on political languages include: Jay M. Smith, *Nobility Reimagined: The Patriotic Nation in Eighteenth-Century France*, Ithaca, NY, Cornell University Press, 2005; Marisa Linton, *The Politics of Virtue in Enlightenment France*, Houndmills, Palgrave, 2001; John M. Burney, 'History, Despotism, Public Opinion and the Continuity of the Radical Attack on Monarchy in the French Revolution, 1787–1792', *History of European Ideas*, 1993, vol. 17, pp. 245–63.
8 Mary Ashburn Miller, *A Natural History of Revolution: Violence and Nature in the French Revolutionary Imagination, 1789–1794*, Ithaca, NY, Cornell University Press, 2011; and Dan Edelstein, *The Terror of Natural Right: Republicanism, the Cult of Nature, and the French Revolution*, Chicago, IL, University of Chicago Press, 2009.
9 Jonathan Israel, *Revolutionary Ideas: An Intellectual History of the French Revolution from* The Rights of Man *to* Robespierre, Princeton, NJ, Princeton University Press, 2014, pp. 20–1. Historians of the French Revolution who have been strongly critical of Israel's thesis include: David A. Bell, in *New York Review of Books*, 10 July 2014; Lynn Hunt, in *New Republic*, 27 June 2014; and in 2015 Jeremy Popkin, in *H-France Review*, www.h-france.net/vol15reviews/vol15no66popkin.pdf.
10 See Roger Chartier, *The Cultural Origins of the French Revolution*, Durham, NC, Duke University Press, 1991 (French edition, 1990). On the intellectual origins of the Revolution, see Marisa Linton, 'The Intellectual Origins of the French Revolution', in Peter Campbell (ed.), *The Origins of the French Revolution*, Houndmills, Palgrave, 2005, pp. 139–59; and, most recently, Censer, 'Intellectual History'.

11 By contrast, the words 'terrorism' (*terrorisme*) and 'terrorist' (*terroriste*) were coined after the fall of Robespierre, as part of a retrospective invention by the Thermidorians of the concept of a system or reign of 'terror'.
12 Jean-François Féraud, *Dictionaire critique de la langue française*, Marseille, Mossy, 1787–1788.
13 *Encyclopédie, ou Dictionnaire Raisonné des sciences, des arts et des métiers*, 1781 edition, 36 vols, Berne and Lausanne, Sociétés Typographiques, 1780.
14 See George Armstrong Kelly, *Mortal Politics in Eighteenth-Century France*, Waterloo, ON, University of Waterloo Press, 1986, p. 294.
15 George Armstrong Kelly, 'Conceptual Sources of the Terror', *Eighteenth-Century Studies*, 1980, vol. 14, pp. 18–36. A revised version of this article was later published in Kelly, *Mortal Politics*, chap. 12; Annie Jourdan, 'Les discours de la terreur à l'époque révolutionnaire (1776–1798): étude comparative sur une notion ambiguë', *French Historical Studies*, 2013, no. 36, pp. 51–81; Ronald Schechter, *A Genealogy of Terror in Eighteenth-Century France*, Chicago, IL, University of Chicago Press, 2018. See, too, Jean-Clément Martin, *La terreur. Vérités et légendes*, Paris, Perrin, 2017, chaps. 10, 11 and 12.
16 Schechter, *A Genealogy of Terror*, Preface, p. ix.
17 Ibid.
18 On terror in the Judeo-Christian tradition, see ibid., chap. 1.
19 Ibid., pp. 18–21.
20 On the *philosophes*' scepticism regarding the terror of eternity, see Kelly, *Mortal Politics*, pp. 298–9.
21 See especially, Dale Van Kley, *The Religious Origins of the French Revolution: From Calvinism to the Civil Constitution, 1560–1791*, New Haven, CT, Yale University Press, 1996. On Jansenism and citizenship, see Marisa Linton, 'Citizenship and Religious Toleration in France', in Ole Peter Grell and Roy Porter (eds), *Toleration in Enlightenment Europe*, Cambridge, Cambridge University Press, 2000, pp. 157–74.
22 Schechter, *A Genealogy of Terror*, p. 37. See too Guilhamou, 'La terreur'.
23 On the concept of kingly virtue and its obligations, see Linton, *The Politics of Virtue*, chap. 1.
24 Guillaume Budé used the kingly virtue of justice (inspired in part by Plutarch's examples of virtuous leaders) to underpin his justification of absolute monarchy in his 1547 work dedicated to François I: *De l'Institution du Prince*, facsimile edition, Farnborough, Gregg Press, 1966, pp. 20–1. A similar argument was later made by Bossuet, 'Sermon sur les devoirs des rois' (1662), in Jacques-Bénigne Bossuet, *Oeuvres oratoires de Bossuet*, J. Lebarq ed., 7 vols, Paris, 1890, vol. 4, p. 273.
25 Jean Bodin, *Les six livres de la République. Un abrégé du texte de l'édition de Paris de 1583*, Gérard Marais (ed.), Paris, Librairie générale française, 1993, pp. 124–5. See, too, Schechter, *A Genealogy of Terror*, p. 40.

26 See Schechter, *A Genealogy of Terror*, p. 57.
27 On terror in the context of military campaigns in antiquity, see Jourdan, 'Les discours de la terreur', p. 54.
28 On this military language of terror, see Kelly, 'Conceptual Sources of the Terror'; Jourdan, 'Les discours de la terreur'; Schechter, *A Genealogy of Terror*; and Martin, *La Terreur. Vérités*.
29 Schechter, *A Genealogy of Terror*, p. 342.
30 Martin, *La Terreur. Vérités*, pp. 80–1. On the war of the Camisards, see W. Gregory Monahan, *Let God Arise: The War and Rebellion of the Camisards*, Oxford, Oxford University Press, 2014.
31 Schechter, *A Genealogy of Terror*, p. 45.
32 See Martin, *La Terreur. Vérités*, p. 82.
33 Schechter, *A Genealogy of Terror*, p. 58; and Martin, *La Terreur. Vérités*, p. 85.
34 See Schechter, *A Genealogy of Terror*, pp. 75–7.
35 Ibid., p. 77.
36 Ibid., chap. 6.
37 On the aesthetics of terror, see Jourdan, 'Les discours de la terreur'; and Schechter, *A Genealogy of Terror*, chap. 4.
38 On cathartic natural violence and terror in the revolutionary imaginary, see Ashburn Miller, *A Natural History of Revolution*.
39 George-Louis Leclerc, comte de Buffon, 'Séptième et dernière époque', *Les époques de la nature*, in *Oeuvres complètes de Buffon*, vol. 1, Paris, F.D. Pillot, 1837, p. 560. See too, Kelly, *Mortal Politics*, pp. 296–7.
40 Jourdan notes that the term 'terror' appears no fewer than thirty-four times in the course of Burke's book: Jourdan, 'Les discours de la terreur', p. 56.
41 Cited in Martin, *La Terreur. Vérités*, p. 87.
42 Jacques-Pierre Brissot de Warville, *Mémoires*, ed. Claude Perroud, 2 vols, Paris, Picard et fils, 1912, vol. 1, p. 71.
43 Ibid.
44 Studies of classical republicanism in eighteenth-century France include: J.G.A. Pocock, *The Machiavellian Moment: Florentine Political Thought and the Atlantic Republican Tradition*, Princeton, NJ, Princeton University Press, 1975; Baker, *Inventing the French Revolution*, notably chap. 6; Johnson Kent Wright, *A Classical Republican in Eighteenth-Century France: the Political Thought of Mably*, Stanford, CA, Stanford University Press, 1997. On the relationship between classical republicanism and the Revolution, see Linton, *Choosing Terror*, chap. 1; and Keith Michael Baker, 'Transformations of Classical Republicanism in Eighteenth-Century France', *Journal of Modern History*, 2001, vol. 73, pp. 32–53.
45 On the different ways in which the revolutionary leader Saint-Just used models adapted from antiquity as a basis for his political identity, see Marisa Linton, 'The Man of Virtue: The Role of Antiquity in the Political Trajectory of L.A. Saint-Just', *French History*, 2010, vol. 24,

pp. 393–419. See, too, Maxime Rosso, 'Les réminscences spartiates dans les discours et la politique de Robespierre de 1789 à Thermidor', *Annales historiques de la Révolution française* [henceforth *AHRF*], 2007, vol. 349, pp. 51–77.
46 On Robespierre's equivocal response to the story of Lucius Junius Brutus, see Ariane Fichtl, *Antiquités imaginaires de Robespierre. La transformation de l'idéal républicain dans la France du XVIIIe siècle entre l'Ancien Régime et la Révolution*, PhD thesis, Universities of Lille and Augsburg, 2018, pp. 62–5.
47 Cited in Fichtl, ibid., p. 448. See, too, her discussion of terror in the context of antiquity, pp. 448–9.
48 Cicero, *Philippics*, London, W. Heinemann, 1957.
49 See Linton, *The Politics of Virtue*, chaps 1 and 2; and Raymonde Monnier, 'Montesquieu et le langage républicain: l'argumentaire de *l'Esprit des lois*', *La Révolution française*, 2013, 5.
50 *Avertissement de l'auteur*, édition de 1757 de *De l'Esprit des lois*, Charles-Louis de Secondat, Baron de Montesquieu, *De l'Esprit des lois*, Paris, Ernest Flammarion, 1924, 2 vols, vol. I, p. 6.
51 *De l'Esprit des lois*, vol. 1, book IV, chap. V, p. 42.
52 *Considérations sur les causes de la grandeur des Romains et de leur décadence* (1734), in Montesquieu, *Oeuvres complètes*, Roger Caillois (ed.), Paris, Bibliothèque de la Pléiade, 2 vols, 1949–1951, vol. 1, p. 266.
53 Ibid., p. 132.
54 R.R. Palmer, *The School of the French Revolution. A Documentary History of the College of Louis-le-Grand and its Director, Jean-François Champagne 1762–1814*, Princeton, NJ, Princeton University Press, 1975. See, too, Harold Talbot Parker, *The Cult of Antiquity and the French Revolutionaries*, New York, Octagon Books, 1965 [1937], pp. 8–36; and Jacques Bouineau, *Les Toges du pouvoir: ou la Révolution du droit antique*, Toulouse, Éditions Eché, 1986, pp. 21–31. On the influence of classical antiquity on the imaginations of revolutionaries, see Fichtl, *La Radicalisation de l'idéal républicain*.
55 See Thomas E. Crow, *Painters and Public Life in Eighteenth-Century Paris*, New Haven, CT, Yale University Press, 1985; Thomas E. Crow, '"The Oath of the Horatii" in 1785: Painting and Pre-Revolutionary Radicalism in France', *Art History*, 1978, vol. 1, pp. 424–71; and Philippe Bordes, *Le Serment du Jeu de Paume de David: Le peintre, son milieu et son temps de 1789 à 1792*, Paris, Réunion des Musées Nationaux, 1983.
56 Saint-Just, 'Rapport sur la conjuration ourdie pour obtenir un changement de dynastie, et contre Danton . . .', 11 germinal an II (31 March 1794), Louis-Antoine Saint-Just, *Oeuvres complètes*, Michèle Duval (ed.), Paris, Éditions Ivrea, 1989, p. 760.
57 Montesquieu, *De l'esprit des lois*, vol. 1, book VI, chap. IX, p. 93.
58 Montesquieu, *Lettres persanes*, Paris, Garnier-Flammarion, 1964, Letter 148, pp. 243–4.

59 Robespierre, *Discours sur les peines infamantes*, Amsterdam, 1785, p. 9. On Robespierre's debt to Montesquieu, see too chap. 1 of this book. See also Marisa Linton, 'Robespierre's Political Principles', in Colin Haydon and William Doyle (eds), *Robespierre*, Cambridge, Cambridge University Press, 1999, pp. 37–53; and Hervé Leuwers, 'Robespierre et la théorie du gouvernement révolutionnaire', in Elsa Forey, Jean-Jacques Clère and Bernard Quiriny (eds), *La pensée constitutionnelle de Robespierre*, Paris, La mémoire du droit, 2018, pp. 183–98.
60 On public opinion, see Chartier, *The Cultural Origins*, chap. 2.
61 On *patriot* ideology during the Maupeou coup, see Durand Echeverria, *The Maupeou Revolution: A Study in the History of Libertarianism*, Baton Rouge, LA, Louisiana State University Press, 1985, part I.
62 Chrétien-Guillaume Lamoignon de Malesherbes, 'Très humble et très respectueuses Remontrances que présentent au Roi ... les gens tenant sa Cour des Aides', *Oeuvres inédites de Chrétien-Guillaume Lamoignon de Malesherbes*, Paris, Hénée, Buisson, Giguet et Michaud, 1808, p. 48. On the recourse of the *parlements* under Louis XV to the language of political terror, see Kelly, *Mortal Politics*, pp. 300–4.
63 On disgrace as terror, see Kelly, *Mortal Politics*, pp. 303–4.
64 On imprisonment, execution and disgrace as instruments of control by the monarchy between 1610 and the Revolution, see Julian Swann, *Exile, Imprisonment or Death: The Politics of Disgrace in Bourbon France, 1610–1789*, Oxford, Oxford University Press, 2017.
65 Schechter, *A Genealogy of Terror*, p. 187.

Chapter 3: Terror in the Heart: The Weight of Fears and Emotions

1 Classic studies of collective emotions and revolutionary mentalities amongst people of the lower orders, include: Georges Lefebvre, *La grande peur de 1789*, Paris, Armand Colin, 1932; and Michelle Vovelle, *La mentalité révolutionnaire: Société et mentalités sous la Révolution française*, Paris, Messidor, Éditions sociales, 1985. On the emotions of the Parisian *sans-culottes* and the influence of their fears on the genesis of 'the Terror', see Sophie Wahnich, *In Defence of the Terror: Liberty or Death in the French Revolution*, New York, Verso, 2016 (French edition, 2003).
2 For extended studies of the role of emotions amongst the revolutionary leaders and the part this played in the genesis of 'terror', see Linton, *Choosing Terror*; and Tackett, *The Coming of the Terror*. A classic study of the emotional sensibility of revolutionary leaders, is Pierre Trahard, *La Sensibilité révolutionnaire, 1789–1794*, Paris, Boivin, 1936.
3 The phrase is used in a recent analysis of the emotional dynamics of contemporary protests and revolutions: James M. Jasper, *The Emotions of Protest*, Chicago, IL, University of Chicago Press, 2018, p. 14.
4 Preface to the French edition of Tackett, *Anatomie de la Terreur*, p. 11.

5 This phrase is used in a study of how literary forms of 'sentimentalism' suffused and constrained revolutionary politics: William Reddy, *The Navigation of Feeling: A Framework for the History of the Emotions*, Cambridge, Cambridge University Press, 2001.
6 On this subject in relation to judicial practices during 1793–4, see Carla Hesse, 'La Preuve par la lettre: pratiques juridiques au tribunal révolutionnaire de Paris (1793–1794)', *Annales: Histoire, Sciences Sociales*, 1996, vol. 3, 629–42; and Laura Mason, 'The "Bosom of Proof": Criminal Justice and the Renewal of Oral Culture during the French Revolution', *Journal of Modern History*, 2004, vol. 76, 29–61.
7 On tears in the Convention as part of a panoply of bodily signs of emotions, see Marisa Linton, '"The Tartuffes of Patriotism": Fears of Conspiracy in the Political Language of Revolutionary Government, France 1793–94', in Barry Coward and Julian Swann (eds), *Conspiracies and Conspiracy Theory in Early Modern Europe: From the Waldensians to the French Revolution*, Farnham, Ashgate, 2004. Laughter as a strategy in the Convention is the subject of a study by Jacob Zobkiw, 'Political Strategies of Laughter in the National Convention, 1792–1794', PhD, University of Hull, July 2015.
8 Peter R. Campbell, Thomas E. Kaiser and Marisa Linton (eds), *Conspiracy in the French Revolution*, Manchester, Manchester University Press, 2007; Timothy Tackett, 'Conspiracy Obsession in a Time of Revolution: French Elites and the Origins of the Terror, 1789–1792', *American Historical Review*, 2000, vol. 105, 691–713; and Tackett 'Collective Panics in the Early French Revolution, 1789–1791: A Comparative Perspective', *French History*, 2003, vol. 17, pp. 149–71.
9 See Coward and Swann, *Conspiracies and Conspiracy Theory in Early Modern Europe*. In November 2018, the 'Conspiracy and Democracy' research project based at CRASSH, University of Cambridge, published its finding that 60 per cent of people in contemporary Britain believe in conspiracy theories about politics: http://www.conspiracyanddemocracy.org/
10 For a longer-term perspective on the interconnectedness of mass violence, trauma and fear, see Howard G. Brown, *Mass Violence and the Self: From the French Wars of Religion to the Paris Commune*, Ithaca, NY, Cornell University Press, 2018.
11 On the 'Famine Plot', which would become a driving force for the *sans-culottes*, see the works of Steven Kaplan, above all Steven D. Kaplan, *Le complot de famine. Histoire d'une rumeur au XVIIIe siècle*, Paris, Éditions de l'EHESS, 1995.
12 On the revolutionary rhetoric of denunciation as a civic virtue and its links to classical Rome, see Colin Lucas, 'The Theory and Practice of Denunciation in the French Revolution', *Journal of Modern History*, 1996, vol. 68, pp. 768–85.
13 Thomas E. Kaiser, 'Who's Afraid of Marie-Antoinette? Diplomacy, Austrophobia, and the Queen', *French History*, 2000, vol. 14,

pp. 241–71; and Thomas E. Kaiser, 'From the Comité autrichien to the Foreign Plot: Marie-Antoinette, Austrophobia, and the Terror', *French Historical Studies*, 2003, vol. 26, pp. 579–617.
14 14 January 1792, *AP*, vol. XXXVII, pp. 413–16.
15 For March 1793 as a pivotal moment in the genesis of the 'Terror', see Tackett, *The Coming of the Terror*, chap. 10.
16 18 November 1793, *AP*, vol. LXXIX, p. 460.
17 On fear of the Foreign Plot as a meta-text for the 'Terror', see Kaiser, 'From the Comité autrichien to the Foreign Plot'.
18 On this factional struggle, see chapter 6.
19 Albert Mathiez, *La Conspiration de l'étranger*, Paris, Armand Colin, 1918; and *L'Affaire de la compagnie des Indes: un procès de corruption sous la Terreur*, Paris, Félix Alcan, 1920.
20 On the links between fear of conspiracy and terror, see Linton, *Choosing Terror*. See also Thomas E. Kaiser, 'Catilina's Revenge: Conspiracy, Revolution, and Historical Consciousness from the Old Regime to the Consulate', and Linton, '"Do You Believe That We're Conspirators?" Conspiracies Real and Imagined in Jacobin Politics, 1793–94', both in Campbell, Kaiser and Linton, *Conspiracy in the French Revolution*.
21 Marie-Jeanne Roland, *Mémoires de Madame Roland*, Paul de Roux (ed.), Paris, Mercure de France, 1966, p. 134.
22 Letter to Marc-Antoine Jullien son, Commissioner of War at Toulouse, Paris, 24 December 1792, in Rosalie Jullien, *'Les Affaires d'État sont mes affaires de coeur'. Lettres de Rosalie Jullien, une femme dans la Révolution 1775–1810*, Annie Duprat (ed.), Paris, Belin, 2016, pp. 219–20.
23 Camille Desmoulins, 'Jean-Pierre Brissot démasqué', in Camille Desmoulins, *Œuvres de Camille Desmoulins*, J. Claretie (ed.), 2 vols, Paris, Charpentier & Cie, 1874, vol. 1, p. 268. Saint-Just in turn used this expression against Danton and Desmoulins when he denounced them as part of the 'Foreign Plot': Saint-Just, 'Discours sur les factions de l'étranger' delivered at the Convention, 23 Ventôse (13 March 1794), Saint-Just, *Œuvres complètes*, p. 725.
24 29 October 1792, *AP*, vol. LIII, pp. 52, 57.
25 Claude-Antoine Prieur, known as Prieur de la Côte-d'Or, cited in Hippolyte Carnot, *Mémoires sur Carnot par son fils*, Paris, Pagnerre, 1861–3, p. 528.
26 Howard G. Brown, *Revolution, and the Bureaucratic State: Politics and Army Administration in France, 1791–1799*, Oxford, Clarendon Press, 1995.
27 On the question of whether the assassination of a deputy constituted a crime of 'lèse-nation', or that of 'parricide', see Michel Biard, *La Liberté ou la mort. Mourir en député 1792–1795*, Paris, Tallandier, 2015, chap. 6. On Jacobin leaders' fear of assassination, see Linton, 'The Stuff of Nightmares'.
28 René Levasseur, *Mémoires de R. Levasseur (de la Sarthe)*

Ex-Conventionnel, 1829–31: this edition, Paris, Messidor/Editions Sociales, 1989, p. 347. Note that it is difficult, however, to distinguish between what Levasseur wrote and what Achille Roche added when he published Levasseur's memoirs in the nineteenth century. On the degree of reliance we can place in the memoirs of *conventionnels*, see Sergio Luzzato, *Mémoires de la Terreur. Vieux Montagnards et jeunes républicains au XIXe siècle*, Lyon, Presses Universitaires de Lyon, 1991.
29 Ibid.
30 Pierre-Victorin Vergniaud, Speech to the Convention, 13 March 1793, *AP*, vol. LX, p. 162.
31 'On the principles of political morality that should guide the National Convention', 17 Pluviôse (5 February 1794), *OMR*, vol. XI, p. 357. See also Linton, 'Commentary on Maximilien Robespierre'.
32 1 April 1793, *AP*, LXI, p. 63.
33 For a statistical analysis of verdicts given by the Revolutionary Tribunal, see James Logan Godfrey, *Revolutionary Justice: A Study in the Organisation and Procedures of the Paris Tribunal, 1793–95*, Chapel Hill, NC, University of North Carolina Press, 1951, pp. 136–50.
34 See Lucas, 'The Theory and Practice of Denunciation'.
35 On the language of political virtue, and its derivations, see Linton, *The Politics of Virtue*.
36 Saint-Just, *Œuvres complètes*, pp. 534–5.
37 On revolutionary transparency, see Lynn Hunt, *Politics, Culture and Class in the French Revolution*, Berkeley, CA, University of California Press, 1984, pp. 39–44; also Jean Starobinski, *Jean-Jacques Rousseau: Transparency and Obstruction*, Chicago, IL, University of Chicago Press, 1988 (French edition, 1971).
38 On the level of scrutiny given to the authenticity of Robespierre's virtue, see Marisa Linton, 'Robespierre et l'authenticité révolutionnaire', *AHRF*, 2013, no. 371, pp. 153–73.
39 On the politics of Jacobin friendship, see Linton, *Choosing Terror*; and Linton, 'Fatal Friendships: The Politics of Jacobin Friendship', *French Historical Studies*, 2008, vol. 31, pp. 51–76.
40 On the risks that deputies incurred as a result of their dining choices, see Marisa Linton and Mette Harder, '"Come and Dine": The Dangers of Conspicuous Consumption in French Revolutionary Politics', *European History Quarterly*, 2015, vol. 45, pp. 615–37.
41 On anxieties over where revolutionary leaders lived, see Marisa Linton, 'Friends, Enemies and the Role of the Individual', in Peter McPhee (ed.), *Companion to the History of the French Revolution*, Oxford, Wiley-Blackwell, 2013.
42 James Matthew Thompson, *Leaders of the French Revolution*, Oxford, Basil Blackwell, 1968 [1929], pp. 196–200. Notwithstanding, this assertion should be put into national perspective, due to their very small share in the total number of overall death sentences.
43 'Report made in the name of the Committee of Public Safety on the

necessity of declaring the government revolutionary until the peace', 10 October 1793, Saint-Just, *Œuvres complètes*, p. 521.
44 Ibid., p. 529.
45 See Linton, *Choosing Terror*, chap. 11 on 'achieving authenticity'.
46 Saint-Just, 'Fragments on republican institutions', *Œuvres complètes*, p. 1008. He put the last two lines into his undelivered speech on 9 Thermidor, ibid., p. 908.
47 Marc-Antoine Baudot, *Notes historiques sur la Convention nationale, l'Empire et l'exil des votants*, Paris, D. Jouaust, 1893, p. 260.
48 Ibid., p. 293.
49 25 February 1792, *OMR*, VIII, p. 198.
50 On Robespierre's physical and mental depletion, Peter McPhee, '"Mes forces et ma santé ne peuvent suffire". Crises politiques, crises médicales dans la vie de Maximilien Robespierre, 1790–1794', *AHRF*, 2003, no. 371. See also Peter McPhee, *Robespierre. A Revolutionary Life*, New Haven, CT, Yale University Press, 2012; and Hervé Leuwers, *Robespierre*, Paris, Fayard, 2014.
51 *Mémoires de Levasseur*, p. 412.
52 François Boissy d'Anglas, *Discours préliminare au projet de constitution pour la République française, prononcé par Boissy-d'Anglas, au nom de la Commission des Onze, dans la séance du 5 messidor, an III*.

Chapter 4: The Revolution and its Opponents: Clashes and the Intensification of Repression

1 For a useful distinction between 'anti-Revolution' and 'counter-Revolution', see Jean-Clément Martin (ed.), *Dictionnaire de la Contre-Révolution XVIIIe–XXe siècle*, Paris, Perrin, 2011, pp. 60–1. See also Roger Dupuy and François Lebrun (eds), *Les résistances à la Révolution*, Paris, Imago, 1987.
2 See Jean-Clément Martin, *Violence et Révolution. Essai sur la naissance d'un mythe national*, Paris, Seuil, 2006.
3 See Stéphane Baciocchi and Philippe Boutry, 'Les "victims" ecclésiastiques de la Terreur', in Biard, *Les politiques de la Terreur*. Note that map 1 is taken from this work. On clerical victims in Lyon, see Côme Simien, *Les massacres de septembre 1792 à Lyon*, Lyon, Aléas, 2011; and Paul Chopelin, *Ville patriote et ville martyre. Lyon, l'Eglise et la Révolution (1788–1805)*, Paris, Letouzey et Ané, 2010, pp. 264–8. Chopelin shows that priests condemned to death in Lyon included some who had taken the oath and even renounced their priestly functions. This shows that convictions were sought for reasons other than religious ones – in Lyon for having taken part in the uprising there – and that there was a desire, after Thermidor, to unite all clergymen into a narrative of religious martyrdom.
4 See the major study by Timothy Tackett, *Religion, Revolution, and*

Regional Culture in Eighteenth-Century France: The Ecclesiastical Oath of 1791, Princeton, NJ, Princeton University Press, 1986.
5 *AP*, vol. XXV, p. 653.
6 Ibid., p. 643.
7 Ibid., vol. XXXV, p. 313 (session of the Assembly on 23 November 1791).
8 Ibid., pp. 436–7.
9 Ibid., vol. XXXVI, p. 258.
10 Ibid., vol. XLIV, pp. 168–9.
11 Ibid., vol. XLV, p. 393.
12 Ibid., vol. XLIV, p. 111.
13 Ibid., vol. XLVII, p. 91.
14 Ibid., vol. XLIX, p. 8.
15 The map is taken from Baciocchi and Boutry, 'Les "victims" ecclésiastiques'.
16 *AP*, vol. XI, pp. 74–5.
17 Figures taken from the as yet unpublished thesis by Benoît Carré, defended at the University of Lille III in April 2018, under the supervision of Marie-Laure Legay, and entitled, *Pensions et pensionnaires de la monarchie, de la grâce royale au système de redistribution de l'Etat au XVIIIe siècle*.
18 *AP*, vol. XXI, pp. 557–9.
19 Ibid., vol. XXVII, pp. 563–4.
20 Ibid., p. 563.
21 Ibid., vol. XXIX, pp. 84–9.
22 Ibid., vol. XXX, p. 632.
23 Ibid., vol. XXXIV, pp. 724–5; vol. XXXV, pp. 27, 103–4.
24 Ibid., vol. XLVIII, p. 181.
25 Ibid., vol. LII, p. 246.
26 Ibid., pp. 408–9.
27 Ibid., p. 635.
28 Ibid., vol. LIII, p. 350.
29 Ibid., vol. LX, p. 495.
30 On the debates within the Legislation Committee, see Jean d'Andlau, 'Penser la loi et en débattre sous la Convention: le travail du comité de Législation et la loi sur les émigrés du 28 mars 1793', *AHRF*, 2019, no. 2, pp. 3–19. Members of this committee remarked that 'the slightest particular exception allowed would provoke, would cause an infinity of others that the Convention would have to judge' (ibid., p. 10).
31 Ibid.
32 *AP*, vol. LIX, p. 518.
33 See d'Andlau, 'Penser la loi'.
34 Jean Vidalenc, *Les émigrés français 1789–1825*, Caen, Association des Publications de la Faculté des Lettres et Sciences Humaines de l'Université de Caen, 1963, p. 35. The total number of *émigrés* was at least 150,000, perhaps as many as 180,000. The Archives nationales now makes

available to researchers, as well as amateur genealogists, invaluable online tools to track the traces of *émigrés*, at https://www.siv.archives-nationales.culture.gouv.fr/mm/media/download/FRAN_ANX_011692.pdf.

35 On imprisonment, see Donald Greer, *The Incidence of the Terror during the French Revolution. A Statistical Interpretation*, Cambridge, MA, Harvard University Press, 1935, pp. 27–33. He estimates a total of 500,000 people were arrested as suspects. Matharan's thesis, defended in 1985, is unpublished, but see Jean-Louis Matharan, 'Suspects', in Albert Soboul, Jean-René Suratteau and François Gendron (eds), *Dictionnaire historique de la Révolution française*, Paris, PUF, 1989, pp. 1004–8; and Matharan: 'Les arrestations de suspects en 1793 et en l'an II, professions et répression', *AHRF*, 1986, no. 263, pp. 74–85. See also Antoine Boulant, 'Le suspect parisien en l'an II', *AHRF*, 1990, no. 280, pp. 187–97; Louis Jacob, *Les suspects pendant la Révolution, 1789–1794*, Paris, Hachette, 1952; Anne Simonin, *Le déshonneur dans la République. Une histoire de l'indignité 1791–1958*, Paris, Grasset, 2008; finally, many recent references are in Philippe Bourdin, 'Les suspects dans le Puy-de-Dôme et la Creuse', in Danièle Pingué and Jean-Paul Rothiot (eds), *Les comités de surveillance. D'une création citoyenne à une institution révolutionnaire*, Paris, Société des études robespierristes, 2012, pp. 63–96.
36 Issue of 26 December 1789–2 January 1790, p. 12.
37 *AP*, vol. XVIII, pp. 645–6.
38 Biard, *Missionnaires*, chap. 1.
39 *AP*, vol. XXVIII, p. 372.
40 Ibid., vol. XLIX, p. 90.
41 Biard, *Missionnaires*.
42 *AP*, vol. LXIX, pp. 594–5.
43 Ibid., vol. LXXIV, pp. 303–5.
44 Ibid., vol. LXXII, p. 102. It was at this moment that Danton spoke of an 'initiative of terror' (cf. above, chap. 1).
45 Indeed, the word 'federalism' did not appear in the first statement of the project presented on 30 August 1793 (ibid., vol. XXIII, p. 246).
46 For instances of wealthy merchants in Nantes and Bordeaux being pressured to 'give gifts' to help the indigent, in hope of securing their own release, see Charles Walton, 'Between Trust and Terror: Patriotic Gift Giving in the French Revolution', in Andress, *Experiencing the French Revolution*, pp. 63–4.
47 Greer, *Incidence of the Terror*, p. 29.
48 This sobriquet was taken up by Claude François Beaulieu, *Essais historiques sur les causes et les effets de la révolution de France*, Paris, Maradan, an XI–1803, vol. 3, p. 56. See too, Hervé Leuwers, *Un juriste en politique. Merlin de Douai (1754–1838)*, Arras, Artois Presses Université, 1996.
49 Pingué and Rothiot, *Les comités de surveillance*.

50 The extensive historiography on 'federalism' includes: Paul R. Hanson, *The Jacobin Republic Under Fire. The Federalist Revolt in the French Revolution*, University Park, PA, The Pennsylvania State University Press, 2003; and Anne de Mathan, *Girondins jusqu'au tombeau. Une révolte bordelaise dans la Révolution*, Bordeaux, Éditions Sud-Ouest, 2004.

51 It is also worth noting that, in the heat of the moment, Hébert openly congratulated himself that the days of 31 May and 2 June went off without bloodshed. Better still, he claims that the Girondins almost wished they had been killed in such a way as to pass for martyrs in order to better stir up certain departments and cities against Paris: 'that beautiful day which saved the republic would have been lost if a single drop of blood had been shed. The Brissotins, who wanted only wounds and bruises, could not have asked for more; it was then that they would have called to their aid all the sugar merchants of the Gironde, Marseille, Lyon and Rouen. The real way to kill these rascals is to let them live. Let's leave to Charlot what belongs to Charlot; the gallows never loses its prey' (*Le Père Duchesne*, no. 244. Charlot was a sobriquet for the executioner of Paris, Charles-Henri Sanson).

52 Hanson, *The Jacobin Republic*, pp. 69–70.

53 The Address is reproduced in Jean Lethuillier, *Le Calvados dans la Révolution. L'esprit public d'un département*, Condé-sur-Noireau, Éditions Charles Corlet, 1990, pp. 20–1.

54 Michel Biard, *Procès-verbaux de la Société populaire de Honfleur (1791–1795)*, Paris, Éditions du CTHS, 2011.

55 Michel Biard, *1793. Le siège de Lyon. Entre mythes et réalités*, Clermont-Ferrand, Lemme édit, 2013, pp. 16–17.

56 Ibid., pp. 17–18.

57 De Mathan, *Girondins*, p. 137.

58 'Hébert repeated this accusation several times in his diary, ironically calling him "milord Brissot", and, just after the execution of the twenty Girondins on October 31, 1793, invented a so-called "Testament of Jean-Pierre Brissot, formerly a spy in England . . . heavily paid . . . by the emperors, kings and other powers of Europe . . . to muddy the waters and put the French to shame, in order to prevent them from becoming republicans"' (*Le Père Duchesne*, no. 305).

59 Biard, *1793*, chap. 1.

60 Paul Chopelin, *Ville patriote et ville martyre*.

61 Biard, *1793*, chap. 2.

62 Ibid., chap. 3. See also William D. Edmonds, *Jacobinism and the Revolt of Lyon, 1789–1793*, Oxford, Clarendon Press, 1990; and Edouard Herriot, *Lyon n'est plus*, Paris, Hachette, 4 vols, 1939, vol. 3.

63 *AP*, vol. LXXII, p. 26.

64 Herriot, *Lyon n'est plus*.

65 *AP*, vol. LXXVI, p. 458.

66 Raymond Curtet, 'Lyon n'est plus: le décret et la réalité. Les démolitions

de Lyon (1792–1795)', in *1793: l'année terrible à Lyon*, Lyon, Musée de l'Imprimerie et de la Banque, 1993, pp. 89–105.
67 Antoine Boulant, *Le Tribunal révolutionnaire. Punir les ennemis du peuple*, Paris, Perrin, 2018, pp. 127–30.
68 See Biard, *La Liberté*, pp. 104–5.
69 Issue of 10 December 1793.

Chapter 5: Creating Revolutionary Law: A Time of Political Exception

1 Heading VII, article 92.
2 Carl Schmitt, *La dictature*, Paris, Seuil, 2000 [1921], see notably, pp. 142–65.
3 The Convention was a Constituent Assembly for as long as its members debated a future draft constitution. From 24 June 1793, once the Constitution had been adopted, the Convention was no longer constituent and it did not become so again in the autumn, contrary to the notion of 'dictatorship of constituent power' proposed by Albert Mathiez, unless one follows the analysis proposed by Yannick Bosc, for whom revolution and exception are one and the same. See Yannick Bosc, 'Albert Mathiez, la guerre, la "dictature" et le pouvoir constituant', in Michel Biard and Jean-Numa Ducange (eds), *L'exception politique en révolution. Pensées et pratiques [1789–1917]*, Rouen, PURH, 2019.
4 Biard, *Missionnaires*, chap. 5.
5 Replaced by twelve executive commissions on 12 Germinal Year II (1 April 1794), which strengthened the control of the Committee of Public Safety.
6 On the role of the surveillance committees, see Jacques Guilhaumou, 'La *loi en acte* dans les comités de surveillance des Bouches-du-Rhône en l'an II', in *Dictionnaire des usages socio-politiques (1770–1815)*, fascicule 6 (*Notions pratiques*), Paris, Publications de l'INALF collection Saint-Cloud – Klincksieck, 1999, pp. 99–125; and Pingué and Rothiot, *Les comités de surveillance*.
7 Simonin, *Le déshonneur*, pp. 291–2.
8 Françoise Brunel and Jacques Guilhaumou, 'Pour une fin des analogies: "gouvernement révolutionnaire" et "état d'exception" dans la Révolution française', in Biard and Ducange, *L'exception*.
9 Michel Biard, 'La "Convention ambulante". Un rempart au despotisme du pouvoir exécutif?', *AHRF*, 2003, no. 2, pp. 55–70.
10 François Saint-Bonnet, *L'état d'exception*, Paris, PUF, 2001. Bonnet notes on his first page that 'the state of exception is found in all times', and devotes nearly half his book to antiquity and the Middle Ages; Giorgio Agamben, *État d'exception. Homo sacer, II, 1*, Paris, Seuil, 2003. Agamben evokes the state of exception as 'a space devoid of law' (p. 86). Armed with this definition, we should note that the members of

the Convention always took great care not to forget the law, for ordinary or 'revolutionary' measures; the always very legalistic functioning of the Revolutionary Tribunal offers an effective example. For a critique of Agamben's book, see Guillaume Paugam, 'L'état d'exception: sur un paradoxe d'Agamben', *Labyrinthe*, 2004, no. 19, pp. 43–58. For yet another approach, see Ninon Grangé, *L'urgence et l'effroi. L'état d'exception, la guerre et les temps politiques*, Paris, ENS Editions, 2018.
11 Féraud, *Dictionnaire*.
12 *AP*, vol. IX, p. 475 (21 October 1789).
13 10 November 1789.
14 *AP*, vol. IX, p. 474.
15 *L'Ami du peuple*, 2 October 1789.
16 *AP*, vol. XLV, pp. 325–7.
17 Edna Lemay (ed.), *Dictionnaires des Législateurs, 1791–1792*, Ferney-Voltaire, Publications du Centre international d'étude du XVIIIe siècle, 2007, vol. II, p. 763.
18 *AP*, vol. XLIX, pp. 12–13.
19 Debry would take a long time to shake off the memory of this radical proposal (cf. Laurent Brassart, 'Un échec devant l'Histoire: Les mémoires de Jean Debry', in Michel Biard, Philippe Bourdin, Hervé Leuwers and Yoshiaki Ōmi, *L'écriture d'une expérience. Histoire et mémoires de Conventionnels*, Paris, Société des études robespierristes, 2016, pp. 167–81).
20 *Courier de l'égalité*, 27 August 1792. Emphasis added.
21 *AP*, vol. LIII, pp. 36–7. Emphasis added.
22 Book IV, chap. VI.
23 To cite just one example, on 5 July 1792, Torné stated before the Legislative Assembly that 'the true Constitution of a nation that is about to perish is entirely in these words: the safety of the people is the supreme law' (*AP*, vol. XLVI, p. 140). See Fichtl, *Antiquités imaginaires*, chap. VI. This work includes illuminating passages on the influence of Cicero and the model of the 'ultimate senatus-consult' used as a weapon against the enemies of the republic (with the possibility of extra-judicial executions). See too, her recently published book, drawn from her doctoral thesis: Fichtl, *La Radicalisation de l'idéal républicain*.
24 *AP*, vol. LVII, p. 707. Emphasis added.
25 Ibid., vol. LX, p. 65.
26 Ibid., vol. LXX, p. 102.
27 Ibid., vol. LXXIII, p. 19 (25 August 1793).
28 Ibid., vol. LXXVI, p. 642.
29 Ibid., p. 315.
30 On the Committee of Public Safety, see the classic study by Robert Roswell Palmer, *Twelve who Ruled. The Year of the Terror in the French Revolution*, Princeton, NJ, Princeton University Press, 1973 [1941].
31 The Committee of General Defence took its cue from the commission of

Twelve instituted by the Legislative. Its primary function was to simplify and accelerate the common work between seven committees, each of which assigned three of their members to the Committee of General Defence. These were the committees of: War, Finances, Colonies, Marine, Diplomacy, Constitution, and Commerce – the essential committees to take responsibility, 'along with the ministers, for the actions required for the coming campaign and the present state of affairs' (*AP*, vol. LVI, pp. 116–17).

32 Raphaël Matta-Duvignau, *Gouverner, administrer révolutionnairement: le comité de salut public*, Paris, L'Harmattan, 2013.
33 Michel Biard, *Missionnaires*.
34 Richard Cobb, *Les armées révolutionnaires, instrument de la Terreur dans les départements. Avril 1793–floréal an II*, Paris, Mouton, 1961–1963, 2 vols.
35 Ibid., vol. I, p. 2.
36 Cf. above, note 6.
37 Jean-Christophe Gaven, *Le crime de lèse-nation. Histoire d'une invention juridique et politique (1789–1791)*, Paris, SciencesPo Les Presses, 2016.
38 Heading III of the Constitution of 1791 ('Des pouvoirs publics'), chap. V ('Du pouvoir judiciaire'), article 23.
39 *AP*, vol. XLVIII, p. 291.
40 Ibid., p. 298.
41 In the order of citations, the Montagnards Garrau, Bentabole and Danton (*AP*, vol. LX, pp. 59–63).
42 Ibid., p. 60 (Vergniaud) and p. 63 (Danton).
43 Ibid., p. 93.
44 Boulant, *Le Tribunal révolutionnaire*.
45 See Annie Jourdan, 'Les journées de Prairial an II: le tournant de la Révolution?', *La Révolution française. Cahiers de l'Institut d'histoire de la Révolution française*, 2016, no. 10.
46 See Anne Simonin, 'Les acquittés de la Grande Terreur. Réflexions sur l'amitié dans la République', in Michel Biard (ed.), *Les politiques de la Terreur, 1793–1794*, Rennes, Presses Universitaires – Société des études robespierristes, 2007, pp. 183–205; and Godrey, *Revolutionary Justice*.
47 Eric de Mari, *La mise hors de la loi sous la Révolution française (19 mars 1793–an III). Une étude juridictionnelle et institutionnelle*, Paris, LDGJ, 2015.
48 Donald Greer, *The Incidence of the Terror during the French Revolution*. Despite their age, Greer's statistics remain the standard ones referred to, in the absence of a new national survey. Several studies carried out in one department or in several neighbouring departments tend to prove that, barring exceptions, few corrections are needed to Greer's figures. As for Eric de Mari's statistics, which concern only those condemned to death judged to be 'outlawed' under the 19 March decree, they reveal here and there discrepancies with Greer's figures, but without overturning Greer's

principal findings. Some examples of these discrepancies: in Lozère, 87 executions according to Greer, whereas de Mari finds 128 for those condemned to death judged to be 'outlawed'; other comparative figures show 17/28 for the Puy-de-Dôme and 52/77 in Haute-Loire.)
49 *AP*, vol. LX, p. 331.
50 De Mari, *La mise*, pp. 279–90.
51 See Biard, *1793*; and Herriot, *Lyon n'est plus*.
52 For works on the war in the Vendée, see chapter 7. See also Bruno Hervé, 'Noyades, fusillades, exécutions: les mises à mort des brigands entre justice et massacres en Loire-Inférieure en l'an II', *La Révolution française. Cahiers de l'Institut d'Histoire de la Révolution française*, 2011, no. 3 (http://journals.openedition.org/lrf/209); and Corinne Gomez-Le Chevanton, *Carrier et la Révolution française en 30 questions*, La Crèche, Geste éditions, 2004.
53 See de Mari, *La mise*.
54 In the end, this *armée révolutionnaire* remained unformed, but its 'revolutionary court', functioning as a kind of 'free electron' in the words of the historian Claude Betzinger, sent thirty-one condemned men to their deaths (Claude Betzinger, *Le tribunal révolutionnaire de Strasbourg. 25 octobre–13 décembre 1793*, Strasbourg, Presses Universitaires de Strasbourg, 2017).
55 According to Michelet's beautiful image: 'Looking at the enormous accumulation of what the Convention did, one is tempted to believe that time, in those years, changed its nature, that its ordinary measures lost all meaning. The days were at least doubled; one can name this Assembly, *the Assembly that did not sleep*' (*Histoire de la Révolution française*, Paris, Gallimard – La Pléiade, 2019, vol. II, p. 867 (book XVI, chap. III).
56 Cf. above, chapter 4.

Chapter 6: Terror in the Convention: Political Conflict as an Engine of 'Terror'

1 On divisions in the National (later Constituent) Assembly, see Timothy Tackett, 'Nobles and the Third Estate in the Revolutionary Dynamic of the National Assembly, 1789–1790', *The American Historical Review*, 1989, vol. 94, pp. 271–301.
2 On the divisions within the Jacobin Club from 1790–1791, see Linton, *Choosing Terror*, chap. 3.
3 On the gradual erosion of the inviolability of deputies, see Biard, *La Liberté ou la mort*, chap. 3.
4 See Georges Michon, *Robespierre et la guerre révolutionnaire 1791–1792*, Paris, Marcel Rivière, 1937; on the war debate and its impact in the Jacobin Club, see Linton, *Choosing Terror*, chap. 4.
5 Lemay, *Dictionnaire des Législateurs*, vol. 2, p. 787.

6 Michael Sydenham, *The Girondins*, London, The Athlone Press, 1961, p. 196; and Alison Patrick, *The Men of the First French Republic*, Baltimore, MD, Johns Hopkins University Press, 1972. See also Jacqueline Chaumié, 'Les Girondins', in Albert Soboul (ed.), *Actes du Colloque Girondins et Montagnards (Sorbonne, 14 décembre 1975). Sous la direction d'Albert Soboul*, Paris, Société des études Robespierristes, 1980; also François Furet and Mona Ozouf (eds), *La Gironde et les Girondins*, Paris, Payot, 1991.

7 See Michael Sonenscher, *Sans-culottes; an Eighteenth-Century Emblem in the French Revolution*, Princeton, NJ, Princeton University Press, 2008, pp. 338–61. On Vergniaud's defence of the patriot perpetrators of a massacre at Avignon in October 1791, see *AP*, vol. XL, pp. 152–3.

8 On the importance of friendship to Girondins and Montagnards, see Linton, *Choosing Terror*, chaps 3–9; and Linton, 'Fatal Friendships'. On the *Cercle Social* and the formation of a Girondin press, see Gary Kates, *The* Cercle Social, *the Girondins and the French Revolution*, Princeton, NJ, Princeton University Press, 1985, chap. 7. On *sans-culotte* networks and relations between *sans-culottes* and Jacobins, see Haim Burstin, *L'Invention du sans-culotte: regard sur le Paris révolutionnaire*, Paris, Odile Jacob, 2005.

9 Brissot, *Mémoires*, vol. 1, p. 176.

10 See Siân Reynolds, *Marriage and Revolution: Monsieur and Madame Roland*, Oxford, Oxford University Press, 2012.

11 See Françoise Brunel, 'Les Députés montagnards', in Soboul, *Actes du Colloque Girondins et Montagnards*, pp. 343–61; and Patrick, *The Men of the First French Republic*, pp. 17–33, 105–7.

12 For the classic social distinction between the Girondins and Montagnards as representing different class interests, see Soboul's introduction to *Actes du Colloque Girondins et Montagnards*.

13 14 December 1793, Aulard, *Société des Jacobins*, vol. 5, p. 559. See Linton, 'Friends, Enemies'.

14 Joseph Guadet, nephew of the revolutionary Guadet, wrote of the extent to which Girondins were connected by personal ties: Joseph Guadet, *Les Girondins. Leur vie privée, leur vie publique, leur proscription et leur mort*, Paris, Librairie académique, 1862, vol. 1, Preface, pp. xiii–xvii.

15 On these accusations, see Linton, *Choosing Terror*, chaps 4 and 5.

16 See Marcel Dorigny, 'Violence et Révolution: les Girondins et les massacres de septembre', in Soboul, *Actes du Colloque Girondins et Montagnards*, pp. 102–20. On the lack of any evidence that Robespierre attempted to secure the arrests of Brissot and Roland by the Commune with the intention of bringing about their deaths, see Peter McPhee, *Robespierre – a Revolutionary Life*, New Haven, CT, Yale University Press, 2012, pp. 133–4; although, as McPhee makes clear, the fact that Brissot and Roland came genuinely to *believe* that Robespierre had done this was the most significant outcome, as it made any future reconciliation impossible.

17 See Tackett, *Coming of the Terror*, pp. 228–33.
18 Anne de Mathan, 'Le fédéralisme Girondin. Histoire d'un mythe national', *AHRF*, 2018, no. 393, pp. 195–206.
19 See Reynolds, *Marriage and Revolution*; and Marc Bouloiseau, 'Robespierre d'après les journaux Girondins', in Albert Soboul (ed.), *Actes du colloque Robespierre*, Paris, Société des études Robespierristes, 1967.
20 See Charles Walton, *Policing Public Opinion: The Culture of Calumny and the Problem of Free Speech*, Oxford, Oxford University Press, 2009.
21 12 December 1792, Aulard, *Société des Jacobins*, vol. 4, pp. 574–5.
22 Biard, *La liberté ou la mort*, pp. 74–5.
23 See Michel Biard and Pascal Dupuy (eds), *La Révolution française: Dynamique et ruptures, 1787–1804*, Paris, Armand Colin, 2008, pp. 89–90.
24 See Albert Soboul (ed.), *Le procès de Louis XVI*, Paris, Gallimard, 1973; and Michael Walzer (ed.), *Regicide and Revolution: Speeches at the Trial of Louis XVI*, New York, Columbia University Press, 1993.
25 Tackett makes a strong case for March 1793 as a turning point marking the moment that begins the descent into terror: *Coming of the Terror*, chap. 10.
26 Greer, *The Incidence of the Terror*, pp. 14–15, 153.
27 On this failure to distinguish, and its consequences, see Biard, *La liberté ou la mort*, p. 74.
28 On the problematic legal definition of treason, see Carla Hesse, 'The Law of the Terror', *Modern Language Notes*, 1999, no. 114, pp. 702–18.
29 14 March 1793, *Le Moniteur*, vol. 15, p. 688.
30 See Linton, *Choosing Terror*, pp. 164–5.
31 1 April 1793, *AP*, vol. LXI, p. 63. See too, Biard, *La liberté ou la mort*, pp. 74–6; and Linton, *Choosing Terror*, pp. 163–4.
32 5 April 1793, *AP*, vol. LXI, p. 335.
33 3 April 1793, ibid., pp. 300–1. 6 April 1793, ibid., p. 381.
34 Levasseur, *Mémoires*, pp. 106–7. See also 'L'Immunité parlementaire sous la Révolution', in Albert Mathiez, *La Conspiration de l'étranger*, Paris, Armand Colin, 1918.
35 Cited in Tackett, *Coming of the Terror*, p. 282.
36 Ibid., pp. 270–6.
37 See Sydenham, *The Girondins*, pp. 166–7.
38 See Morris Slavin, *The Making of an Insurrection: Parisian Sections and the Gironde*, Cambridge, MA, Harvard University Press, 1986, pp. 62–3, 88.
39 Slavin concludes not only that the militants in the sections took a leading role in events, but that their threats to Montagnards, should they too fail to fulfil the militants' demands, was not an idle one: ibid., p. 162.
40 See Hanson, *The Jacobin Republic*; and Mathan, *Girondins jusqu'au tombeau*.

41 'Rapport au nom du Comité de salut public sur les trente-deux membres de la Convention détenus en vertu du décret du 2 juin', Saint-Just, *Oeuvres complètes*, pp. 459, 472, 474, 476–7.
42 Ibid., p. 459.
43 Ibid., pp. 476–7.
44 Ibid., p. 476.
45 Ibid., p. 459.
46 On the embargo against depicting individual living revolutionaries in ways that glorified them, see Marisa Linton, 'Virtue or Glory? Dilemmas of Political Heroism in the French Revolution', *French History and Civilisation: Papers from the George Rudé Seminar*, 2015, no. 6, pp. 83–102.
47 On fear of assassination, see Linton, 'The Stuff of Nightmares'. On the commemoration and 'panthéonization' of dead deputies, see Biard, *La liberté ou la mort*, chap. 8.
48 Neither Fauchet nor Deperret, nor the Girondin Barbaroux who had recommended Corday from Caen, seems to have had any idea of what she intended. Fauchet vehemently denied having even met Corday, but his protests were ignored. See his letter to the Convention, in E.B. Courtois, *Papiers inédits trouvés chez Robespierre, Saint-Just, etc., supprimés ou omis par Courtois*, Paris, 1828, vol. 3, pp. 255–7.
49 15 July 1793, *Le Moniteur*, vol. 17, pp. 198–9. The number of those included under the category of 'traitors to the *patrie*' on 8 July rose from nine to eighteen when the Saint-Just report was transformed into a decree on 28 July.
50 Cited in Tackett, *Coming of the Terror*, pp. 295–6.
51 See Biard, *La Liberté ou la mort*, chap. 3, p. 70.
52 Sydenham, *The Girondins*, pp. 20–38.
53 See the powerful account of the arrests, and the subsequent trial of the Girondin leaders, in Tackett, *Coming of the Terror*, pp. 306–11.
54 Cited in Biard, *La Liberté ou la mort*, pp. 87–8.
55 3 October 1793, *AP*, vol. LXXV, p. 534.
56 Ibid., p. 533.
57 Ibid., pp. 535–7; *OMR*, vol. X, pp. 134–6. On the men who signed the protest and whether they can be categorized as 'Girondin sympathizers', see Sydenham, *The Girondins*, pp. 41, 44–8, 219.
58 3 October 1793, *AP*, vol. LXXV, pp. 535–7; *OMR*, vol. X, pp. 133–6.
59 Hébert, *Le Père Duchesne*, no. 296, p. 7.
60 Cited in Biard, *La Liberté ou la mort*, p. 89.
61 'Projet de Défense de Vergniaud', in Henri Wallon, *Histoire du Tribunal révolutionnaire*, Paris, Hachette, 1880–1882, 6 vols, vol. 1, pp. 480–2.
62 Walter, *Actes du Tribunal révolutionnaire*, pp. 338–40.
63 Ibid., p. 338.
64 Patrick, *The Men of the First French Republic*, p. 32.
65 Jordan points out that a quarter of Robespierre's constitutional proposals were 'devoted to forcing officials to be virtuous, or at least outwardly

honest'. See David Jordan, *The Revolutionary Career of Maximilien Robespierre*, New York, The Free Press, 1985, p. 156.
66 On financial corruption amongst the Jacobins, see Albert Mathiez, *La Corruption parlementaire sous la Terreur*, Paris, Armand Colin, 1927; Olivier Blanc, *La Corruption sous la terreur (1792–1794)*, Paris, Robert Laffont, 1992; and Arnaud de Lestapis, *La Conspiration de Batz*, Paris, Société des études robespierristes, 1969. On conspiracy, corruption and the 'Foreign Plot', Linton, *Choosing Terror*, chap. 7.
67 See Morris Slavin, *The Hébertistes to the Guillotine: Anatomy of a 'Conspiracy' in Revolutionary France*, Baton Rouge, LA, Louisiana State University Press, 1994.
68 Soboul attributed the motivation of the Hébertist leaders principally to ambition and personal spite; Albert Soboul, *Les Sans-culottes parisiens en l'an II*, Paris, Librairie Clavreuil, 1958, pp. 149, 726–7, 723–59. See also Norman Hampson, *Danton*, London, Duckworth, 1978, p. 127; and Slavin, *The Hébertistes*, pp. 100–1.
69 Linton, *Choosing Terror*, chap. 8. Hervé Leuwers also takes the view that Robespierre's decision to support other Committee of Public Safety members, most notably Billaud-Varenne and Collot d'Herbois, in attacking Danton was taken for pragmatic reasons, and to preserve the unity of the Committee of Public Safety: Hervé Leuwers, 'Danton et Robespierre. Le duel réinventé', in Biard and Leuwers, *Danton, le mythe et l'Histoire*, pp. 141–53.
70 On Danton's attitude, see Linton, *Choosing Terror*, chap 8. On Danton's close relations with Rousselin, a keen advocate of terror tactics when serving as an agent in Troyes in late 1793, see Jeff Horn, *The Making of a Terrorist: Alexandre Rousselin and the French Revolution*, Oxford, Oxford University Press, 2021.
71 See Hampson, *Danton*, pp. 55–66.
72 Robespierre denied that Danton inclined towards 'treason', on 13 Frimaire (3 December 1793): *OMR*, vol. X, p. 223.
73 Leuwers, *Robespierre*, p. 308.
74 This account of the destruction of the factions is largely taken from Linton, *Choosing Terror*, chap. 8.
75 9 Thermidor (27 July 1794), *Le Moniteur*, vol. 21, p. 332. On Desmoulins, see Hervé Leuwers, *Camille et Lucile Desmoulins: Un rêve de république*, Paris, Fayard, 2018.
76 One of them, Robert Lindet, is reported to have said that his role was to feed patriots, not to kill them. Palmer, *Twelve who Ruled*, pp. 297–8.
77 P.A. Taschereau-Fargues, *à Maximilien Robespierre aux enfers*, Paris, Year III, 1795. The author of this pamphlet said that Vadier gave him this account two days after the events, though, like everything written about Robespierre in Thermidorian literature, its veracity must be approached with some caution.
78 *OMR*, vol. X, p. 414.
79 See Linton, 'Do You Believe That We're Conspirators?'.

80 Antoine-Claire Thibaudeau, *Mémoires sur la Convention et le Directoire*, Paris, Baudouin, 1824, 2 vols, vol. 2, p. 58.
81 See Biard, *La Liberté ou la mort*, p. 71; and Linton, *Choosing Terror*, chap. 11.
82 Baudot, *Notes historiques*, pp. 202–4.
83 Michel Biard lists 96 representatives of the people who died unnatural deaths before 1799 (a higher number than Baudot, though it includes some deaths after the separation of the Convention). Others died as a result of imprisonment, deportation or a mission (*La Liberté ou la mort*, pp. 317–20, 344).
84 On arrests of deputies as 'purging' of the Convention, see Mette Harder, 'Crisis of Representation: The National Convention and the Search for Political Legitimacy, 1792–1795', PhD thesis, University of York, July 2010.
85 On purges after Thermidor, see Françoise Brunel, 'L'épuration de la Convention nationale en l'an III', in Michel Vovelle (ed.), *Le tournant de l'an III. Réaction et terreur blanche dans la France révolutionnaire*, Paris, CTHS, 1997, pp. 15–26; Mette Harder, 'A Second Terror – The Purges of French Revolutionary Legislators after Thermidor', in 'Forum: Thermidor and the French Revolution', Laura Mason (ed.), special issue, part 1, *French Historical Studies*, 2015, vol. 38, pp. 33–60; Mette Harder, '"Elle n'a pas même épargné ses membres!" Les épurations de la Convention nationale entre 1793 et 1795', *AHRF*, 2015, no. 3, pp. 77–105.
86 Thibaudeau, *Mémoires*, vol. 1, p. 50.

Chapter 7: Paris and the Vendée at the Heart of the 'Terror'

1 On the difficulties in accurately estimating this number, see chap. 3 of vol. 11 of the *Atlas de la Révolution française*, Paris, EHESS, 2000, dedicated to Paris.
2 Michel Biard, Philippe Bourdin, Hervé Leuwers and Pierre Serna (eds), *1792. Entrer en République*, Paris, Armand Colin, 2013.
3 Hervé Leuwers, 'Ces représentants qui ont choisi la république: les Conventionnels des 20 et 21 septembre 1792', ibid., pp. 241–54.
4 See the works of Jean-Clément Martin, including *La Vendée de la mémoire (1800–1980)*, Paris, Seuil, 1989 (new edition in 2019, published by Perrin).
5 George Rudé, *The Crowd in the French Revolution*, Oxford, Clarendon Press, 1959.
6 On the origins of the designation, see Annie Geffroy, 'Sans-culotte(s) (novembre 1790–juin 1792)', in *Dictionnaire des usages sociopolitiques, 1770–1815*, fasc.1, Paris, Klincksieck, 1985, pp. 159–86; and Sonenscher, *Sans-culottes*. On the genesis of the *sans-culottes*, see Robert Barrie Rose, *The Making of the Sans-culottes: Democratic Ideas*

    and Institutions in Paris, 1789–92, Manchester, Manchester University Press, 1983.
7 If those with responsibilities have for the most part been identified, it is much harder to estimate the number of militants without official responsibilities: see the invaluable work of Albert Soboul and Raymonde Monnier, *Répertoire du personnel sectionnaire parisien en l'an II*, Paris, Publications de la Sorbonne, 1985.
8 In addition to the monumental work of Soboul, *Les sans-culottes parisiens*; see studies on two of the Parisian *faubourgs*: Raymonde Monnier, *Le Faubourg Saint-Antoine (1789–1815)*, Paris, Société des études robespierristes, 1981; Haim Burstin, *Le Faubourg Saint-Marcel à l'époque révolutionnaire. Structure économique et composition sociale*, Paris, Société des études robespierristes, 1983; Haim Burstin, *Une révolution à l'œuvre: le faubourg Saint-Marcel (1789–1794)*, Seyssel, Champ Vallon, 2005.
9 See Arlette Farge, *La vie fragile. Violence, pouvoirs et solidarités à Paris au XVIIIe siècle*, Paris, Hachette, 1986; Daniel Roche, *Le peuple de Paris. Essai sur la culture populaire au XVIIIe siècle*, Paris, Aubier-Montaigne, 1981; David Garrioch, *Neighbourhood and Community in Paris, 1740–1790*, Cambridge, Cambridge University Press, 1986; and David Garrioch, *The Making of Revolutionary Paris*, Berkeley, CA, University of California Press, 2002.
10 Burstin, *L'Invention du sans-culotte*.
11 See Kaplan, *Le complot de famine*. On rumour, denunciation and conspiracy fears, see Tackett, *Coming of the Terror*, chap. 5; on rumour on the streets of Paris, see Lindsay Porter, *Popular Rumour in Revolutionary Paris, 1792–1794*, Basingstoke, Palgrave Macmillan, 2017.
12 Richard M. Andrews, 'Social Structures, Political Elites and Ideology in Revolutionary Paris, 1792–4', *Journal of Social History*, 1985–86, vol. 19, pp. 71–112; and David Andress, 'Politics and Insurrection: The Sans-culottes, The "Popular Movement", and the People of Paris', in David Andress (ed.), *The Oxford Handbook of the French Revolution*, Oxford, Oxford University Press, 2015, pp. 401–17.
13 A classic example is the image by James Gillray, 'un petit souper à la parisienne' (1792). The contrasting image of 'Le bon *sans-culotte*' can be seen on the website 'Liberté, Egalité, Fraternité: Exploring the French Revolution', at: hnm.gmu.edu/revolution/exhibits/show/liberty--equality--fraternity/item/2714
14 See Bernard Conein, 'Le tribunal et la terreur du 14 juillet 1789 aux massacres de septembre', *Les révoltes logiques*, 1979–1980, no. 11, pp. 2–42; Pierre Caron, *Les Massacres de septembre*, Paris, Maison du livre français, 1935. See also David Andress, *The Terror: Civil War in the French Revolution*, London, Little, Brown, 2005, pp. 93–115.
15 On the fears roused by rumours of conspiracy in Paris and beyond, and the extent to which these emotions were an inciting factor in the massacres, see Côme Simien, 'Rumeurs et Révolution: la saison des massacres de Septembre 1792', *AHRF*, 2020, no. 402, pp. 3–31; and

Timothy Tackett, 'Rumor and Revolution: The Case of the September Massacres', *French History and Civilisation*, 2011, vol. 4, pp. 54–64.
16 Duprat, *Les affaires d'Etat*, pp. 196–200.
17 10 March 1793, *Le Moniteur*, vol. 15, p. 683.
18 See Annie Jourdan, 'Terroriste avant la lettre ou terroriste à temps partiel?' in Biard and Leuwers, *Danton*, pp. 99–111.
19 Micah Alpaugh, *Non-Violence and the French Revolution: Political Demonstrations in Paris, 1787–1795*, Cambridge, Cambridge University Press, 2014.
20 Colin Lucas, 'The Theory and Practice of Denunciation in the French Revolution', *Journal of Modern History*, 1996, vol. 68, pp. 768–85.
21 Hébert was the son of a goldsmith, and had attended a *collège*, though the family had since fallen on hard times. Marat, who had had a long career as a writer, scientist and medical practitioner, was also from the class of 'gentlemen'; whilst Varlet, the *Enragé* leader, received a private income and had no need to work. Others, such as François Hanriot, were from genuinely humble origins. See Robert Barrie Rose, *The Enragés: Socialists of the French Revolution*, Melbourne, Melbourne University Press, 1965, pp. 10–11.
22 Madame Roland, *Mémoires*, pp. 169–70.
23 See Linton, *Choosing Terror*, pp. 105–6.
24 See Burstin, *L'Invention du sans-culotte*, pp. 95–112. On Robespierre, the Duplays and the surrounding network, there is much information in Stéfane-Pol [Paul Coutant] (ed.), *Autour de Robespierre: le Conventionnel Le Bas, d'après des documents inédits et les mémoires de sa veuve*, Paris, Ernest Flammarion, 1901. On the networks of Robespierre and Saint-Just, see Linton, *Choosing Terror*, pp. 231–8.
25 See Colin Lucas, 'Revolutionary Violence, the People and the Terror', in Keith Michael Baker (ed.), *The French Revolution and the Creation of Modern Political Culture*, vol. 4 *The Terror*, Oxford, Pergamon Press, 1994, pp. 57–79; and Wahnich, *In Defence of the Terror*.
26 Jacques Roux, 'Manifesto of the Enragés', presented on behalf of the Gravilliers section to the Convention, 25 June 1793, *AP*, vol. LXVII, pp. 457–9.
27 Walter Markov, *Jacques Roux, le curé rouge*, Montreuil, Libertalia, 2017 (German edition, 1967); and Albert Soboul, 'Sur les "curés rouges" dans la Révolution française', *AHRF*, 1982, no. 249, pp. 349–63. See also Rose, *The Enragés*, pp. 40–1.
28 Dominique Godineau, *Citoyennes tricoteuses. Les femmes du peuple à Paris pendant la Révolution française*, Aix-en-Provence, Alinea, 1988; English edition: *The Women of Paris and Their Revolution*, Berkeley, CA, University of California Press, 1998.
29 For a recent account of *sans-culottes* and the popular movement in 1793, see McPhee, *Liberty or Death*, pp. 222–7.
30 See Marie Cerati, *Le club des citoyennes républicaines révolutionnaires*, Paris, Éd. sociales, 1966.

31 Godineau, *Citoyennes tricoteuses*, pp. 149–77; and Françoys Larue-Langlois, *Claire Lacombe. Citoyenne révolutionnaire*, Paris, Punctum, 2005.
32 Cobb, *Les armées révolutionnaires*.
33 Farge, *La vie fragile*, pp. 218–23.
34 Godineau, *Citoyennes tricoteuses*, pp. 227–33.
35 Nicole Bossut, *Chaumette, porte-parole des sans-culottes*, Paris, CTHS, 1998.
36 5 September 1793, *AP*, vol. LXXII, pp. 419–20.
37 Katie Jarvis, 'The Cost of Female Citizenship: How Price Controls Gendered Democracy in Revolutionary France', *French Historical Studies*, 2018, vol. 41, pp. 647–80.
38 On dechristianization, see Michel Vovelle, *La Révolution contre l'église. De la raison à l'être suprême*, Paris, Éditions complexe, 1988; and Vovelle, *Religion et Révolution. La déchristianisation de l'an II*, Paris, Hachette, 1976.
39 Soboul, *Les Sans-culottes parisiens*, pp. 726–7; and Slavin, *The Hébertistes*, pp. 87–8, 101–2, 225–6.
40 14 Ventôse (4 March 1794), Session of the Cordeliers Club, *Le Moniteur*, vol. 19, p. 630, and footnote. On Hébert's threats to Robespierre and other members of the Committee of Public Safety, and Hébert's probable use of the Cordeliers to promote his own ambitions, see Slavin, *The Hébertistes*, pp. 100–2, 112, 117–20; Louis Jacob, *Hébert Le Père Duchesne, Chef des sans-culottes*, Paris, Gallimard, 1960, pp. 305–24; Soboul, *Les Sans-culottes parisiens*, pp. 149, 723–59; and Linton, *Choosing Terror*, pp. 215–18.
41 Boulant, *Le Tribunal révolutionnaire*, p. 109. On the imprisoned suspects, see Charles-Aimé Dauban, *Les prisons de Paris sous la Révolution d'après les relations de contemporains*, Paris, Henri Plon, 1870; and Jacob, *Les suspects*.
42 Michael Rapport, 'Political Trials, Terror and Civil Society: The Case of the Revolutionary Tribunal in Paris, 1793–94', in M.T. Davis, E. Macleod and G. Pentland (eds), *Political Trials in an Age of Revolutions: Britain and the North Atlantic, 1793–1848*, Houndmills, Palgrave, 2019.
43 Alex Fairfax-Cholmeley, 'Defence, Collaboration, Counter-attack: The Role and Exploitation of the Printed Word by Victims of the Terror', in Andress, *Experiencing the French Revolution*, pp. 137–54. See also Alex Fairfax-Cholmeley, 'Creating and Resisting the Terror: The Paris Revolutionary Tribunal, March–June 1793', *French History*, 2018, vol. 32, pp. 203–25, which shows that opportunities to mount a legal defence were written into the procedures of the Revolutionary Tribunal.
44 Jonathan Smyth, *Robespierre and the Festival of the Supreme Being: The Search for a Republican Morality*, Manchester, Manchester University Press, 2016. On other fêtes in Paris orchestrated by David, see David Lloyd Dowd, *Pageant Master of the Republic: Jacques-Louis David and the French Revolution*, New York, Books for Libraries Press, 1948.

45 On Robespierre and the Law of Prairial, see Leuwers, *Robespierre*, pp. 336–42. On Robespierre's withdrawal from public life, see McPhee, *Robespierre*, pp. 207–13. On assassination fears as a factor, see Linton, 'Stuff of Nightmares'.
46 Jourdan, 'Les journées de Prairial'.
47 On the demeanour of revolutionary leaders on their way to the scaffold as a means of asserting their authentic identities, see Linton, *Choosing Terror*, chap. 11.
48 On the culture around the deployment of the guillotine, see Daniel Arasse, *The Guillotine and the Terror*, London, Penguin, 1991; and, recently, Guillaume Debat, 'La guillotine révolutionnaire: de l'incarnation de l'humanisme pénal à une machine effroyable? (1789–1794)', *AHRF*, 2020, no. 402, pp. 33–57.
49 Erin-Marie Legacey, *Making Space for the Dead. Catacombs, Cemeteries, and the Reimagining of Paris, 1780–1830*, Ithaca, NY, Cornell University Press, 2019. The Madeleine cemetery was succeeded, at the height of the 'terror', by those of Errancis, Sainte-Marguerite and Picpus (cf. map 6).
50 Vergniaud and the Montagnards accused one another of wanting to stir up a civil war, 31 December 1792: *AP*, vol. LVI, p. 93.
51 And even this should be qualified, because, if the construction of a nation-state and the indivisibility attributed to the First Republic argue in this sense, in conformity with the rhetoric of the time, it is not certain that all the Republican soldiers sent to the territories affected by the rebellion were aware that they were fighting other Frenchmen, no more than the 'Vendéens' were all aware of being engaged in a fight to the death with their fellow French. (See the pages devoted to this question of the civil war by Jean-Clément Martin, *La Vendée et la Révolution*, Paris, Perrin, 2007, notably chap. 5.)
52 The bibliography on the 'Vendée War' is vast. One should refer to the various works and other texts by Jean-Clément Martin, including his recent synthesis, *La guerre de Vendée 1793–1800*, Paris, Le Seuil, 2014 (a new, entirely revised version of *La Vendée et la France, 1789–1799*, Paris, Le Seuil, 1987).
53 Cf. Jean-Clément Martin, 'Histoire et polémique, les massacres de Machecoul', *AHRF*, 1993, no. 1, pp. 33–60.
54 For further geographical details, see the list of the '735 communes of the military Vendée' proposed in Jacques Hussenet (ed.), *'Détruisez la Vendée!'. Regards croisés sur les victimes et destructions de la guerre de Vendée*, La Roche-sur-Yon, Centre vendéen de recherches historiques, 2007, pp. 575–621.
55 *AP*, vol. LXII, p. 188.
56 There are many examples. One need only consult two 'witnesses', often used by historians in the nineteenth century and from opposite political sides: the Montagnard Lequinio, who takes up the theme of a conspiratorial Vendée, and the Marquise de La Rochejaquelein, who describes

a 'Vendée' enjoying idyllic social relations, rising up spontaneously, without any prior conspiracy. (Lequinio, *Guerre de la Vendée et des Chouans*, Paris, Pougin, an III, pp. 161–2; *Mémoires de Mme la marquise de La Rochejaquelein*, Paris, Michaud, 1815, pp. 44–5 and 55–6.)
57 On the roots of the insurrection in the 'Vendée', in addition to the very numerous scholarly works published in the twentieth century, notably those of Jean-Clément Martin, see Alain Gérard, *Pourquoi la Vendée?*, Paris, Armand Colin, 1990.
58 It is estimated that 60,000–100,000 'Vendéans' crossed the Loire, including some 30,000 fighters, or even more, with plans to seize a port, there to await British aid.
59 Anne Rolland-Boulestreau, *Les colonnes infernales. Violences et guerre civile en Vendée militaire (1794–1795)*, Paris, Fayard, 2015.
60 See Jean-Clément Martin, 'A propos du "génocide vendéen". Du recours à la légitimité de l'historien', *Sociétés contemporaines*, 2000, no. 39, pp. 23–38.
61 Annie Jourdan provides some comparative examples in Jourdan, *Nouvelle histoire*.
62 Anne Rolland-Boulestreau, *Guerre et paix en Vendée (1794–1796)*, Paris, Fayard, 2019.
63 See the often-illuminating pages by Anne Rolland-Boulestreau, *Les colonnes*.
64 Jean-Clément Martin, *Blancs et Bleus dans la Vendée déchirée*, Paris, Gallimard, 2001 (1st edn, 1986), p. 49.
65 He writes that the 'Vendée' was less affected by 'terror' than by extremely severe repressive tactics, which he compares to those implemented in other territories in the eighteenth century, such as those of Corsica in 1769 or Ireland in 1798–1799: Martin, *La terreur. Vérités*, p. 144.

Chapter 8: Who Lived and Who Died? The Difficult Balance Sheets of Terror

1 These victories were all the more decisive because, far from the 'Vendean' front, the armies of the Republic won in December other major successes: the recapture of Toulon (19th), the victory of Geisberg (26–29th) which led to the recovery of Wissembourg, the lifting of the siege of Landau and the end of the threats that weighed on Alsace.
2 Brown, 'The Thermidorians' Terror'.
3 Greer, *The Incidence of the Terror*, notably pp. 135–47.
4 Jean-Clément Martin, 'A propos du "génocide vendéen"'; Jacques Hussenet (ed.), *'Détruisez la Vendée!'* (notably the major contribution of this author, 'Quel bilan?', pp. 107–48). Another figure is proposed for Republican losses, this time estimated at up to 50,000 men (ibid., pp. 317–420). In any case, these losses were heavy and, as in other battlefields, casualty figures were not confined to those killed outright,

since many of the wounded died in hospitals, either as a result of their wounds or from disease (in the vast majority of cases infectious diseases, those of the respiratory tract and intestinal ailments; see Pierre Contant, 'Dans les hôpitaux de l'armée de l'Ouest', ibid., pp. 395–414).

5 And to which, according to a decree of 26 Germinal Year II (15 April 1794), all 'conspiracy suspects' arrested throughout the national territory were to be transferred. The Law of Prairial (10 June), by modifying the functioning of this extraordinary court, considerably increased the number of executions in the capital between that date and the fall of Robespierre at the end of July (cf. above, chap. 6 and 7.1).

6 Vendée, Loire-Inférieure, Maine-et-Loire, Ille-et-Vilaine, Mayenne and Sarthe. To which could also be added the neighbouring departments of Orne (nearly 200 death sentences), Charente-Inférieure and Deux-Sèvres (both suffered more than 100 executions).

7 There were nearly 500 death sentences in these two cities, more than two-thirds of them in Arras between March and July 1794. This proximity of the enemy armies was also used as an argument by Barère to defend Lebon before the Convention when, on 11 Messidor Year II (29 June 1794), he announced the victory of Fleurus (*AP*, vol. XCII, pp. 277–8); cf. below, conclusion).

8 Created by a decree of the Committee of Public Safety of 21 Floréal Year II (10 May 1794), in response to a request from the Montagnard representative Maignet, and at a time when the other extraordinary courts of justice in the departments were suppressed in order to concentrate the judgements of 'conspiracy defendants' at the Revolutionary Tribunal in Paris, this commission was to be composed of five members charged with judging the enemies of the Revolution who were to be found in the surrounding countries, particularly the departments of Vaucluse and Bouches-du-Rhône (Alphonse Aulard, *Recueil des actes du comité de Salut public avec la correspondance officielle des représentants en mission et le registre du Conseil exécutif provisoire*, Paris, Imprimerie Nationale, 1889–1999, 32+4 vols). It condemned to death 332 of the 595 defendants who appeared before it in only 47 days. Prison sentences were handed down on 116 others, while 147 acquittals were pronounced. In addition, a few days before the committee creating the commission was arrested, a terrible repression, again ordered by Maignet, descended on the commune of Bédoin, a small town of about 2,000 inhabitants at the foot of Mont Ventoux, where on the night of the 12 Floréal (1 May) the tree of liberty was uprooted, the red bonnet above it thrown into a well, and the decrees of the Convention that had been posted destroyed. As the Orange Commission was not yet in place, the criminal court of Vaucluse moved from Avignon to Bédoin to judge 140 accused, or nearly 7 per cent of the population, 63 of whom were sentenced to death, while 10 fugitives were declared outlawed (Jacques Guilhaumou and Martine Lapied, 'La mission Maignet', *AHRF*, 1995, no. 2, pp. 283–94).

9 Anne-Marie Duport, *Terreur et Révolution. Nîmes en l'an II 1793–1794*, Paris, J. Touzot, 1987.
10 Robert Allen, *Les tribunaux criminels sous la Révolution et l'Empire, 1792–1811*, Rennes, Presses Universitaires de Rennes, 2005, p. 255.
11 Marie-Hélène Froeschlé-Chopard and Michel Froeschlé, *La République à visage humain. Jean-François Ricord, maire de Grasse, conventionnel, représentant en mission dans le Var et les Alpes-Maritimes*, Nice, Serre Editeur, 2019.
12 Claude Betzinger, *Le tribunal révolutionnaire de Strasbourg*.
13 Cf. above, chap. 1 for the case of Valenciennes.
14 Michel Biard, 'Les représentants du peuple en mission et la Loire (1793–1795)', in Jean-Pierre Bois (ed.), *La Loire, la guerre et les hommes. Histoire géopolitique et militaire d'un fleuve* [Colloquium at Angers, March 2012], Rennes, Presses Universitaires de Rennes, 2013, pp. 131–54. In the same work, see also the contributions of Claude Petitfrère, Jacques Boislève and Anne Rolland-Boulestreau.
15 Donald Greer counts 3,548 executions for this department, of which 2,905 for the Bignon commission alone (*The Incidence of the Terror*, p. 141). Bruno Hervé, on the other hand, has 2,665 'rebels' judged by the military commissions of Loire-Inférieure (Bruno Hervé, 'Les archives de la justice révolutionnaire, une source majeure de l'histoire politique de la Révolution française?', *L'Atelier du Centre de recherches historiques* (online review), http://journals.openedition.org/acrh/1654). The Bignon commission was also active in several other cities in the West.
16 *AP*, vol. LXXXIII, p. 145.
17 A total of 1,160 according to Greer (*The Incidence of the Terror*, p. 141).
18 During the conquest of the island by the 'Vendéens' in the autumn of 1793, some 200 Republican soldiers taken prisoner were shot.
19 Bruno Hervé, 'Les archives de la justice révolutionnaire'.
20 Valin, 'La commission militaire de La Rochelle', pp. 105–6.
21 De Mari, *La mise hors de la loi*, p. 541.
22 Ibid., pp. 539–40.
23 *Tableau des prisons de Lyon, pour servir à l'histoire de la tyrannie de 1792 et 1793, par A.F. Delandine, ci-devant Bibliothécaire à Lyon, l'un des prisonniers*, Lyon, Daval, 1797.
24 Ibid., pp. 10, 29.
25 *Mémoires d'un détenu pour servir à l'histoire de la tyrannie de Robespierre*. This text was recently republished by Anne de Mathan, *Histoires de Terreur. Les Mémoires de François Armand Cholet et Honoré Riouffe*, Paris, Honoré Champion, 2014.
26 Rolland-Boulestreau, *Les colonnes infernales*.
27 Ibid., chap. 2.
28 Even so, the question of how to distinguish between combatants and civilians in the midst of a civil war is a difficult subject. See Claude Petitfrère, 'La Vendée en l'an II: défaite et répression', *AHRF*, 1995,

no. 2, pp. 173–85, esp. p. 177. There is also the nagging question of the distinction between civilians and combatants in a conflict in which civilians who have taken up arms or are suspected of having carried them are considered combatants, when there is uncertainty regarding the very nature of the weapons. A rifle, a pistol, a sword leave little room for doubt in a territory plagued by civil war, but what about the knives, agricultural tools and iron sticks then omnipresent in the countryside?

29 See Rémi Dalisson, 'La célébration de la fête de la Fédération au XIXe siècle. Entre mémoire, subversion et raison (1815–1890)', in Pascal Dupuy (ed.), *La Fête de la Fédération*, Rouen, Publications des Universités de Rouen et du Havre, 2012, pp. 139–50.

30 Decree of 16 August 1793, article 6 (Alphonse Aulard, *Recueil des actes du comité de Salut public*, vol. VI, p. 4).

31 Georges Lefebvre, one of the great historians of the French Revolution, commented on these appointments by writing that the municipality had been replaced by 'a commission of *sans-culottes*' (*Études Orléanaises*, Paris, CHESR, 1963, vol. II, p. 98).

32 Alphonse Aulard, *Recueil des actes du comité de Salut public*, vol. IX, pp. 149–61.

33 Circular letter from the Committee of Public Safety sent to the representatives in charge of these purges as part of a collective mission decided on 9 Nivôse (29 December) and affecting all the departments (ibid., p. 162).

34 Recent works have demonstrated how misleading the term 'machine' is with regard to the methods of proceeding of the popular societies. See, particularly, vol. 6 of l'*Atlas de la Révolution française* which is dedicated to them (Jean Boutier, Philippe Boutry and Serge Bonin (eds), Paris, EHESS, 1992).

35 Purification minutes of the constituted authorities Gondrecourt (AN, AF II 123 plaq. 935 pièce 23). For other examples of these purifications with few, if any, changes, because the chosen ones emerged 'pure' from the purifying crucible, see Biard, *Missionnaires*, chap. 5, p. 3.

36 Unfortunately, the archives of the Parisian sections were partially destroyed by the fires of the Commune in 1871.

37 The expression is that of Laurent Brassart, *Gouverner le local en Révolution. État, pouvoirs et mouvements collectifs dans l'Aisne (1790–1795)*, Paris, Société des études robespierristes, 2013, p. 338.

38 The phrase is that of Côme Simien, author of a remarkable doctoral thesis, as yet unpublished, entitled, *Des maîtres d'école aux instituteurs: une histoire de communautés rurales, de République et d'éducation, entre Lumières et Révolution (années 1760–1802)* (under the direction of Philippe Bourdin, Université Clermont-Auvergne, 2017, 2 vols).

39 On the issue of social and legal rights that women received, see, for example, Suzanne Desan, *The Family on Trial in Revolutionary France*, Berkeley, CA, University of California Press, 2004.

40 See Biard, *Missionnaires*.

41 Ibid., chap. VI.

42 Ibid. See also Jean-Pierre Gross, *Égalitarisme jacobin et droits de l'Homme, 1793–1794 (la Grande famille et la Terreur)*, Paris, Arcanteres, 2000, pp. 343–4 (English edition in 1997 entitled *Fair Shares for All, Jacobin Egalitarianism in Practice*, Cambridge, Cambridge University Press).
43 See Nathalie Alzas, *La liberté ou la mort. L'effort de guerre dans l'Hérault pendant la Révolution*, Aix-en-Provence, Publications de l'Université de Provence, 2006.
44 Albert Mathiez, *La vie chère et le mouvement social sous la terreur*, Paris, Payot, 1927, third part, chap. 3.
45 See the extensive bibliography on subsistence struggles and 'tax' movements during the Revolution, but also their links to popular demands under the Ancien Régime and what Edward P. Thompson called 'the moral economy of the crowd' (Edward P. Thompson, 'The Moral Economy of the English Crowd in the Eighteenth Century', *Past and Present*, 1971, vol. 50, pp. 76–136.
46 See, amongst others, Gross, *Égalitarisme*. On Jacobin egalitarianism, see also Patrice Higonnet, *Goodness Beyond Virtue: Jacobins During the French Revolution*, Cambridge, MA, Harvard University Press, 1998.
47 *AP*, vol. LXIV, pp. 114–15.
48 Ibid., vol. LXIX, pp. 594–5.
49 See Henri Calvet, *L'accaparement à Paris sous la Terreur. Essai sur l'application de la loi du 26 juillet 1793*, Paris, Ernest Leroux, 1933.
50 *AP*, vol. LXXV, pp. 321–2.
51 Letter of Jeanbon Saint-André to Barère, dated 26 March 1793 (Alphonse Aulard, *Recueil des actes du comité de Salut public*, vol. II, p. 534).
52 On these public relief policies, see Catherine Duprat, *Le temps des philanthropes*, Paris, Éditions du CTHS, 1993, vol. 1; for support for injured combatants and families of the slain, see Michel Biard and Claire Maingon, *La souffrance et la gloire. Le culte du martyre de la Révolution à Verdun*, Paris, Vendémiaire, 2018.
53 *AP*, vol. LXXIV, pp. 46–7.
54 See Bernard Bodinier and Éric Teyssier, *L'événement le plus important de la Révolution. La vente des biens nationaux*, Paris, Éditions du CTHS et Société des études robespierristes, 2000.
55 *AP*, vol. LXXXV, pp. 516–20 (8 Ventôse); and vol. LXXXVI, pp. 22–3 (13 Ventôse).
56 See the analysis by Françoise Brunel, *1794. Thermidor. La chute de Robespierre*, Brussels, Complexe, 1989, pp. 59–71; and Jourdan, 'Les journées de Prairial'.
57 See Hesse, 'Terror and the Revolutionary Tribunals'. She points to the fact that article 1 of the decree of 8 Ventôse empowered the Committee of General Security to release patriots who have been detained as counter-revolutionary suspects, providing that they can give a satisfactory account of themselves.
58 Biard, *Missionnaires*.

59 Jean-Pierre Gross, *Saint-Just, sa politique et ses missions*, Paris, Bibliothèque nationale, 1976, pp. 166–8.
60 Letter of 8 Frimaire Year II (28 November 1793), cited by Gross (ibid., p. 169).
61 See Michaël Cufi, *Le glaive de la loi. La justice révolutionnaire à l'armée des Pyrénées Orientales. 22 nivôse–3 prairial an II (12 janvier–22 mai 1794)*, Master's thesis, under the supervision of M. Cadé, Université de Perpignan, 1998.
62 Michelet, *Histoire de la Révolution française*, vol. II, p. 868 [in the original, vol. 7, book XVI, chap. II].
63 *Le Vieux Cordelier*, no. IV (30 Frimaire Year II [20 December 1793]).
64 Ibid.
65 See Biard, *La liberté ou la mort*.
66 *AP*, vol. LX, p. 162 (session of the Convention of 13 March 1793).

Conclusion: How the Convention Reconstructed Itself After Thermidor

1 Duprat, *Le temps*.
2 Report of 8 Ventôse Year II (26 February 1794).
3 Hannah Arendt, *La liberté d'être libre. Les conditions et la signification de la révolution*, Paris, Payot, 2019, p. 65 (text that dates back to the 1960s and remained unpublished until its discovery in 2017).
4 Ibid., p. 68.
5 Loris Chavanette, *Quatre-vingt-quinze. La Terreur en procès*, Paris, CNRS Ed., 2017.
6 In sub-series D III. See Biard, *Missionnaires*, chap. 7.
7 Louis-Eugène Poirier, *Toi ou moi, ou Le dernier coup de massue, en réponse aux impostures que Joseph Lebon s'est permises (...)*, Paris, Maret, messidor an III (June 1795), p. 3. Thanks to Véronique Mathis who drew our attention to the links between Poirier and Lafitte, the artist to whom she devoted her doctoral thesis: *Louis Lafitte (1770–1828), un peintre entre la Révolution et la Restauration* (under the direction of Michel Biard, defended at the University of Rouen Normandie autumn 2019). The following passage on Lafitte belongs to him.
8 http://parismuseescollections.paris.fr/fr/musee-carnavalet/oeuvres/les-formes-acerbes-0.
9 On the political uses of hell, see Biard, *La Révolution hantée*.
10 See, for example, the cover of Ronen Steinberg, *The Afterlives of the Terror. Facing the Legacies of Mass Violence in Postrevolutionary France*, Ithaca, NY, Cornell University Press, 2019.
11 Michel Biard, 'Les fantômes d'une Assemblée décimée. Commémorer et réparer', in Hervé Leuwers, Virginie Martin and Denis Salas (eds), *Justice transitionnelle et Révolution française. L'an III (1794–1795)*, colloquium held in Paris, October 2019, forthcoming.

12 The invention of this sentence seems to be attributed to Thibaudeau (*Mémoires sur la Convention et le Directoire, Paris*, Ponthieu, 2nd edn, 1827 [1st edn, 1824], vol. I, p. 142). Thanks to Françoise Brunel for having indicated this possible source to us.
13 *Moniteur*, 20 Frimaire Year III (10 December 1794). As we have seen (chapter 5) there were more than 73.
14 For details, see Biard, 'Les fantômes'.
15 *Moniteur*, 21 Frimaire Year III (11 December 1794).
16 *Moniteur*, 29 Frimaire Year III (19 December 1794).
17 Ibid.
18 Ibid., 21 Ventôse Year III (11 March 1795).
19 Ibid., 24 Germinal Year III (13 April 1795).
20 See Biard, 'Les fantômes'.
21 AN, F^7 4729.
22 *Discours prononcé par le représentant du peuple J.B. Louvet, dans la séance du 14 prairial an III, pour célébrer la mémoire du représentant du peuple Féraud, assassiné dans ses fonctions le premier de ce mois*, Paris, Imprimerie de la République, an III. Louvet was one of the Girondins reintegrated in Ventôse.
23 *Moniteur*, 15 Vendémiaire Year IV (7 October 1795).
24 Françoise Brunel, 'Les Derniers Montagnards et l'unité révolutionnaire', in Soboul, *Actes du Colloque Girondins et Montagnards*, pp. 297–316; Françoise Brunel, 'L'épuration'.
25 *Moniteur*, 15 Vendémiaire Year IV (7 October 1795).

Index

Addison, Joseph 192n12
Agamben, Giorgio 209n10
Alpaugh, Micah 124
Amar, Jean-Pierre-André 77, 109, 127
American Revolution 6, 7
Ancien Régime 46, 56, 78
  antiquity and 37
  executions 32–3, 130
  friendship 100
  justice 27
  natural right 28
  religion 29–31
  terror 9, 27, 28–35
  venality 46, 57
antiquity 14, 15, 35–7, 46
Antonelle, Pierre-Antoine 112
Aoust, Eustache-Charles 154
Arendt, Hannah 157
Aristotle 33
armaments production 147–8
armées départementales 104–5
armées révolutionnaires 21, 85, 89, 93–4, 126, 127, 129, 182, 183
Artois, Charles-Philippe, comte d' (Charles X) 47, 66
assassination 118
  fear of 51, 107, 130
  of Féraud 162
  of Marat 19–20, 107, 109
Austrian Committee 47, 50

Baker, Keith 26–7
Barère, Bertrand 10–11, 13, 14, 17, 19, 84, 106, 132
Barras, Paul 139
Barruel, Augustin, abbé 26
Barry, Jeanne Bécu, comtesse du 78
Baudot, Marc Antoine 59, 118
Beccaria, Cesare 33
Bernardin de Saint-Pierre, Jacques-Henri 44
Bertier de Sauvigny, Ferdinand de 123
Biard, Michel 108
Bible 29–30
Bignon commission 93, 140
Billaud-Varenne, Jacques-Nicolas 13, 48, 59, 81, 107, 109, 114–15
Birottcau, Jean 54, 74, 104, 110, 195n49
Blanc, Louis 191n2
Bodin, Jean 31
Bossuet, Jacques-Bénigne Ligne 30
Bouquier law 146–7

Index

Bourbon monarchs 15, 31, 32, 35, 40, 102
Bourbotte, Pierre 140
Bourdon, Léonard 111
Boyer-Fonfrède, Jean-Baptiste 104, 109
Brissot, Jacques-Pierre 28, 34–5, 47, 50, 97, 98, 99, 101, 102, 104–5, 107
Brissotins 98, 208n51
Brival, Jacques 148
Brown, Howard 137–8, 191n7
Brunel, Françoise 81
Brutus, Lucius Junius 35–6
Brutus, Marcus 37
Budé, Guillaume 198n24
Bulletin du tribunal révolutionnaire 128–9
Burke, Edmund 8, 34
Burstin, Haim 5, 122

Cabet, Etienne 190n1
Calvinist Protestants 30
Cambacérès, Jean-Jacques-Régis de 72
Cambon, Pierre-Joseph 14
capital punishment 12, 18, 33, 71
 the Great Terror 91
 martial law 82
 see also death penalty; executions
Carnot, Lazare 136, 153
Carnot, Sadi 136
Carrier, Jean-Baptiste 88, 134, 158, 160, 162
catharsis 34, 35, 40
Catholic faith 30
Catiline 14, 46
Censer, Jack 26
Chabot, François 111
Charette, François de 134
Charlier, Louis-Joseph 11
Chaumette, Pierre-Gaspard 112, 126, 127–8
Chopelin, Paul 205n3
Chopin, Augustin 145
Cicero 36, 37, 46

Clavière, Étienne 105
clergy 62, 63–6, 97, 123
 constitutional priests 64
 executions 65, 179
 oath of loyalty 63–4
 refractory/non-juring priests 63–6, 71
 repression 65
Clootz, Anacharsis 48–9, 115
Cobb, Richard 89
Collot d'Herbois, Jean-Marie 13, 88, 100, 130
commissars 79, 80–1, 145
Commission of Twelve 19, 83, 104–5
Committee of General Defence 86
Committee of General Security 10, 85–6, 108, 109, 115, 127, 161
Committee on Legislation 68, 71, 72, 161
Committee of Public Safety 56, 85–7, 106, 136, 143, 161
 attacks on 108, 114, 128
 denunciations 14, 88, 115
 deputies on mission 87, 88, 152–3
 economic dictatorship 149
 members 10, 12, 51
 Robespierre and 115, 117, 128, 129
 surveillance role 80, 86
Committee of Surveillance 86
Committee of War 153
Common Sense (Paine) 8
Conciergerie prison 108, 128, 142
Condé, Louis-Joseph, prince de 66
Condorcet, Jean-Antoine-Nicolas, marquis de 59, 155
confiscation of property 69, 152
conspiracy
 in antiquity 14, 15, 36
 aristocratic conspiracy 66–7
 definitions of 103
 famine conspiracy 17
 fears of 3, 45–9, 51, 55, 66, 118
 Foreign Plot 48–9, 113, 115, 116
 friendship and 100–1

Girondin conspiracy 99, 106–8, 111
Lyon revolt 66
Constituent Assembly 8
  committees 85
  criminal tribunals 92
  deputies *see* deputies; deputies on mission
  émigré repression 66, 67
  factions 96–7
  language of political will 26–7
  martial law 81–2
  non-juring priests 63–6
  revolutionary law 81–2
  'suspects' 70
Constitution 20, 46, 94
  1791 67, 90, 97
  1793 80–1, 127, 143–4, 155
  1795 60, 158
  1799 79
  1804 156
  clergy and 63, 64
  oath to maintain 47, 63
  supremacy of 79
  suspension of 79, 80
  Year VIII 79
Convention 4, 10, 14, 18, 20, 21, 22, 54, 84, 94, 96, 120, 161, 162
  amnesty 5, 14–15
  deputies *see* deputies
  disbanded 163
  divisions in 11, 18
  émigrés 68
  factions 97–105
  jealousy in 59
  Lyon revolt 74–7
  the Maximum 127, 149–51
  Montagnard control 73, 74–5
  revolutionary laws 80–1, 83–4
  'terror as order of the day' 22
  'terror' as policy 5
  'Thermidorian' 9, 12, 147, 156
Corday, Charlotte 19–20, 107
Cordeliers/Cordeliers Club 20, 48–9, 81, 108, 113, 119, 126, 128
  see also Hébertists

corruption 49, 57, 141
  Ancien Régime 46
  in antiquity 36
  Danton 114, 115
  financial 71, 113, 114, 115, 116, 141
  political 113
Council of Elders 163
Council of Five Hundred 163
counter-revolutionaries 17, 20, 21, 22, 45, 47, 51, 103
  see also clergy; *émigrés*; Vendée uprising
countryside 17, 22, 42, 90
  access to land 151
  democracy in 146
  maintaining order in 133
  politicization in 146
  popular societies 146
  purges 144–5
  requisitions from 151
Couthon, Georges 10, 11, 14, 15, 105, 117, 129
la crainte (dread) 28, 29, 38
criminal tribunals 23, 68, 84, 85, 90–2, 103, 138, 139, 150
Cruikshank, George 122

Damiens, Robert-François 9, 32–3
Danton, Georges 59, 60, 97, 100, 105, 156
  arrest and trial 115–17
  Doumouriez and 104
  financial corruption 114, 115
  on political crime 91
  Revolutionary Tribunal and 124
  Riouffe on 142
  Robespierre and 114–16
  terror and 20–1
Dantonists 38, 49, 98, 113–17
  denunciation by Saint-Just 37–8, 115–16
  trial and executions 54, 115–17
Dartigoeyte, Pierre-Arnaud 22, 88
David, Jacques-Louis 107

death penalty 47, 67, 103
  émigrés 68
  monopolistic behaviour 150
  see also capital punishment;
    executions
Debry, Jean 82–3, 84
Decemviral tyranny 162, 163
dechristianization 113, 128, 129
Declaration of the Rights of Man 5,
  14, 64, 143, 155
Delandine, Antoine-François 141
Delattre, Louis-Pierre-François 154
democracy
  local 147
  popular societies/clubs 144
  pure/direct 121, 145
  rural France 146
  sans-culottes and 60, 124, 147
  suspension of Constitution of 1793
    143, 155
  violence and 60
  virtue and 53
  women's right to vote 147
denunciation 46, 50, 54–5, 88, 159
  in antiquity 36
  as civic duty 124–5
  culture of 124–5
  terror of 36
  virtue and 118, 124
Deperret (Lauze de Perret), Claude-
  Romain 107
deputies 18, 54, 87–8, 101–5
  amnesty 5
  arrest of 54, 73, 105–6, 108, 136,
    160
  declared outlaws 108–9
  execution of 14, 108–12, 117,
    118, 160
  inviolability of 97, 100, 102–3,
    104–5
  political independence 112
  political virtue 96
  vulnerability of 20
deputies on mission 71, 80–1,
  152–5
  armée révolutionnaire 93

  to the armies 14, 22, 87, 153
  checks on 88
  Committee of Public Safety 86, 87,
    88, 152–3
  denunciations of 158–9
  by department 180
  institutionalization of system 144,
    152–3
  Legislative Assembly 87
  local purges 144–5
  Lyon revolt 76–7
  military missions 152–4, 181
  numbers of 87
  powers 87–8
  recall to Paris 88
  role in the 'terror' 88
  Vendée uprising 133–4
  war production 147–8
Desmoulins, Camille 50, 68, 97
  arrest 115
  as Dantonist 114
  as Montagnard 100, 101, 102
  rehabilitation 156, 161, 163
  rejection of terror 155
  Robespierre and 101, 114
  Le Vieux Cordelier 114
despotism 9, 10, 31, 36, 38, 156
Devérité, Louis-Alexandre 161
Dherbez-Latour, Pierre-Jacques 76
dictatorship
  of commissars 79, 80
  economic 149
  Rousseau on 83–4
  show trials 114
Diderot, Denis 34
Dietrich, Philippe-Friedrich 84
the Directory 5, 134, 141, 158,
  163
disgrace 40
dragonnades 32
dread (la crainte) 28, 29, 38
Ducos, Jean-François 65, 109
Dulaure, Jacques-Antoine 109, 161
Dumouriez, Charles-François 47–8,
  103–4, 132
Duplay, Maurice 125

Index 233

Edelstein, Dan 27–8
Edict of Nantes 68
education
  classical 37, 46
  political 39, 58, 124
  schools 37, 146–7
Elbée, Maurice 140
elections 131, 144, 145
émigrés 23, 47, 48, 66–9, 71
  banishment 68
  criminal tribunal 68
  criminalization of emigration 67
  death penalty 68
  executions 68, 134, 135
  Lyon revolt 77
  repression 66–9, 156
  seizure/confiscation of property 69, 151
  Vendée Wars 134
  wives and children 67–8
emotions 24, 34, 42–61
  cult of sensibility 44
  dangers of 50
  emotion of terror 53
  fear *see* fear
  jealousy 59
  laughter 44
  loss 61
Encyclopédie 29
Enlightenment
  discourse of reason 27
  philosophes 28, 30, 33
  Rousseau's 'general will' 27
  the Terror and 26–8
Enragés 125–6, 127, 128
exagérés see Hébertists
executions 13, 57, 78
  Ancien Régime 32–3, 130
  clergy 65, 179
  collective 13
  Convention opponents 108–12
  coup of Thermidor 117, 118
  criminal tribunals 138, 139
  Damiens 9, 32–3
  deputies 14, 108–12, 117, 118, 160
  émigrés 68, 134, 135
  factions 108–12, 115–18
  geographical distribution 138, 185
  the Great Terror 91, 129
  guillotine *see* guillotine
  Louis XVI 18, 103
  Lyon revolt 93
  military commissions 138–40
  of military leaders 153
  noyades (mass drownings) 88, 134
  number of 92, 137–43, 185
  outlaws 92
  public executions 32–3, 130
  revolutionary commission 93
  women spectators 126–7
  see also capital punishment; death penalty
extraordinary justice 90–5
extraordinary law 21, 69, 79–80, 81–5, 91
  see also revolutionary law

Fabre d'Églantine, Philippe-François-Nazaire 111
Fabre de l'Herault, Claude-Dominique-Côme 154
factions 96–7
  arrests/political trials 105–18
  Constituent Assembly 97
  Convention 97–105
  coup of Thermidor 117, 118
  elimination of 112–18
  executions 108–12, 115–18
  Foreign Plot and 113
  political strife 98–105
  women members 126
  see also Girondins; Hébertists; Montagnards
Farge, Arlette 122
farmers-general 39
Fauchet, Claude 107
Favras, Thomas de Mahy, marquis de 70
fear 51–3
  of assassination 51, 107, 130
  of conspiracy 3, 45–9, 51, 55, 66, 118

fear (*cont.*)
  definitions 29
  Great Fear 17, 42
  of *sans-culottes* 51, 74, 122, 125
federalists 72, 101, 144
  Lyon revolt 74–7, 93
  repression 73–8
Fénelon, François 37
Féraud, Jean-François 29
Festival of Reason 129
Festival of the Supreme Being 129
First Republic 94, 143
Fléchier, Esprit 30
Flesselles, Jacques de 123
Foreign Plot 48–9, 113, 115, 116
foreigners 48–9, 89, 115, 116
Foullon, Joseph 123
Fouquier-Tinville, Antoine-Quentin 78, 116
Fréteau de Saint-Just, Emmanuel-Marie-Michel-Philippe 67
friendship 99, 100–1, 109, 114, 116
Furet, François 5, 26, 27

Garrioch, David 122
Gensonné, Armand 47, 59, 98, 195n41
Gillray, James 122
Girondins 18–19, 20, 28, 84, 91
  anti-Paris stance 101, 102
  arrests/political trials 48, 105–12, 155
  Commission of Twelve 19, 104–5
  conflict with Montagnards 18–19, 75, 91, 100, 105–8, 155
  execution of king 103
  executions of 54, 108–12
  imitating *sans-culottes* 125
  Lyon revolt 74–7
  Marat on 50
  Montagnards compared 100, 101
  political strife 98–105
  rehabilitation 156, 160–1, 163
  repression 73–8, 105–8
  September massacres 124
Glorious Revolution 8

Godineau, Dominique 126–7
Gorsas, Antoine-Joseph 74, 99, 110, 162
Gossuin, Eugène-Constant-Joseph-César 20, 110
grain prices 46, 149–50
Great Fear 17, 42
Great Terror 91, 129
Greer, Donald 72, 92, 138, 139
Grégoire, Henri 161
Greuze, Jean-Baptiste 44
Guadet, Marguerite-Élie 59
Guilhaumou, Jacques 19, 22, 81
guillotine 17, 112, 155
  collective executions 13
  locations 119, 129, 130, 184
  as public spectacle 130
  as symbol of terror 6, 21, 129, 159
  women spectators 126–7
  see also executions

Hanriot, François 127
Hébert, Jacques-René 19, 101, 108, 112, 114
  arrest 104
  death 142
  Paris Commune 127
  Le Père Duchesne 73, 108, 125, 128
  sans-culottes and 110, 125, 126, 127–8
Hébertists 22, 86, 89, 98, 108, 114, 116, 142, 155
  dechristianization policy 113, 128, 129
  Énragés and 128
  executions 49, 115
  sans culottes and 127–8
  see also Cordeliers/Cordeliers Club
Henry, Patrick 7
Henry-Larivière, Pierre 74
Hérault de Séchelles, Marie-Jean 90
Herriot, Edouard 77
Hesse, Carla 6, 7, 152
High Court 90

Hoche, Louis-Lazare 134
Houchard, Jean-Nicolas 153

Indulgents *see* Dantonists
Israel, Jonathan 28

Jacobins/Jacobin Club 4, 23, 97, 105, 112
  associated societies/clubs 145–6
  centralization 145–6
  corruption 49, 57, 113
  deaths of 53, 76, 112
  Desmoulins and 101
  fear of conspiracy 45, 48
  Montagnards and 99–100
  political virtue 113
  terror as system 25
  'white terror' 24, 161
Jansenists 30
Jaucourt, Louis, chevalier de 29
Jourdan, Annie 29, 31, 130
Julius Caesar 29, 37
Jullien, Madame Rosalie 50, 123
Jullien, Marc-Antoine 50
justice
  Ancien Régime 27
  monarchy and 31, 32
  natural 31
  parlementaires and 27
  terror and 9, 10, 11, 18, 20–1, 27, 32–3
  transitional 158, 159, 163

Kaplan, Steven 191n3
Kelly, George Armstrong 29
Kingly terror 31–3

Lacombe, Claire 126
Lacoste, Ellic 151
Lafitte, Louis 159
language of terror 40–1
Lanjuinais, Jean-Denis 161
LaPlanche, Jacques Léonard 22
laughter 44
Law of Prairial 54, 117, 129–30, 138, 152, 158

Law of Suspects 23, 57, 69, 70, 71, 72–3, 114, 127, 151
Lazowski, Claude-François 124
Le Bas, Philippe 10, 11, 14, 117, 153
Le Peletier de Saint-Fargeau, Louis-Michel 19, 20, 107
Lebon, Joseph 88, 138, 159, 162
Lebrun, Charles-François 105
Leclerc, Jean-Théophile-Victor 127
Lecointre, Laurent 13
Lefebvre, Georges 225n31
Legendre, Louis 14, 116
Legislative Assembly 47, 64, 68, 82–3, 86, 87, 97, 98, 120
Lenoir commission 140
Léon, Pauline 126
Lequinio, Joseph 221n56
Lescure, Louis Marie de 16
lèse-nation 23, 47, 90
lettre de cachet 40
Leuwers, Hervé 59, 216n69
Levasseur, René 52, 60
Lindet, Jean-Baptiste 75–6
Lindet, Robert 216n76
Linton, Marisa 24
Livy 35, 37
Louchet, Louis 11
Louis XIV 32, 68
Louis XV 9, 32, 39, 78
Louis XVI 8, 15, 18, 42
  coronation 32
  flight to Varennes 17, 47, 66, 70, 99
  trial 103
  veto 65, 67
Louvet, Jean-Baptiste 18–19, 50
Lyon revolt 66, 74–7, 88, 93, 114

McPhee, Peter 59
Maistre, Joseph-Marie, comte de 26
Malesherbes, Guillaume-Chrétien de Lamoignon de 39
Mallarmé, François-René 145
Marais (the marsh) *see* the Plain
Marat, Jean-Paul 18, 19, 38, 89, 97, 101, 104, 125

Marat, Jean-Paul (*cont.*)
  assassination 19–20, 107, 109
  David painting 107
  martial law 82
  as Montagnard 100, 102
  Revolutionary Tribunal 50, 104, 111
Mari, Eric de 92, 140–1, 187, 211n48
Marie-Antoinette 47
Mark Antony 36
martial law 81–2
Martin, Jean-Clément 29, 135
Massillon, Jean-Baptiste 30
Mathan, Anne de 73
Matharan, Jean-Louis 69
Mathiez, Albert 149
Mathis, Véronique 227n7
Maupeou, René-Nicolas-Charles-Augustin de 39
Maure, Nicolas 163
the Maximum 127, 149–51
memoirs 44, 52, 59, 99, 118, 141–2
Merlin de Douai, Philippe-Antoine 72, 161
Michelet, Jules 1, 94, 121, 154–5
Milhaud, Jean-Baptiste 22, 154
military commissions 23, 68, 77, 85, 92–4, 138–40, 163, 186
military missions 152–4, 181
military recruitment 92, 131–2
military terror 16–17, 31–2
Miller, Mary Ashburn 27
Mirabeau, Honoré-Gabriel Riqueti, comte de 28
monarchy
  absolute monarchy 35
  Bourbon monarchs 15, 31, 32, 35, 40, 102
  Kingly terror 31–3
  Montagnard support 75
  parlements and 38–40
  use of public disgrace 40
Monck, George 107
monopolist behaviour 126, 149–50

Montagnards 4, 10, 20, 28, 98, 99–100
  arrests/political trials 105–12
  attack on Robespierre 11
  conflict with Girondins 18–19, 75, 91, 100, 105–8, 155
  corruption 57
  deputies on mission 147–8
  emotions 50
  execution of king 103
  Girondins compared 100, 101
  members 100
  'Montagnard' Convention 73–5
  National Convention and 73, 74–5
  political strife 98–105
  representatives on missions 87
  right to property 149
  sans-culottes and 100
  terror and 11, 18, 19, 52
Montesquieu, Charles-Louis de Secondat, baron de 9, 28, 36–8, 40, 55
monument to the martyrs of liberty 18

Napoleon Bonaparte 72, 79, 191n9
National Assembly *see* Constituent Assembly
National Convention *see* Convention
National Guard 127, 131, 133, 145
national holidays 143
natural justice 31
natural right
  Ancien Régime concept of 28
  to life 94, 149
nature 27, 33–5
Neerwinden, Battle of 103, 132
New Testament 30
newspapers 16, 22, 102, 119, 142, 153
Nicolas, Charles-Léopold 125
Noël, Jean-Baptiste 78
noyades (mass drownings) 88, 134

Old Testament 29–30
ordinary law 37, 68–9, 80, 158

Orléans, Louis-Philippe-Joseph, duc d' [also known as Philippe-Equality] 102–3, 104
outlaws 68, 92, 106
　annulment of decrees 161
　armed rebels 103, 133
　deputies 108–9, 160
　executions 92, 135, 141
　number of 141, 187
　representatives 161
　traitors to the *patrie* 109, 110

Paine, Thomas 8–9
pamphlets 8, 15, 102, 108, 128, 142, 159
panic terror 17, 31–2
Paris 101
　capital of *sans-culotte* movement 120–7
　epicentre of *the Terror* 119, 127–30
Paris Commune 18, 21, 70, 81, 108, 119, 127
parlements/parlementaires 27, 38–40
Patrick, Alison 99
Pénières-Delzors, Jean-Augustin 161
Le Père Duchesne 73, 108, 125, 128
Philippeaux, Pierre 161, 163
philosophes 26, 28, 30, 33
the Plain 19, 72, 83, 101–2, 160
Plutarch 37
Pointe, Noel 147–8
Poirier, Louis Eugène 159
political crimes 90–1, 94, 103
　lèse-nation 23, 47, 90
political societies 145, 146, 147
political terror 18–19, 35–6
political theory 35–41
political trials 105–18
political virtue 36–7, 55, 96, 101, 113, 126
politicians' terror 52–3
popular societies/clubs 122, 126, 127, 144–6
popular tribunals 123
Précy, Louis François Perrin 162

priests *see* clergy
Prieur [de la Marne], Pierre-Louis 140
Prieur [de la Côte-d'Or], Claude-Antoine 51, 76
prisons 128, 130, 184
　Conciergerie 108, 128, 142
　conditions in 72
　floating prisons 65
　memoirs 141–2
　popular tribunals 123
　September Massacres 18, 19, 22–3, 65, 74, 101, 123–4, 130
property rights 94, 149, 151
　confiscation of property 69, 152
　reparations 158, 162
　restitution of property 162
Protestants 30, 32, 68
public disgrace 40
public good 35–6, 53–5, 96, 103, 151
　kingly virtue and 31, 32
　Robespierre and 53–4, 55, 116
　self-sacrifice 37, 55, 58
public opinion 39, 46, 56, 129
public safety 67, 89, 106

Quinet, Edgar 191n2

Ramel, General 154
Reflections on the Revolution in France (Burke) 8, 34
reparations 158, 162
republicanism
　classical 35–6
　Montesquieu on 36–7
restitution of property 162
Revocation of the Edict of Nantes 68
revolutionary institutions 85–90
revolutionary law 69, 80, 81–5
　see also extraordinary law
Revolutionary Tribunal 24, 78, 85, 91–2, 93, 103
　Bulletin du tribunal révolutionnaire 128–9

Revolutionary Tribunal (*cont.*)
  Committee of General Security and 86
  creation of 23, 68
  Danton and 124
  Law of Prairial 152
  Marat acquitted 50, 104, 111
  politicians brought before 54, 117–18
  Robespierre and 21
  setting-up of 124
  trial of Dantonists 116–17
  trial of the Girondins 111–12
  women and 126, 127
revolutionary tribunals 85, 91, 93, 94, 139
Révolutions de Paris 70
Richet, Denis 5
Riouffe, Honoré 141–2
Robespierre, Augustin 10, 11, 14, 15, 25, 69, 117
Robespierre, Maximilien 51, 84, 85, 99
  arrest and execution 4, 10, 23, 117, 118
  Barère on 10, 13, 14
  blackening of reputation 4, 10–16, 23, 142
  Committee of Public Safety 115, 117, 128, 129
  on conspirators 103
  Danton/Dantonists and 114–16
  declining health 59–60
  denunciations of 10–16, 18–19, 50, 115, 128
  Desmoulins and 101, 114
  Discours sur les peines infamantes 38
  Enlightenment 28
  exhaustion 59–60
  Festival of the Supreme Being 129
  Girondins and 43, 105, 109–10, 128
  Jacobin Club 97
  Law of Prairial 129
  legislative centralization 81
  as man of virtue 114
  martial law 82
  as Montagnard 100, 102, 105
  Montesquieu and 9, 38
  monument to the martyrs of liberty 18
  political virtue 113
  public good and 53–4, 55, 116
  queue (tail) 15
  'reign of terror' 4, 14, 15, 25, 138, 141, 194n27
  Revolutionary Tribunal and 21
  Riouffe on 142
  Saint-Just and 136, 152
  sans-culottes and 105, 125
  as scapegoat 14, 69, 162
  Tallien on 10, 11–13
  terror and justice 9, 10, 11, 20–1
  terror and virtue 9, 11, 53–4, 57
  virtue as principle of republics 38
  war and 50, 97
Roche, Daniel 122
Rochejaquelein, Victoire, marquise de la 221n56
Roland, Jean-Marie 18, 98, 99, 102, 107
Roland, Marie-Jeanne, Madame 50, 99, 125
Rolland-Boulestreau, Anne 142
Romme, Charles-Gilbert 148
Ronsin, Charles-Philippe 89, 127–8
Rousseau, Jean-Jacques 26, 28, 44, 55
  on capital punishment 33
  dictatorship 83–4
  the 'general will' 26, 27
  Social Contract 83–4
Rousselin, Alexandre 216n70
Roux, Jacques 126, 127
Roux-Fazillac, Pierre 148
royalists 19, 23, 72, 108, 138, 162
Royer, Claude 25, 30
Rudé, George 121
Rühl, Philippe 163
rural areas *see* countryside

Saint-André, Jeanbon 151
Saint-Bonnet, Françoise 209n10
Saint-Domingue 6
Saint-Just, Louis-Antoine 10, 11, 14, 15, 28, 100, 117, 125
　anticipation of death 58
　death 117, 136–7, 152
　denunciation of Dantonists 37–8, 115–16
　loyalty to Robespierre 136
　military operations 137, 153
　posthumous reputation 136
　on public service 55, 57–8
　report on the Girondins 19, 106–7, 109, 110
　revolutionary laws 84
　Robespierre and 136, 152
　sees himself as a powerless and innocent man 58–9
　Ventôse decrees 152, 157
Sallust 35, 46
saltpetre harvest 148–9
sans-culottes 22, 75, 98, 99, 127–8
　caricatures 122
　democracy and 60, 124, 147
　denunciations 124–5
　Enragés 125–6, 127, 128
　fear of 51, 74, 122, 125
　Girondins and 105
　Hébert and 110, 125, 126, 127–8
　historians and 121, 122
　identifying 121–2
　imitation of 125
　mass demonstrations 127, 156
　Montagnards and 100
　murders/executions 122–3
　Paris as centre of movement 120–7
　popular tribunals 123
　Robespierre and 105, 125
　September Massacres 18–19, 22–3, 65, 74, 75, 101, 123–4, 130
　terror and 127
　violence 122–4
　women *sans-culottes* 126–7
Sautayra, Barthélemy 76
Schama, Simon 5

Schechter, Ronald 29–30, 41
Schmitt, Carl 79, 80
schools 37, 146–7
　see also education
September Massacres 18, 19, 22–3, 65, 74, 101, 123–4, 130
Sextus Roscius 36
show trials 114
Sillery, Charles-Alexis Brulart, marquis de 104
Simien, Côme 225n38
Simonin, Anne 81
slavery 6, 99, 151
Slavin, Morris 214n39
Smyth, Jonathan 129
Soboul, Albert 123, 144
Society of Revolutionary Republican Citizenesses 126, 127, 147
Soubrany, Pierre 154
Staël, Germaine, Madame de 194n27
Stalinism 25
Stofflet, Jean-Nicolas 134
suicides 14, 53, 118, 155, 163
surveillance committees 72–3, 89–90, 127
suspects 69–73
　arrests 71
　chronology 69–70
　imprisonment 72
　Law of Suspects 23, 57, 69, 70, 71, 72–3, 114, 127, 151
　statistics 69
　surveillance committees 89
　use of term 70
Sydenham, Michael 99

Tacitus 35, 37
Tackett, Timothy 2–3, 24, 43
Taine, Hippolyte 121
Tallien, Jean-Lambert 10, 11–16
taxation 39, 149–50
terror 3, 5–6
　Ancien Régime 9, 27, 28–35
　beginning of 25
　cathartic 34, 35, 40
　la crainte (dread) 28, 29, 38

terror (*cont.*)
   definitions 29
   despotism and 9, 10
   economic terror 149
   emotions and 34, 42–61
   female terror 126–7
   of God's judgement 29–30
   the Great Terror 91, 129
   guillotine as symbol of 6, 21, 129, 159
   ideology and 26, 27, 77
   justice and 9, 10, 11, 18, 20–1, 27, 32–3
   Kingly terror 31–3
   language of 40–1
   meaning pre-Revolution 25–41
   military terror 16–17, 31–2
   Montesquieu on 38
   nature and 27, 33–5
   as 'order of the day' 5, 11, 16, 17, 19–24, 25, 30, 151
   Paine on 8–9
   panic terror 17, 31–2
   passive 9
   political terror 18–19, 35–6
   politicians' terror 52–3
   public disgrace and 40
   public executions 32–3
   'reign of terror' 1, 2, 4, 14, 25, 138, 141
   religious dimensions 29–31
   Robespierre as scapegoat 14, 69, 162
   role in political theory 35–41
   as sacred 29–30
   state terror 25
   as sublime 34–5
   'system' of 5, 9, 10–16, 18, 19, 25, 52, 79, 156, 157, 162
   Tallien's definition 11
   theatrical tragedy 33, 35
   use of terror 1789–94 16–19
   virtue and 9, 11, 35–6, 37–8, 53–61
   as weapon of the weak 6
   'white terror' 24, 161

terrorism, origin of term 11, 198n11
terrorist, origin of term 13, 198n11
the Terror
   beginning of 5, 23, 25
   capitalization 1–2, 3
   chronological period 2, 5, 23–4
   definite article 1, 3
   ending of 4–5, 23
   Enlightenment and 26–8
   Paris as epicentre of 119, 127–30
   personification 1
   virtue and 9, 11
Thermidorian Convention 9, 12, 147, 156
Thermidorian moment 4, 10
Thibaudeau, Antoine-Claire 117, 228n12
Thompson, Edward Palmer 226n45
Thompson, James Matthew 57
Torné, Bishop Pierre-Athanase 210n23
transitional justice 158, 159, 163
treason 47–8, 54, 90, 103–4, 116
truth commissions 158
Tuileries palace 18, 20, 22, 65, 90

Vadier, Marc-Guillaume-Alexis 14, 115
Valazé, Charles-Éléonor Dufriche de 112
Van Kley, Dale 30
Varlet, Jean-François 127
Vatar-Delaroche, Aimé 75
Vendée uprising 32, 47, 73, 88, 89, 131–5
   deaths 130, 138, 142–3
   terror in 16, 120, 134–5
   women in 126
Ventôse decrees 152, 157
Vergniaud, Jean-Baptiste 19, 53, 59, 83, 98, 105, 109, 111, 155
Le Vieux Cordelier 114
Vincent, François-Nicolas 127–8
virtue
   denunciation and 118, 124

kingly virtue 31
the man of virtue 35, 56–7, 114
Montesquieu on 9, 36–7
political 36–7, 55, 96, 101, 113, 126
republic of virtue 35, 38
Robespierre and 9, 11, 38, 53–4, 55, 57, 113, 114
terror and 9, 11, 35–6, 37–8, 53–61
transparency and 55–6

war economy 147–9
War Office 51
weapons production 147–8
Westermann, François-Joseph 16
'white terror' 24, 161
women
   attendance at executions 126–7
   clubs 126, 127
   Dames des Halles 127
   popular societies/clubs 126
   right to vote 147
   sans-culottes 126–7
   Society of Revolutionary Republican Citizenesses 126, 127, 147
   Vendée uprising 126